Timely Assets

School for Advanced Research
Advanced Seminar Series

James F. Brooks
General Editor

Timely Assets

Contributors

Courtney Childs
Class of 2005, University of Virginia

Paul K. Eiss
Department of History, Carnegie Mellon University

Elizabeth Emma Ferry
Department of Anthropology, Brandeis University

Richard Handler
College of Arts and Sciences, University of Virginia

Mandana E. Limbert
*Department of Anthropology, Queens College and the Graduate Center,
City University of New York*

Celia Lowe
Department of Anthropology, University of Washington

Erik Mueggler
Department of Anthropology and American Indian Studies, University of Michigan

Paul E. Nadasdy
Department of Anthropology, University of Wisconsin, Madison

Huong Nguyen
Class of 2005, University of Virginia

Karen Strassler
Department of Anthropology, Queens College, City University of New York

Timely Assets

The Politics of Resources and Their Temporalities

Edited by Elizabeth Emma Ferry and Mandana E. Limbert

School for Advanced Research Press

Santa Fe

School for Advanced Research Press

Post Office Box 2188
Santa Fe, New Mexico 87504-2188
www.sarpress.sarweb.org

Co-director and Editor: Catherine Cocks
Manuscript Editor: Margaret J. Goldstein
Designer and Production Manager: Cynthia Dyer
Proofreader: Kate Whelan
Indexer: Catherine Fox
Printer: Cushing Malloy, Inc.

Library of Congress Cataloging-in-Publication Data:

Timely assets : the politics of resources and their temporalities / edited by Elizabeth Emma Ferry
and Mandana E. Limbert.
    p. cm. — (School for Advanced Research advanced seminar series)
  Includes bibliographical references and index.
  ISBN 978-1-934691-06-9 (pa : alk. paper)
1. Economic anthropology. 2. Value. 3. Natural resources. 4. Cultural property. 5. Finite, The.
6. Time—Sociological aspects. I. Ferry, Elizabeth Emma. II. Limbert, Mandana E. III. School for
Advanced Research (Santa Fe, N.M.)
  GN448.2.T56 2008
  306.3—dc22
                2008011558

Cover illustration: Oil Well at Sunset © Lushpix, 2008.

Contents

CONTENTS

Figures

Acknowledgments

We would like to thank all the participants in the SAR seminar for their engaged and sustained contribution to this project both in Santa Fe and in the process of writing the volume. We would especially like to thank Karen Strassler for her invaluable suggestions. Many thanks as well to the two anonymous readers for SAR Press and to Catherine Cocks for her help and encouragement. Of course, we take full responsibility for any misrepresentations that may appear.

Timely Assets

1

Introduction

Elizabeth Emma Ferry and Mandana E. Limbert

Oil is running out. What's more, its final depletion, once relegated to a misty future, now seems imminent. A report commissioned by the United States Department of Energy's National Energy Technology Laboratory in February 2005 states, "The world has never faced a problem like this.... Previous energy transitions (wood to coal and coal to oil) were gradual and evolutionary; oil peaking will be abrupt and revolutionary."[1] Such apocalyptic predictions, as well as denials and pragmatic mechanisms for managing the anticipated shortfall, reverberate from the pages of the *New York Times*, numerous books and articles, and environmental and oil industry conferences and publications.[2] Despite their differences, in all these discussions, nature, labor, and time converge, as people and states create and contest *resources*—objects and substances produced from "nature" for human enrichment and use. This volume focuses on how resources, resource-making, and resource-claiming are entangled with experiences of time. Although individual studies have long noted the temporal aspects of resources, few have brought resources and time together with the explicit goal of comparing and theorizing their relationships.

This was the aim of the fall 2005 seminar at the School for Advanced Research in Santa Fe from which this volume emerges. The anthropologists who participated in that seminar and whose work forms the basis of this volume had encountered objects, substances, people, and ideas that were seen as "resources" by our subjects: silver in Mexico, "diversity" in the United States, and historical documents in Indonesia, to name but three examples. Yet for many of us, thinking explicitly about a range of resources raised a set of new questions: Under what conditions and with what consequences do people find something to be a resource? What kinds of temporal experiences, concepts, or narratives does thinking of things as resources entail? How do the making and imagining of resources assume or condition particular understandings of past, present, and future? How do understandings of time shape the ways resources are named, managed, or allocated?

We began with the premise that nothing is essentially or self-evidently a resource. Resource-making is a social and political process, and resources are concepts as much as objects or substances. Indeed, to call something a resource is to make certain claims about it, and those claims participate in an ideational system (not always a completely coherent system, but a system nonetheless) that has a history, perhaps multiple histories. To call something a resource is to presuppose a set of interactions between "nature" and "society" that creates goods, products, and values. Moreover, particular expressions of this ideational system, what we might call resource imaginations, often have a strongly temporal aspect: they frame the past, present, and future in certain ways; they propose or preclude certain kinds of time reckoning; they inscribe teleologies; and they are imbued with affects of time, such as nostalgia, hope, dread, and spontaneity.

Two issues have arisen to make our task more difficult and more intriguing. First, the connections between resources and time can go in either direction: we can think about how resources affect time and about how time affects resources. Rather than seek causal relationships (for instance, through identifying either given resources or time as independent or dependent variables), we hope to trace multiple paths between the two domains. Second, although many of us noted an expansion in the kinds of things that could plausibly be called resources, we do not want to conclude that everything is or can be called a resource. Our impulse was toward specifying the conditions under which people make and think about resources—including those moments when they claim new things as resources—rather than generalizing the category itself.

In most of the cases in this volume (those studied by Ferry; Childs, Nguyen, and Handler; Limbert; Lowe; and Nadasdy), certain people or objects are explicitly described by our informants as resources (or the equivalent), although some of these may not be things normally thought of as such (Childs, Nguyen, and Handler; Lowe). The range of cases reflects our recognition that the kinds of "things" that are called resources include not only land, plants, and oil but also people, knowledge, and history itself.

However, in several of the cases we examined (Eiss; Mueggler; Strassler), people did not use an explicit language of resources. We were therefore faced with the question of whether and how the concept of resources was relevant, given that our informants were not framing the question explicitly in those terms. In these cases, it seemed either that processes taking place mirrored or paralleled processes of resource-making (Strassler) or that participants deployed alternative views of nature, society, knowledge, and property, helping us clarify what resource-making is and what it does (Eiss; Mueggler). The presence of these cases clarifies one of the central claims of the volume: our concern is not simply resources as things, but the practices of making and imagining resources. We argue that the concept of resources engages particular constellations of nature, society, and economy, with far-reaching implications for how collectivities (such as nations) conceive of their possessions and how relations between past, present, and future are understood. Often, these implications frame understandings and practices, even when participants do not use the word *resources* or its equivalent. In this introduction, we trace a few genealogies of the concept of resources.

"THE STONE UNQUARRIED"

The first definition of *resource* in the *Oxford English Dictionary (OED)* is "a means of supplying some want or deficiency; a stock or reserve upon which one can draw when necessary." The first part of this definition emphasizes a forward movement toward some purpose or destination; the second emphasizes a backward or prior movement. As John Yeats, author of *The Natural History of the Raw Materials of Commerce* wrote:

> in describing the natural resources of any country we refer to the
> ore in the mine, the stone unquarried, the timber unfilled, the
> native plants and animals—to all those latent elements of wealth
> only awaiting the labour of man to become of use, and therefore
> of value. (Yeats 1887:2)

The word *resource* is related to the French word *source*, meaning a spring of water, and like a spring of water, the concept implies dynamism. It suggests both the continuous generation of something from an originary point, as water emerges from a spring, and the potential for creating something else, as water nourishes growing plants.[3] Making this potential actual, however, creates another potential, for resources are commonly used to make or do something else (as oil is used to make things go, silver is used for coin and plate, or "diversity" in the university is used to make a just society). It is as if to define something as a resource is to suspend it between a past "source" and a future "product."[4]

Thus it appears that the concept of resource is intimately connected to notions of generativity, which we can divide into three moments. First is the moment of conception, when the original source generates the resource. This moment often occupies the misty realms of the past or is seen as an "always already" condition from the perspective of those engaged in the recognition, classification, and exploitation of resources. Descriptions of the formation of petroleum, coal, diamond, and other mineral deposits that emphasize the serendipitous confluence of forces ages ago are good examples. Such descriptions emphasize the primordial moment of resource generation. In Erik Mueggler's chapter, the romance of the primordial source becomes a point of encounter between two very different "archival regimes" concerned with the origins of rhododendrons.

The second generative moment is the human, cultural act of naming or appropriation that constitutes the "birth" of the resource. This act is a kind of midwifery, as the resource becomes available for use within the human, cultural world and is often intimately tied to naming practices.[5] For instance, Paul Nadasdy's chapter demonstrates the ways in which designating wildlife as "renewable resources" immediately creates a set of social relations and bureaucratic practices within a new temporal frame.

The third generative moment is the future orientation of resources themselves. Their quality as potential wealth generates a possible future or futures, as well as the futures of those collectivities that lay claim to them or grapple with their limits and scarcity. In Elizabeth Ferry's chapter, silver producers in Guanajuato, Mexico, attempt to avoid a dismal, depleted future by resuscitating the glorious past, whereas mineral collectors follow their specimens to a future that seems limitless. In discussing oil-based prosperity in Oman, Mandana Limbert demonstrates that the temporality created through resource-making is not always teleological: it may appear as a prosperous interregnum between an impoverished past and a threatening or redemptive future.

To speak of the generation of possible futures is to raise the question of resource scarcity. The link between resource-making endeavors and the idea of scarcity is by no means simple, however. To begin with, although scarcity often appears to be an essential quality of things, it may be more profitably seen as an expression of a social relationship, culturally defined.

As David Harvey notes, "It is often erroneously accepted that scarcity is something inherent in nature, when its definition is inextricably social and cultural in origin" (1974:272; see also Sahlins 1972). Furthermore, in some cases people deny scarcity of those resources or postpone their anxiety by displacing resource exhaustion to a far-enough-distant future.[6]

Nevertheless, the moment when something (water, air, virgin forest) becomes conceptualized as a resource, the issue of its finitude is raised (or perhaps the converse: only those things for which scarcity is at issue are conceptualized as resources in the first place). Although resources such as mines are implicitly (or explicitly) recognized as scarce, even renewable resources such as agricultural land and forests are also understood as limited. Resources seem to have a natural life span, which threatens the life span of the collectivities dependent on them. And bonanzas and the busts that succeed them come to define particular epochs, such that a prosperous past often contrasts with a straitened present, or a prosperous present with a straitened future. The projected depletion of resources often frames people's everyday experiences of their past, present, and future and conditions the state's representation of national time and the temporal trajectories of development initiatives.

Faced with the fear that a resource might run out, people often try to counter with plans for renewal or replacement by another resource. People regularly uphold technology and "human ingenuity" as the resolution to scarcity, as Julian Simon does in his popular business text *The Ultimate Resource* (1981). Indeed, technocratic high-modern states, as described by James Scott (1998), specialize in the use of planning to override or bracket questions of scarcity. A tension emerges here, however, between technological innovation and human obsolescence: like the old couple whose house is razed by Faust (Berman 1982), the scarcity of resources is death to some people and some places but also feeds the relentless future of a generalized resource-based economy. Neo- and anti-Malthusian debates also reveal this tension—between resource scarcity and the presumed limitlessness of growth (Meadows et al. 1972; Simon 1981; see Harvey 1974). Invoking the language of resources, therefore, entails the question of their future exhaustion and thus their temporality.

THE MEETING PLACE OF THE NATURAL AND THE SOCIAL

The path of a resource from origin to future needs an external agent, something outside of "nature" to appropriate and exploit it. Thus the idea of "resource" implies a distinction—perhaps even confrontation—between the human and nonhuman world. In this sense, the generative movement by which nature becomes "natural resources" is seen to be a movement from the realm of nature to the realm of culture. The object or substance in question changes from something external and even alien to the human social world into something that takes its meaning from its interaction with and utility for humans. Resource-making, indeed, might be said to refer to those transformations in which active human labor converts the passive ground of nature into usable, productive wealth. In this view, resources appear as those natural materials and objects that are available for transformation through labor. However, the fact that resources themselves participate in the organic process of generation suggests that the divide is not as strict as it appears, that the boundaries between the natural and the social are continually being crossed and, like national borders, must also continuously be policed.

In John Locke's discussion of the origin of property, he expressed the centrality of labor to this process:

> Though the earth, and all inferior creatures, be common to all men, yet every man has a property in his own person: this nobody has a right to but himself. The labor of his body and the work of his hands, we may say, are properly his. Whatsoever then he removes out of the state that nature hath provided, and left it in, he hath mixed his labor with, and joined to it something that is his own, and thereby makes it his property. (Locke 2003 [1690]:111–112

This moment of appropriation, of "remov[al] out of the state that nature hath provided," is also the actualization of nature in a form useful to humans—thus the moment in which it becomes possible for "nature" to be claimed as a "natural resource." Although property, not resources, was Locke's primary concern, ideas of the world as available for human use, and of that use as the basis of proper human society, underwrite the concept of resources.[7]

Marx refines the concept of labor as appropriation, saying, "We see, then, that labour is not the only source of material wealth, of use-values produced by labor. As William Petty puts it, labor is its father and the earth its mother" (1967[1867]:50). This captures the generative (and often gendered) quality of the movement from nature to natural resources, for natural resources, as we have argued, are values in potential form. The inseminating power of labor makes it possible for the earth to produce value in the form of resources. Put another way, the point at which labor and nature are brought together is the domain of the resource.[8]

As should be clear, not all acts of appropriation (and thus not all encounters between labor and nature) make resources; rather, the creation and imagination of resources are products of particular ways of organizing labor and nature. For instance, the fact that under capitalism the labor power of workers is sold as a commodity seems aligned with a frame of mind that objectifies the products of labor and nature as resources. As Marx stated in *The Grundrisse*, capitalism entails not only the alienation of the worker from his own labor, which he now sells as a commodity, but also "the negation of the situation in which the working individual relates to land, the soil, to the earth itself, as his own" (Marx 1993[1857]:498). Under such conditions, nature appears as the nonhuman ground on which alienated human labor is expended to make resources. Just as the Lockean view of appropriation makes thinking about resources possible, so too does the objectification of labor and nature that helps to define capitalism.[9]

Furthermore, the fact that labor's commodification often takes a temporal mode has significant effects on resource-making. As E. P. Thompson (1967) argued, the constitution of abstract categories of time and space is necessary for industrial capitalism to function smoothly. In capitalist contexts, abstract and homogenous time often frames the production and distribution of resources as well. In these contexts, the "homogenous empty time" of the nation-state (Anderson 1991; W. Benjamin 1968) can become the temporal foundation for creating resources. Yet, as the chapters by Nadasdy, Lowe, Limbert, and Strassler point out, the multiple forms of time that coexist in projects of constituting and maintaining collectivities also affect practices of making resources.

If resources are produced by labor, they are also tightly linked to nature. Conceiving of something as a resource underscores its "naturalness," even while bringing it into a cultural domain. Indeed, synonyms for *resources* among economists include both *natural capital* and *natural commodity*. Recently, the idea of nature as the self-evident source of value has been the object of many discussions within social theory.[10] Such discussions often begin with an ambiguity in the concept of nature noticed by Raymond Williams (1976): the universe of nature may include or exclude humans, depending on the context. Indeed, as Williams noted, ambivalence over whether the natural world includes or is external to humanity is fundamental to many of the complexities in the way the concept of nature is deployed.

These discussions tend to take one of two directions. One approach dedicates itself to exploring the social qualities of apparently natural things. The basic premise, as the ecological historian William Cronon has neatly expressed it, is that "'nature' is not nearly as natural as it seems. Indeed, it is a profoundly human construction" (1995:25). Anthropologists, environmental historians, and geographers have been especially effective in demonstrating the social production of nature in various contexts (Cronon 1983, 1991; Eder 1996; Harvey 1974, 1996; D. Mitchell 1996; N. Smith 1984; Spirn 1995; Worster 1993).[11]

Bruce Braun and Noel Castree describe this "production of nature" approach as "captur[ing]…the way in which 'first nature' is replaced by an entirely different produced 'natural' landscape. The competitive and accumulative imperatives of capitalism bring all manner of natural environments and concrete labor processes upon them together in an abstract framework of market exchange which, literally, produces nature[s] anew" (Braun and Castree 1998). Resource-making and resource imaginations are central to this process.

A second approach is inspired by science studies (Callon, Law, and Rip 1986; Haraway 1991; Latour 1987; Shapin and Schaffer 1989). Rather than commit itself either to the socialness of the seemingly natural or to the naturalness of the seemingly social,[12] this approach treats the agency of nonhuman and human actors together and assumes that neither is reducible to the other (compare Callon 1979; Latour 1988; T. Mitchell 2002). This approach aims to transcend the (human) subject and (nonhuman) object distinction entailed within the "modern Constitution" (Latour 1993).[13]

Recently, we have seen the emergence of a field within political ecology that draws on science studies, as well as other critical work on knowledge, society, and agency. Scholars working within this arena combine the two approaches above by focusing on the political and social dimensions of nature and its uses and at the same time interrogating the epistemological bases of the nature–society relation (see, among others, Brosius 1999; Escobar 1999; Nadasdy 2003; Raffles 2002; Watts 1998).[14] This volume aims to contribute to these discussions in two ways. First, by focusing on the temporal dimension of making and imagining resources, we illuminate further the politics of such practices and their epistemological underpinnings. Second, we bring together discussions of the concept of resources and temporality so as to examine time's material, affective presence in the world.

(MODERN) NATION-STATES AND "NATURAL" RESOURCES

The OED's second definition of the word *resource*, which came into use in English in the eighteenth century, is "the collective means possessed by any country for its own support or defence."[15] Here, the stress falls not on a material product but on a national collectivity, defined and maintained though the existence of resources and the wealth they generate.[16] It is not surprising that resources come to be associated with "support of a country" at the end of the eighteenth century, for resources, especially "natural resources," are intimately tied to the history of the nation-state as a modern political form.[17] This is certainly why we often see pictures of waterfalls, forests, mines, and indeed "native peoples" on national currencies.[18] These natural resources ground the political body of the nation by demonstrating its emergence or growth from that territory and its "natural" endowments (Anderson 1991; Coronil 1997; Delaney 1995). The seemingly essential relationship between a people and a territory, with all its potential wealth, became, in principle at least, a taken-for-granted frame for ownership.

As states name and appropriate resources in order to define national communities, they often rely on "expert" techniques to insert their practices into multiple realms. In chapter 5, Celia Lowe shows how debates among Indonesian and foreign conservation biologists help produce a popular sense of biodiversity and ethnic diversity as "national resources" while also aligning Darwinian and nationalist temporalities.[19] Such expertise often underscores the notion that the efficient use of resources is what enables and maintains political legitimacy.[20] Within national and international policy circles, for example, states are judged as "strong" or "weak" based on their perceived ability to manage natural resources. This is why resource management is so deeply embedded in ideas of sovereignty and why contemporary protests against the United States, the World Trade Organization, and the International Monetary Fund so often focus on the question of whether resources should be privatized or nationalized.[21]

Nevertheless, the connection between nation-state and resources often seems "natural." It is often tied not only to claims for sovereignty but also to claims about economic (and social) hardship. Identifying a nation with its natural resources allows states to portray economic problems solely as problems of resources, natural rather than social in origin, drawing attention away from the social and political causes of poverty (Alonso 1994; Gupta 2004; T. Mitchell 2002; A. Sen 1983).

The processes of making and managing resources also regularly shape the ways in which "modernity" is experienced and projected. Nations often base claims to modernity on their abilities to manage their resources appropriately. In classic modernization theory, the trajectory to modernity begins with takeoff, fueled in part by the efficient exploitation of natural resources (Rostow 1960). If these expectations are not realized, however, development and modernization can come to be "experienced not as a liberation but as a betrayal" (Ferguson 1999:249). Furthermore, the modern management of resources requires not only expertise and efficiency but also planning, an orientation to the future that, as Koselleck argues, projects a temporal frame of the "new" or "unique" (Koselleck 2002). Modernity is also often an explicit concern for actors and institutions engaged in creating resources.[22] In Strassler's chapter in this volume, for example, the ways in which history is documented and archived for future generations are understood to reaffirm Indonesia's place as a modern nation. These futures are also anything but morally neutral; indeed, the nation-state, its temporalities, and its resource-making projects tend to be suffused with senses of morality and propriety. Thus practices of resource-making and managing often serve national ideologies of efficiency, progress, development, and morality.

However, just as there is no one "modernity" (Gaonkar 2001; Özyürek 2006; Rofel 1999), there are also multiple temporal experiences of nature and resources. Although a linear, teleological path of national modernization is often associated with the proper management of resources, other temporal understandings of nature use and nature relationships also exist and clash in the contemporary world. For instance, in chapter 8, Eiss's discussion of the multiple resources that have underwritten *el pueblo* (the people) in Hunucmá demonstrates how successive claims to "communal resources" are best seen as moments in an ongoing narrative of dispossession and repossession. This narrative, and the notion of el pueblo constituted through it, continues to be salient, even as the "resources" in question have changed completely. This volume foregrounds the tensions between multiple and overlapping temporalities that suffuse the making and imagining of resources, as well as those between and within national projects and everyday life.

AFFECT, FUTURE, AND MATERIALITY

The chapters in this volume contribute to the venerable anthropology of time, with its focus on the ways in which temporal experience is embedded in culture (Bourdieu 1963; Durkheim 1994[1912]; Geertz 1973; Gell 1992; Munn 1992; Thompson 1967) and its exploration of multiple temporal modalities (Birth 1999; Bloch 1977; Evans-Pritchard 1940; Traweek 1988). At the same time, our attention to resource-making and resource imaginations also allows us to explore aspects of time that have been less extensively theorized: the affective qualities of and moral sentiments associated with temporal experiences, the future as it is produced and imagined in the present, and the materiality of time.[23] Many of the contributors to this volume analyze how senses of time—of speed and direction, of time's motion as slow, fast, unilinear, or cyclical—are entangled in how people perceive, relate to, and understand "resources." These senses are often extremely subtle, however, and are made apparent not in direct statements but in the ways in which people convey feelings and sentiments of fate, surprise, hope, optimism, pessimism, pride of origin, nostalgia, or the aesthetic pleasure taken in the rationality of homogenous empty time.[24] Thus we often focus on subtle temporal assumptions, senses, and feelings that saturate understandings about resources and the ways that such affective qualities may be tied to particular historical conditions.

We found that senses of time associated with the appropriation of nature often take the form of moral and/or aesthetic norms. For instance, in Locke's chapter "On Property," discussed above, the proper mode of interaction with the natural world is its appropriation for human use.[25] In some contexts, this approach is framed in religious terms; as Locke says, "God, who hath given the world to men in common, hath also given them reason to make use of it to the best advantage of life and convenience" (Locke 2003[1690]:18). The double meaning of the word *waste* as unusable and polluting dross and as those parts of nature that are not made use of underscores this normative aspect of the concept of resources.[26]

For Locke, it is the moral dimension that comes out most strongly, but ideas of proper use also have their aesthetic expression. Drawing on this Lockean tradition, two characters in Jane Austen's novel *Sense and Sensibility*, Marianne Dashwood and Edward Ferrars, dispute alternative notions of beauty with respect to landscape. Marianne champions a picturesque notion of the landscape arranged for visual contemplation, whereas Edward praises the woods "full of fine timber" and "rich meadows" and says, "It exactly answers my idea of a fine country, because it unites beauty with utility" (Austen 1992[1811]:71–72). Edward's perspective on the landscape as beautiful and useful (or perhaps beautiful *because* useful) aptly demonstrates the notion of nature as the repository of resources *in potentia*, as well as the moral injunction for humans to exploit those resources (compare Handler and Segal 1990:20–22).[27] The scripts laid out by Locke and Austen have a decided future orientation, for they locate morality and beauty in the realization of nature's potential, which can be seen even before the land is harvested and the timber is felled. "Waste" refers to those parts of nature where the proper issue in the form of usable human products has been abortively cut off and therefore the proper future has been foreclosed. Thus these moral and aesthetic prescriptions are themselves temporal affects.

In addition to these rather positive, future-oriented perspectives on resources, there are, of course, explicit critiques of the ways in which nature has become constituted as resource, often founded on nostalgia. There is certainly a long history of this nostalgia for untouched nature (Adler 2006; Glacken 1967; Merchant 1980). Indeed, as Raymond Williams (1973) describes in *The Country and the City*, as soon as one imagines that he or she has found the origins of the emergence of this form of nostalgia for the countryside as exemplary nature, one need only look at the literature of a previous generation to find that such images of the country, and the city, persist.

Martin Heidegger's essay "The Question Concerning Technology" provides a good example of this nostalgic mode, this time in a modernist idiom. Heidegger (1977:17) laments how modern technology transforms nature into what he calls a "standing-reserve." Nature is no longer, in Heidegger's terms, brought forth (or revealed) through *techne* as *poiesis*. It is revealed as "a challenging." He writes: "The revealing that rules in modern technology is a challenging, which puts to nature the unreasonable demand that it supply energy that can be stored as such....The earth now reveals itself as a coal mining district, the soil as a mineral deposit" (14–15). Such critiques of the exploitation of nature often rely on a romantic longing for the past and a sense of the present as a point of decline. Nearly all the chapters in this volume explore the moral implications of resource-making projects and their connection to the affective dimensions of temporal experience, particularly the time of the nation-state (chapters 5 and 9), the university (chapter 7), and the pueblo and other collective entities (chapter 8).

Another aspect of the temporality of resource-making and resource-thinking is the production of "other times," both past and future, in the present. The past, both as an object of study and an object of political fixation, has been the focus of much anthropological attention (among many others, Bloch 1977; Hill 1988; Peel 1984; Sahlins 1985; Trouillot 1995),[28] and much of the work in this volume builds on these insights. For instance, many resource-making acts entail a sense of social and political origins as emerging from the land and natural endowments on which and through which people live. Origin myths that incorporate the earth and its resources may be inextricably tied, in complicated ways, to how societies and people frame and enact their modes of belonging. Such claims to origins are always objects of contention, in the form of a monarch with a vexed dynastic history (as in developmentalist Oman) or doubts about evidentiary truth (as in Indonesia) or racial diversity (as in a university in the southern United States). Nevertheless, tensions over the past are imbricated in confrontations and understandings of "resources."

Anthropological attention to the past has, in recent years, been complemented by a growing interest in futures. Daniel Rosenberg and Susan Harding remark in the introduction to their recent edited volume *Histories of the Future*, "We live in a world saturated by future-consciousness as rich and full as our consciousness of the past" (Rosenberg and Harding 2005:9). Similar to and in conversation with recent interest in the future (see, for example, Crapanzano 2003; Douglas and Wildavsky 1982; Guyer 2007; Koselleck 2002; Lupton 1999; Mason 2007; Maurer 2002; Miyazaki 2003b, 2006), several contributors to our volume (particularly Childs, Nguyen, and Handler; Ferry; Limbert; and Strassler) explore "the presence of the future in the present" and its implications.[29] At the same time, because the future "has not yet happened," its materiality has been relatively ignored in scholarly discussions. We hope to take Rosenberg and Harding's call seriously by attending to not only the conceptual richness of the future but also its material presence in the world. Accordingly, many of the chapters explore concepts and sensibilities of risk, hope, dread, fate, and life span as they are grounded in resource-making projects.

Indeed, we explore how resources make time material. The concept of resources, we suggest, tends to objectify and make tangible those "things" understood as such, even incorporeal ones such as a memory of dispossession, as in Paul Eiss's chapter, or biological diversity, as in Celia Lowe's. In paying attention to the experience of time as mediated through and constituted by resources, we hope to emphasize the material aspects of past and future consciousnesses and sensibilities. Several chapters in the book are explicitly concerned with the materiality of the resources they discuss. Even when the resource is removed from the view of those who use and rely on it (such as oil in the Omani state, in Mandana Limbert's chapter), that absence has its own materiality in the golden doors of banks and the smooth asphalt of new roads. Our explorations of materiality aim to ground the study of time and the future in the lived world. An attention to the materiality of resources and its links to time also allows us to unpack the perceived distinction between human subjective action and the passive nature from which resources are produced. Recent literature that examines the agency of objects to overcome or at least call into question the subject/object divide informs our efforts in this respect (Latour 2005; Law and Hassard 1999; see also Miller 2005 for an informative discussion of this issue).

The chapters in this volume thus allow for new purchase on the mutual entanglements of resources and time as they work together to constitute everyday social being.

SUMMARY OF CHAPTERS

The sequence of chapters in this volume traces a movement from objects most commonly understood as "resources," such as oil, minerals, and lumber, to national "biodiversity," which includes fish species, humans, plants, and forms of knowledge about plants, to shifting understandings of social collectivities and historical documents. Simultaneously, this movement considers the various ways in which sources and pasts, as well as hopes, fears, and expectations for the future, are experienced, understood, and contested on the ground of resource-making and management.

In chapter 2, Mandana Limbert explores the place of oil in Oman's national teleology, for both the origins of the modern state and its future. She argues that although oil enabled the massive transformations in infrastructure that marked the emergence of the modern state, oil—and the conflicts that its discovery and export imply—disappears from national discourses on the nation's origins. At the same time, she argues that Oman, unlike most developmentalist states, does not project a hopeful future. Rather, the future, which is expected to be oil-less, appears to be bleak, potentially redemptive, or unknown. This is not, in other words, a story of a progressive modernization that the state projects into the future and about which people become disillusioned. Instead, this "natural resource" becomes a source for a history structured around disappearances, miracles, and surprises.

Elizabeth Emma Ferry's chapter begins by asking why one substance mined in Guanajuato, Mexico—silver—is generally considered to be a non-renewable natural resource but another—mineral specimens, often quite similar in a mineralogical sense—is rarely talked about as such. The chapter examines the different temporal experiences and frames asso-ciated with each substance as a way of looking at how the concept of resources emerges within a particular political and social context (with certain consequences for the experience and structuring of time) and how the act of resource-making (and -unmaking) also produces certain temporal effects. It explores a counterpoint between two "bodies"—the organic, corporeal, and mortal body of the mine and the corporate, self-renewing, and seemingly immortal body of the collection—which provide alternative temporal frames for the substances of silver ore and mineral specimens. These temporal frames both constitute and are constituted through the classification of silver as a resource and of minerals as objects that do not engage the same obligations—to provide the "raw material" and "energy" for a so-called modern collectivity.

In chapter 4, Paul Nadasdy focuses on ideas and debates about nature's "renewability" in the Yukon. Although everyone in the Yukon agrees that fish and wildlife populations are renewable, there is a fundamental disagreement over the concept of renewability itself and the spatiotemporal order it implies. Wildlife biologists view animal populations and human–animal relations as embedded in cyclical time, characterized by the periodic recurrence of similar events of the same type. First Nation people, by contrast, are more likely to view them as embedded in circular time, a temporal framework within which the same event recurs over and over again. This difference has significant implications for how each group conceives of the animal as resource, the proper role of human agency vis-à-vis animals, and what constitutes appropriate management. Although First Nation people can and do assert some control over space and time within the bureaucratic context of wildlife management in the territory, that very context takes for granted the cyclical topology of bureaucratic space-time and is therefore incompatible with their view of proper human–animal relations. To some extent, then, First Nation people's participation in the bureaucratic co-management process (and acquiescence to the spatiotemporal assumptions underlying it) makes it increasingly difficult for them to challenge dominant Euro-Canadian views of wildlife management and human–animal relations.

Whereas chapters 2–4 focus on substances commonly thought of as resources (although the limits of resource-making are also explored), the following chapters explore substances not typically described as resources, such as knowledge, human and animal diversity, and documents, and confront resource-making practices and imaginations.[30] Once we recognize how participants claim these as resources or how the concept of resources sharpens our understanding of the case, temporal processes strikingly similar to those discussed in chapters 2–4 become immediately evident.

In her chapter, Celia Lowe traces connections and tensions between claims about bio- and human diversity as they become defined as national resources and as they are embedded in Darwinian and nationalist temporalities. Debates and tensions between Indonesian and foreign scientists about the discovery of biological species overlap with representations of human diversity, both serving as sources of national pride and origins. Similarly, Lowe draws parallels between the "event" of speciation and the "event" of nationalist awakening. Such a temporality, Lowe argues, is not structured by the fulfillment of a messianic plan but enables an "open and contingent" future. This temporality, however, is not one of official nationalism, with its planned teleology, but of a popular nationalism. Thus evolutionary biology seems not to reinforce official nationalist trajectories, but popular ones.

In chapter 6, Erik Mueggler compares two regimes of gathering and making knowledge focused on the origin and growth of rhododendron plants in Yunnan. The first, carried out by British botanical explorers employed in collecting plant specimens for the British Museum and for various botanical companies, involved mapping, surveying, and cataloging the earth and its products. The second, carried out by Naxi ritual practitioners and evidenced in ritual writings and drawings in the dongba script, took the earth as something to be palpated to its depths, pored over in search of hidden origins. The chapter complicates an understanding of imperial practices as imposing (or failing to impose) a modern sensibility about the earth and its proper relationship with humans by suggesting how the British explorers and their Naxi guides came to be engaged in a mutual search for the origin of the rhododendron in "the vast mountain of Shílo." Although these participants most certainly misrecognized each other's aims and motives at almost every turn, they ended up making an interleaving set of relations with the earth that cannot be reduced either to acts of resource-making or to resistance to those acts. Nor can they be easily reduced only to competing, conflicting, or consensual relations among humans, for the nonhuman actors (plants, mountains, the earth itself) in the story also exert their influence. Although a modernist frame of mind might seem to deny this possibility, a closer look shows multiple contexts in which the human and nonhuman participate in establishing overlapping and hybrid engagements. The modernist settlement thus gives a context for alternative engagements with the earth that both contrast and intersect with a concept of resources.

In chapter 7, Courtney Childs, Huong Nguyen, and Richard Handler— the former two recent graduates (2005) and the latter an anthropology professor and administrator at the University of Virginia (UVA)—connect the politics of "diversity" as a covering term for race, race relations, and racial discrimination to the temporality of the American university, with its model of progress through enlightenment principles of reason and learning. They draw on the work of anthropologist Bonnie Urciuoli on the corporatization of the university and the role of "diversity" within that process. The spatial and temporal dispositions of race are articulated through a language of "diversity as a resource" that helps to place race in a progressive temporal framework that alternately recognizes the links between UVA and slavery and racism in the South and works to erase that history. The concept of resources thus allows for certain ways of framing the university's history, future, and relation to the future lives of the students. Such a framing appears to address the eradication of racism and segregation and at the same time allow for their continuing reproduction.

Paul Eiss's chapter explores the place of resources in the construction of el pueblo in Hunucmá, Yucatán, Mexico. More than simply "the people," el pueblo defies easy definition as it transcends (and unites) place-based, communal, and political identity. Eiss argues that resources are central to the construction of el pueblo in all its senses via a rhetoric of possession. Paradigms of possession, dispossession, and repossession have long been and continue to be critical to el pueblo as a framework of collective belonging, loss, and possible future redemption. A wide variety of resources, in different historical moments, have been substrata for the definition of el pueblo. In recent decades, after the decline of commercial and subsistence agriculture that had made woodlands the most valued communal resource, history itself—whether in the form of historic buildings, the experience and narration of labor struggles, language, tradition, or tales of a virgin's miraculous deeds—has come to be the preeminent resource. Within this context, residents contemplate the manifold possibilities of el pueblo's material, spiritual, and political repossession and of their own re-possession by el pueblo.

In her chapter, Karen Strassler examines the debates about history that took place in Indonesia in the aftermath of President Suharto's resignation in 1998. Focusing on public debates about history rather than on professional historical practice, Strassler argues that documents were conceived as resources to be conserved for the benefit of future generations and mined for the production of new, more "modern" histories based on "authentic" evidence. From the fetishization of Supersemar—the missing founding document of the Suharto regime—to the search for authentic documents that might prove Suharto's manipulations of history, documents were imagined to anchor historical interpretation to authentic, originary sources. At the same time, the production of "public archives" through popular practices of documentation and the "art" of newspaper clipping would generate a more participatory, pluralistic history. As resources of the post-Suharto historical imagination, documents seemed to promise a means to secure the temporal, progressive continuity of the nation by establishing more credible narratives about the past and a more democratic future history.

Resources engage questions of generativity, progress, modernity, risk, hope, and decline; they are saturated with time. Our assumptions about and management of time, meanwhile, inflect how we perceive and govern resources. On the one hand, senses of temporality are often embodied and materialized in and through resources. On the other hand, resources are experienced through assumptions about temporality. Studying these interconnections shows us the ways in which temporal affects, teleologies, and experiences of the past, the future, and "modernity" imbue resource-making and resource imaginations, as well as the ways in which these temporal qualities are immanent in the material world. At a moment when the complacency of unfettered resource-making projects itself is becoming the object of nostalgia and fear of a future defined by the lack of resources grows more immediate every day, understanding the ways in which resources and time bleed into each other becomes urgent indeed.

Notes

1. Quoted in Maass 2005.

2. See, for example, ASPO USA 2007; Goodstein 2004; Lovins et al. 2005; Maass 2005; Roberts 2004.

3. The word *resource* derives from the Latin *resurgere* (to rise again).

4. At the same time, of course, resources are often valued as forms of wealth in and for themselves. For instance, it is true that oil derives its value from the fact that it makes other things go, but it has come to have its own value (of which one expression is price per barrel) that is, or at least appears to be, independent of its ultimate uses. The futures markets that develop around the expected prices for particular commodities exemplify this process (Miyazaki 2003b).

5. Describing Kalimantan, Indonesia, in the 1990s, where loggers, miners, and others spearheaded a new "resource frontier" in the rain forest, Anna Tsing tells how "the wild loggers had introduced the new practice in the area of writing one's name on trees—to claim the tree to hold it or sell it to a logger with a chain saw before somebody else did" (Tsing 2005:61).

6. The current debates over the future of the oil economy are a good example. Many seek to downplay or negate the present or future depletion of petroleum resources.

7. This aspect of our genealogy raises the question of how resources are different from property. It could be argued that in the case of resources, there is always an implied movement beyond appropriation. Resources come from somewhere, but they are also *for* something, thus engaging a sense of (spatio)temporal movement. Property,

in contrast, seems to halt at the moment of appropriation. Furthermore, the argumentative weight of property lies more in its relation to the production of persons and society than in its ability to provide engine or energy for future productive processes (Hann 1998; Maine 1986[1864]; McPherson 1962; Pocock 1985; Strathern 1999). These ideas are also engaged in resource-making projects but may be less clearly emphasized.

8. One issue that arises here is whether Marx intended to describe the production of wealth through the mixing of labor and nature as a particular feature of capitalism (and the resource imaginations and resource-making that go along with it) or whether he saw this interaction of labor and nature as operating transhistorically (Postone 1993). This issue is also connected to discussions within anthropology about noncapitalist "labor theories of value," often focused especially on social reproduction in various forms (Fajans 1997; Graeber 2001; T. Turner 1995).

9. Arturo Escobar (1999) has described arrangements such as these, as well as their visible manifestations on the landscape, as "regimes of nature."

10. Of course, this idea has its own complex genealogy. For instance, in the mid-eighteenth century, the French Physiocrats based their economic system on the premise that agricultural development of land was the only true source of wealth. Their version of laissez-faire depended on the idea that the economy should be organized so as not to interfere with this basic given. Here we see an example of the idea that nature exists as the a priori ground from which wealth is produced. David Ricardo brought to the table an understanding of production as emerging from the triumvirate of land, labor, and capital. His theory of rent—the profits from the ownership of land—writes nature into the economic process from the beginning but does not treat the production of wealth from nature as a self-evident process. At the same time, as Coronil points out, "[classical political economists] came to distinguish between natural riches as invariable givens and labor as a value-creating force. For them, while the wealth of nations results from the combination of nature and labor, only productive labor could expand its existing magnitude" (Coronil 1997:31).

11. Political ecologists drawing on this tradition focus on struggles over resource use and conservation primarily in the global South (Blaikie and Brookfield 1987; Brosius 1999; Cruz-Torres 2004; Gezon 2006; Guha 1990; Peluso 1991; Stonich 1993; Squatriti 2007; Watts 1998).

12. One area where these two philosophical options get played out is in debates between social constructionists and sociobiologists/essentialists (compare Hacking 1999).

13. Emily Martin and others have critiqued this approach on the grounds that it reduces all possible forms of agency, human and nonhuman, to that of a self-maximizing

economic individual and thus "allows room for only one kind of being, who resembles all too closely a Western businessman" (Martin 1995:272).

Other ecologically minded scholars have taken a markedly different approach, rejecting the "anthropocentrism" of both capitalist and socialist exploitation of nature and arguing for nature's "intrinsic value," outside of its uses for humans (Dobson 1990; Eckersley 1992; Gorz 1982). Ecofeminists have argued for the development of more "womanly" engagements with the nonhuman world, because they are more egalitarian and participatory (Plumwood 1986).

14. Paulson, Gezon, and Watts 2003 provides a useful overview of genealogies and recent developments in the field of political ecology.

15. The OED attributes this use of *resource* to the 1770 correspondence of Edmund Burke.

16. The potential quality of resources is evident here as well, for the more completely resources are exhausted, the less security and legitimacy they furnish for the collectivity itself.

17. The process of claiming resources, it should be noted, has been integral to constituting the political for a long time, although what counts as politically constitutive wealth has changed over the years. For instance, we might see the royal treasury, tribute, the right of coinage, and other fiscal practices as integral to the medieval European state. This category expanded to include substances "in the ground" and land as sources of wealth, emerging more clearly by the eighteenth century (the arguments of the Physiocrats being an expression of this shift). Taken together, these helped to create the domain of "nature" as a source of wealth, which both needed to be managed by and helped constitute the state. It is at this point that the word *resource* is linked to "the support of a country."

18. The appellations *indigenous* and *native* place some people and not others as mediators between the natural and the social, with clearly political implications (Conklin and Graham 1995; Krech 1999; Nadasdy 2005b). As Tania Li has discussed the process or constitution—and self-constitution—as indigenous can be intimately involved with claims over resources. She describes how particular Indonesian communities come to be "positioned" and "articulated" as "indigenous people" and others do not. Li argues that the competition and contestation over resources, and their potential benefits, are what help motivate others to define and communities to consider themselves "indigenous" (Li 2000). In this volume, chapters by Eiss, Lowe, and Nadasdy touch on these questions.

19. Timothy Mitchell's discussion (2002) of expertise as a tool for state formation and management in nineteenth- and twentieth-century Egypt provides a good example of the ways in which states deploy expert techniques to arrange particular forms of

activity into a "national economy." Central to this notion of the economy is that of the progressively more expert exploitation of natural resources.

20. For a fine example of the role of "efficiency" in the forging of political legitimacy, see Hays 1959.

21. Nation-states, we note, are not the only polities to be evaluated this way. As Childs, Nguyen, and Handler show in chapter 7, the contemporary American university is judged, in part, on its ability to manage the resource of "diversity."

22. See Marshall Berman's account of Faust the developer, who harnesses the profitless energy of the earth in the interest of production, as a modern protagonist (Berman 1982:60–71).

23. To a great extent, the anthropological literature on time can be traced to Durkheim's discussions of the cultural embeddedness of temporality (Durkheim 1994[1912]; Gell 1992; Munn 1992). It has examined how the experience and perception of time has been nestled in and produced through ecological conditions (Bourdieu 1963; Evans-Pritchard 1940), modes of production (Bloch 1977; Thompson 1967), ritual (Geertz 1973), and linguistic practices and ideologies (Irvine 2004; Parmentier 1985, 2007; Whorf 1956). As the field developed, it moved beyond an assumption that the absence of a linear, progressive sense of time signaled atemporality or detemporalization, to a richer analysis of multiple and overlapping temporalities both "within" and "between" particular cultural contexts.

24. Indeed, Kevin Birth describes the difficulties in studying time in everyday life: "Cultural conceptions of time do not lie by the side of the road waiting for an ethnographer to wander by and pick them up" (2004:70).

25. This tendency exists in productive tension with a conservationist tradition that values the protection of "wilderness" from human use. Leo Marx traces this idea brilliantly in his essay on the counterpoint between industrialism and the pastoral ideal in nineteenth-century America (2000[1964]). Indeed, in nostalgic appeals to an Edenic nature that is outside humankind, the temporality of nostalgia is linked to that of planning and progress, just as conservation (Bugbee 1974; Cronon 1995; Slater 1995) is linked to resource-making.

26. James Tully has pointed out how Locke's arguments were used in the New World to justify the European appropriation of native lands: because nature was given to humans for their use (defined especially as agricultural cultivation), Indians had not established a right to their lands, for they were not actualizing them as resources in a proper manner (Tully 1993).

27. Leo Marx describes Joseph Addison's papers on the "pleasures of the imagination" as "in effect an aesthetic corollary to Locke's system." Addison prefigures the attitude taken by Edward Ferrars in finding most beautiful a landscape with "frequent

plantations, that may turn as much to the profit as to the pleasure of the owner" (L. Marx 2000[1964]:94).

28. This tradition emerged to some extent as anthropology began to take seriously not only the politics of its own past but also the implications of colonialism and capitalism as social formations (Asad 1987; Cooper 2005; Cooper and Stoler 1997; Dirks 1993, 2001; Mintz 1985; Stoler 1985, 2002; Wolf 1982).

29. In the lead article for the forum "Futures We Envision" in *American Ethnologist,* Jane Guyer (2007) points to similarities in monetarist and evangelical views of the future, in particular, the evacuation of the domain of the "near future," which Guyer identifies as the domain of planning and reasoned expectation. The linking of these separate epistemological traditions is especially fascinating, bringing together economic anthropology and anthropologists of evangelism and prophecy. In a different vein, Reinhart Koselleck describes shifts in visions of the future within the Church through the seventeenth century, when interpretations of the future became persecuted and when, with the rise of "modernity," "prognosis became the counterconcept of contemporary prophecy" (2002:18). Anthropological reflections on how views of the future are entailed in prophecy and eschatology include Florida 1995; Harding 2005; and Robbins 2004.

30. For this reason, the labor of bringing nature into the social world is more evident in the first three chapters, for instance, through theories of prediction (as with oil), through the presumed life span of substances (as with silver and minerals), or through bureaucratic practices (as with wildlife). In the following chapters, the labor entailed in resource-making is less immediately evident because it takes other forms: walking through the landscape, discovering new species, the labor of documenting and determining racial "diversity" as a resource, or preserving, archiving, and manufacturing significant documents. Seeing these activities as forms of labor at the meeting point of the natural and the social allows us to see making and imagining resources in new ways.

2

Depleted Futures

Anticipating the End of Oil in Oman

Mandana E. Limbert

The elevator in the building where a wealthy businessman works breaks one day as he gets in. The elevator falls several floors, and the man inside is seriously hurt. He is rushed to a hospital and for several days remains in a coma while we, the viewers of the soap opera, follow the adventures of his family as they vacillate between shock at the prospect of losing him, tension over the inheritance, and anxiety as they search for a briefcase full of money that he had had with him and that mysteriously disappeared. Several days later, the man awakes from the coma but apparently does not remember anything that has happened in the last thirty years. In the next several episodes, viewers follow the businessman's awe at the incredible buildings and infrastructure that have become Oman today: roads, cars, schools, the gold doors of a bank, enormous new mosques. Everything is a shock to this man, who has just "woken up" and cannot believe that what he sees is "real."

In the spring of 1997, as I was conducting fieldwork in the pre-Islamic, walled oasis town of Bahla in the interior region (al-Dakhiliya) of the sultanate of Oman, this popular Omani soap opera (*halqa*) aired on national television. The soap opera, which I watched with my hosts every night during its airing and discussed with our neighbors every day, drew on, tapped into, and explored recurrent themes about Oman's sudden oil wealth and the massive infrastructural transformations that this wealth enabled. As the soap opera made explicit and literal, people often describe Oman's dramatic transformation from isolation and poverty to wealth and prosperity over the last thirty years as Oman's "renaissance" and as "unbelievable." Are all the changes since oil was discovered in 1967 and Qabus bin Said al-Bu Saidi became sultan in 1970 real? Or is this a dream? Will all this apparent wealth and infrastructural glamour disappear, like the briefcase, as mysteriously and suddenly as it appeared?

This chapter explores the doubts evoked in this soap opera and suggests that there is widespread uncertainty about Oman's prosperity and future—uncertainty produced not only in the experiences of the unevenness and failures of development but also in the sense of fleeting, undeserved, and sudden wealth, as well as in a popular understanding, encouraged by national proclamations and initiatives, that oil resources are limited. Not only might the briefcase never be retrieved, but the glamorous infrastructure might disappear as well. Oil reserves, state-run sources have been telling Omanis for at least twenty years, will be depleted in twenty years, a constantly forward-moving and, for many, threatening horizon.[1]

Instead of a set stage in a teleology of progress spurred on by oil wealth that has either succeeded or failed, the present in Oman is understood as temporary and the future as unknowable, bleak, or, for the optimistic, redemptive. The uncertainties evoked by the television series complicate, as well, scholarship on discourses and policies of development and developmentalist states. Although much of this writing has encouraged anthropologists to consider the ways in which everyday encounters with "development" are marked by failings, these failings are often understood as the breakdown of or inequalities produced from development projects that continue to inhabit a discursive field of teleological progress. What struck me as unique in Oman was that development discourses there did not follow neat teleological models of progress. Indeed, the Omani case offers insight into a developmentalist state that presents a different temporal trajectory, one that presumes, or threatens, an end and encourages surprises instead of an unlimited and progressive future. In Oman, and perhaps other oil-rich states, instead of a utopia, the future portends to be a dystopia, where oil reserves are depleted and the golden age of the present has evaporated. States, development policies, and citizens often produce and assume multiple and, at times, contradictory temporalities, sometimes tied to the exploitation of natural resources, often linked to shifts in rule, and, of course, sometimes presumed to follow teleologies of progress and modernization. However, whereas most states, especially authoritarian ones, presume to hold the power of knowledge over a deferred utopian future (Eiss 2002b), other states and their development discourses may encourage not only mysteries, miracles, surprises, and uncertainties but also a deferred possible dystopia.

It should be noted that in Oman, temporal uncertainties about prosperity are accompanied and enhanced by uncertainties about leadership and the potential revival of a theocratic regime. On the one hand, as an example from fieldwork below illustrates, the sultan himself has no heir (although rumors about mysterious sons persist). Although a constitutional provision regarding his successor in the eventuality of his demise has been established, the content of the provision is still a mystery. On the other hand, Oman's past form of theocratic government, based on Ibadism (a third distinct branch of Islam after Shi'ism and Sunnism), remains an imagined, and in some cases hoped-for, future. It is what could be called a preserved possibility. Unlike Shi'ism and Sunnism, in Ibadi political philosophy, the leader of the Muslim community need not be a direct descendant or a member of the tribe (the Quraysh) of the prophet Muhammad, opening the way to a more profane and accessible form of religious governance. Similarly, unlike Shi'ism or Sunnism, in Ibadism, the theocratic state is understood to exist in one of four conditions of manifestation and can, depending on particular political and religious contexts, shift from one to the other, making transition into and out of theocratic rule relatively more available than in most interpretations of Shi'ism and Sunnism.[2] Therefore, although current revivalist discourses in Oman intersect at times with transnational Islamist movements that demand social piety and call for the establishment of an Islamic state, the language of revival in Oman more often draws from memories and understandings of local history and political philosophy. The last Ibadi imamate lasted from 1913 to 1955 and is part of the living memory of many Omanis. In fact, at the beginning of 2005, thirty-one Omanis were arrested, convicted, and then pardoned for plotting to reinstall the Ibadi imamate state.[3]

This chapter, therefore, focuses on the sense of disquiet in Oman, the oil economy that underlies Oman's transformations, and the temporal sensibilities it engenders. It examines also the tension between the negation of oil as a source of infrastructural transformation and the recognition of its finitude, the tension between oil's absences and presences. Paradoxically, oil as a source of transformation is obscured in the official press by an emphasis on the sultan's "miracles" as the primary source and origin of Oman's dramatic late-twentieth-century development, even though oil continues to be projected to end. This contradiction, I argue, enables the glorification of the sultan's miraculous abilities in transforming Oman from poverty to prosperity while deflecting blame from him in the future, when oil reserves are depleted and Oman is no longer wealthy. At the same time that official publications and state-run media downplay Oman's oil as enabling the transformations in the country's prosperity beginning in the 1970s, personal memories and experiences, not surprisingly, continue to remind many Omanis of the links between the establishment of the modern Omani nation-state, the discovery of oil, and the beginnings of "development" (*tatawwur*). The violence of border conflicts and oil discovery and the increasing dependence on and material transformations available through remittances from family members working in the oil industry are hardly separate from the history of modern Oman after 1970, no matter how much the official press ignores these issues. This connection with oil, however, is a connection of instability, ephemeral relations, and limits— all combining to help produce the unease, and uncertainty, about Oman's future.

After exploring the discourses that obscure Oman's oil-generated prosperity and emphasize its future depletion, I focus, in the second half of this chapter, on three examples from my research that highlight some of the future-oriented concerns, doubts, and expectations shaped by the uncertainties of this petro-state. Such examples can hardly come to represent the opinions of an entire population, but as instances of future-oriented comments and actions, they reveal shared yet somewhat different sensibilities about Oman's prospects and history. These three instances include a wealthy man's cynical personal project teasing his nation's and his family's supposed sense of secure opulence, another man's statements about the mysterious possibility of the genealogical continuity of rule in the face of near-certain discontinuity, and, finally, an elderly woman's sense of historical contingency. These examples highlight the different ways in which the future is understood (as possible return and as structured by surprise), and the complex ways in which the past serves as a "preserved possibility" for the future. The present "dream" of Omani prosperity is punctured, therefore, not only by nostalgia for and memories of a simpler and yet difficult past but also by the constant presence of horizons, both the contingent and, as Freud once wrote, the uncanny, the anxiety aroused by the feeling of the secretly familiar.

PRESENT FUTURES

From Walter Benjamin's attention to the fleeting and transitory to David Harvey's exploration of time-space compression, the temporal dimensions of modern life have long and variously fascinated philosophers and scholars of modernity. Indeed, recent scholarship on the temporality of development discourses as a manifestation of this modernity has also highlighted the "myth of permanence" associated with urbanization, modernization theory, and development models in general (Ferguson 1999), as well as the ways in which life-cycle stages—birth and maturity—have served as metonyms for national development, discursively relegating the developing world to the status of the "immature" (Gupta 1998; Ludden 1992; Manzo 1991) and setting the world along a linear teleology. This chapter draws from such attention to temporality in developmentalist states and discourses but considers a situation in which there is no myth of permanence—not to mention a linear teleology—in the first place. Instead of emphasizing permanence, the present is often structured as anomalous or temporary, whereas the past, in its various forms, remains a preserved possibility. Similarly, unlike the optimism characteristic of classic discourses of nationalism, what Anderson has called the "future perfect" and Herzfeld has argued is central to "monumental time," pessimism and the unknowable mark expectations of Oman's future.[4] This case suggests, too, that if life-cycle stages serve as metonyms for national trajectories, then one ought to consider the discursive workings not only of birth and maturation but also of death. It is precisely the impermanence of oil—its finiteness—that emerges as central to official declarations and personal expectations of the future.

Official declarations about the limits of oil, on national television and radio and in state-run newspapers in Oman, are accompanied, to be sure, by attention to economic diversification through the development of LNG (liquefied natural gas) projects, aluminum smelters, tourism, real estate, and fertilizer and petrochemical plants, as well as by growing national proclamations and local incentives regarding saving water, learning to sew, and accepting manual labor. These calls may be interpreted as continued faith in the teleological model whereby "modernization" could be said to be attainable and sustainable through diversification, neoliberalism, and a shift to increased economic privatization. As a *Times of Oman* article from the beginning of October 2003 noted, these kinds of projects "hold the key." Although they hold the key, presumably, to continued prosperity, the outcome is uncertain: one may hold the key, but whether the key fits the lock is another matter. Indeed, instead of producing a sense of security and future prosperity, these calls for and statements about diversification and privatization seem to have produced, among many Omanis at least, the opposite—either the expectation of poverty or the assumption that the future is unknowable. Modernity thus becomes less an irrevocable and penultimate stage in a teleology of development than a contingent and bounded era.

What are the everyday implications of this future-oriented sensibility that is either pessimistic or resigned to the unknowability of the future? And how does this future-oriented sensibility shape understandings and experiences of the present? The expectation of an oil-less (and sultan-less) future could be interpreted as apocalyptic (Baudrillard 1994; Stewart and Harding 1999), as producing a "state of emergency" (Berlant 1996), as entangled in disciplinary technologies and economic conditions that tame chance (Hacking 1999) and manage risk (Mason 2007), or as a future-oriented antonym of the experiential and psychological conditions of "hope" (Crapanzano 2003; Miyazaki 2003a, 2003b). Indeed, as the soap opera suggests, "dreams" not only are the expression of wishes and desires (the psychological rather than metaphysical orientations of hope, as discussed by Crapanzano) but also are signs, if not of the "unreal," then at least of the impermanent or transitory. Although I agree that the production of uncertainty can help manage and discipline Omani expectations, I would also suggest that such uncertainty should be understood as intertwined with distinctive temporalities and historicities. Rather than as part of a linear narrative of progress that has either failed or succeeded as a sensibility produced as a mechanism for disciplining neoliberal subjects, this is a temporality structured around and understood as one of miracles, the secretly familiar, and surprises, as well as limits and ends.

MIRACLE OF THE RENAISSANCE

Omani school textbooks, histories, and the press herald Sultan Qabus bin Said's 1970 accession to power as ushering in Oman's modern era, the "years of the renaissance."[5] To give a sense of the transformations attributed to the new regime, oft quoted statistics cite that between 1970 and 1980 the number of modern schools increased from 3 to 363, the kilometers of asphalt roads increased from 6 to 12,000, and the number of hospitals increased from 1 to 28. Although some of the contours of this discourse have shifted over the years, official speeches, newspaper articles, television programs, and textbooks (all part of the highly controlled media) continue to extol the great abilities of Sultan Qabus in providing modern infrastructure to Oman. Indeed, the introduction to the sultan's royal speeches notes: "The success that has been achieved in Oman during the years of the renaissance amounts to a miracle. It is the achievement of the leader, and his people guided by the wisdom and determination of His Majesty Sultan

Qabus bin Said" (Ministry of Information 1995:5). The overdetermined quality of the sultan's personal abilities in transforming Oman is evident in the official press and much scholarship about Oman.

The time from Sultan Qabus's coup d'état in July 1970 to the present is officially known as the *al-nahda*, often translated into English as "renaissance."[6] The use of the notion of al-nahda to mark a shift in history is not original to the Qabus era or to Oman. Influenced by the Salafiya movements elsewhere in the Middle East, Ibadis also used the notion of "the awakening" in the nineteenth century (Hoffman 2001; Wilkinson 1987: 152–153).[7] The awakening of the nineteenth century, however, unlike that of the late twentieth century, was specifically one of religious revival aimed at synthesizing and explaining features of Ibadism for both Ibadis and non-Ibadis (Wilkinson 1987).[8] And while in other places in the Arab world in the second half of the twentieth century, eras referred to as al-nahda tend to be associated with literary and intellectual revival, the contemporary Omani renaissance tends to be associated with industriousness, cosmopolitanism, piety, and seriousness of purpose. These cultural traits, said to have been awakened by the renaissance, operate in collusion with discourses of development that promote private enterprise and hard work, deemphasizing the politics and violent histories of oil exploration and the sultanate's unification.[9] Thus, although the notion of al-nahda is not new to Oman, to other places in the Arab world, or even to nationalist movements in general, in Oman this language has particular effects—obscuring the place of oil and the wars that oil exploration entailed in the formation of modern Oman.[10]

Nahda suggests awakening, rising, growth, and revival—both a beginning and reentrance into the "real" and "true" spirit of Oman after a time of sleep (or coma) and darkness. The metaphors of waking and sleeping continue to play out in Sultan Qabus's statements, in the official press, and in the popular media, as the soap opera described at the beginning of this article illustrates. Although the notion of the present as a time of reawakening marks many official temporal structures, discourses such as those articulated in the soap opera, where there is much disbelief at the changes, raise the possibility that the present might be the awakening's opposite, a time of sleeping and dreaming, in which the future might be the real, awakened return to poverty.

The trope of sleeping, dreaming, waking, and the *almost* unbelievable also nicely colludes, I would argue, with the Omani state's investment in a discourse about the "miracle" of success: only in a dream, as only by a "miracle," could Oman have changed so dramatically, so quickly. The surprising quality of a miracle echoes the surprises found in a dream; the ultimate inability of humans to control miracles (which are gifts of God to individuals) is similar to generally accepted notions in Oman that humans do not control dreams and that dreams are not symbolic of people's unconscious struggles, worries, desires, and memories. Rather, dreams are often gifts of God or manipulations of the devil. As the excerpt from the introduction to Sultan Qabus's speeches (cited above) suggests, the dramatic changes in Oman—more than an outcome of oil—are more often than not portrayed as due to a miracle. This downplaying of oil as the *source* of the dramatic transformations in Oman since 1970 is similar as well to what Fernando Coronil (1997) describes as the "magic" of the formation of the Venezuelan nation-state. For Coronil, the magic of the Venezuelan state is both its appearance as a unified whole and its apparent ability to turn oil into progress, somehow without productive labor. In Oman, the "miracle" is the sultan's singular (and unified) ability to produce progress, without productive labor or oil.

This "miracle" is furthered by the personalization—and thus apparent unification—of the state in the figure of the sultan. The unification of state apparatus and bureaucracies in the figure of the sultan, as Coronil also noted in regard to Venezuela, obscures the messiness that is "the state," making the state seem more powerful and coherent than it is. One obvious example of the personalization of the Omani state is the placing of the celebration of Omani National Day on Sultan Qabus's birthday in the Gregorian calendar. The first National Day was celebrated on the one-year anniversary of the coup, July 23, 1971. Since 1972 and the second National Day celebration, the event has been marked in November, on the sultan's birthday.[11] In his fourth National Day speech, Sultan Qabus himself noted, "On this immortal landmark day, four years ago, a new sun shone in our beloved land to light the flame of the national spirit and zeal of our citizens." Marking this day on the sultan's birthday, rather than on the political event of the coup, July 23, 1970, has significant symbolic effects. The investment in the person of the sultan and his ability to provide for the nation discursively makes the "miracle" easier—an individual is more likely than an entity such as a state to call for a miracle. This investment also reveals Sultan Qabus's sense that he has made an immortal mark on Omani history. Obscuring its political history, the modern state appears more as a miracle of birth than a product of history.

Despite this emphasis on the sultan's singular powers, oil could hardly be erased from national and personal experiences, memories, and representations. Oil in the mid-1990s accounted for about 80 percent of Oman's

total national revenue (al-Yousef 1995).[12] Similarly, the territorial boundaries of and regions included within modern Oman were established in the
aftermath of a series of oil wars. From the first oil concession given to the
famous D'Arcy Exploration Company in 1925 until the beginning of crude
oil exportation in 1967, Oman witnessed two major wars directly connected
to oil: the Bureimi War in the early 1950s, which was a border war between
Saudi Arabia, the Emirate of Abu Dhabi, and Oman, and the Jebel Akhdar
War in the mid-1950s, which pitted theocratic Ibadi imamate forces against
the British-supported sultan, who was attempting to "protect" oil exploration teams entering imamate territory (India Office Records Archive,
R/15/6/185; R/15/6/186).[13] Both wars are retained in local memory and
continue to mark the landscape of interior Oman in particular. For example, in Bahla, as people describe their life stories, they often refer to where
they were (in what field or in what house) when British planes bombed the
town fort. As I toured mud houses recently abandoned in favor of cement
ones, people often showed me where they used to hide weapons during the
fighting in the 1950s. And as I collected descriptions of the various neighborhoods, people often reminded me that one of the neighborhoods was
built by and made up of people who had fled the neighboring town of
Tanuf, which was completely destroyed in the British bombing campaign.
Finally, Bahla's destroyed fort, which sits on a hill in the middle of town,
overlooking palm groves, continues to stand as a testament to the bombing
and the war.

The 1950s, however, was not the first time that oil exploration and territorial expansion figured into Omani politics. Sultan Said bin Taimur, the
father of the current sultan, had already in the 1940s discussed with British
diplomats the possibility of the sultan's taking control of imamate territory
for access to potential oil fields. Although oil was not, the story goes, actually discovered in interior, northern Oman (excluding the Bureimi oasis)
until the late 1960s, it was earlier expected that oil might be discovered. In
1946, when rumors reached Muscat that Imam Mohammad bin Abdullah
al-Khalili, Ibadi imam from 1920 to 1954, was severely ill, Sultan Said bin
Taimur and British diplomats considered attacking the area. In a telegram
from the government of India at New Delhi to the secretary of state for
India in London on March 10, 1946, the political resident wrote:

> Access to Oman's hinterland has been denied for too long and
> opportunity of opening it for development of oil and other
> resources, which extension of Sultan's control would provide, is
> too good to be missed. We therefore support proposal to supply

> Sultan with 1000 rifles (and ammunition), six (point 3 inch) mortars and four machine guns.[14]

This 1946 proposal to supply and subsidize the sultan's arms purchase was not ultimately realized, however, because the sultan insisted that to venture into interior Oman, he would need support from the Royal Air Force (RAF), which London and New Delhi refused at the time (India Office Records Archive, R/15/6/242).[15] This refusal, as well as the imam's recovery, led the sultan to abandon these plans, at least until the imam died in 1954.

The establishment of modern Oman, through the Bureimi and Jebel Akhdar wars, thus meant the collapse of the theocratic imamate administration and the incorporation of imamate territory into what was first called the Sultanate of Muscat and Oman and then, under Qabus, the Sultanate of Oman. Many people in the town of Bahla, especially those connected to the religious administration, supported the imamate forces in 1954 against the arrival of oil exploration teams "protected" by the sultan. Bahla's incorporation into the Sultanate of Muscat and Oman after 1955, when Bahla and other towns in the region surrendered to the sultan's troops, makes this history particularly relevant locally.[16] References to the imamate administration and to the Jebel Akhdar War, which continued after 1955 when guerrilla fighters moved into the mountains and continued to fight oil exploration teams and military personnel sent to protect them, underlie many personal actions and comments about the imamate in Bahla. This imamate history, which has partially propelled the drive to insist on a new, more or less independent imamate administration, is never far from popular imaginings about the future.[17] Indeed, the history of the imamate remains a preserved possibility and a model for what might happen in the future. And the finite nature of Oman's oil supply makes the past viable as a model for the future in a way it would not be if modernity were seen as irrevocable rather than contingent and limited.

Access to potential oil fields and the incorporation of Oman into the sultanate from the mid-1950s marked a major shift in the establishment of modern Oman. But it should be noted that it was the Dhofar War in southern Oman, starting in 1965, that, in addition to the beginnings of oil exportation in 1967, brought an end to Said bin Taimur's reign and paved the way for the establishment of the bureaucratic and state structures of today's Oman.[18] The Dhofar War, unlike the previous two, was the least overtly connected to oil exploration.[19] Nevertheless, the possibility in 1970 that the Marxist Dhofar rebellion was expanding north to the former imamate territory, where most of the oil fields were located, provided ample reason for the oil companies and Britain to support a change in government.[20] A new government could quell the rebellion in Dhofar militarily and diminish opposition in the north, it was argued, by providing "development."[21]

Probably suspicious of his fate, Said bin Taimur—after sending his son to the British military academy at Sandhurst—attempted to limit his son's relations with British advisers, restricting him for the most part to the palace in Salalah, the capital of the southern Dhofar region. Eventually, on July 23, 1970, Qabus bin Said, with the support of British intelligence, overthrew his father. Said bin Taimur was flown from an RAF base in Salalah to Bahrain and then to England, where he lived at the Dorchester Hotel until his death in 1972.[22] With this coup d'état, "a new era" is said to have begun in Oman.[23] This new era was and has continued to be constructed in direct opposition to the preceding regime, situating its distinctiveness against the supposed "backwardness" and "isolation" of that era.

Oil retains a place locally and nationally not only through the memories of these wars but also through conversations about fluctuations in price and the government jobs and job searches created and destroyed by these fluctuations. As with many other rentier states, the government is by far the primary employer of Omani nationals.[24] The oil-state requires a bureaucracy to manage the extraction and export of oil; oil wealth itself has enabled (and relies on) the massive expansion of state bureaucracy in Oman since 1970. By the middle of the first decade of the 2000s, oil had reached $95 a barrel, but in the mid- to late 1990s, oil fluctuated between $13 and $25 a barrel. Indeed, in 1996, in the aftermath of a decade of oil price volatility, the government embarked on a comprehensive economic reform program whereby "11,000 civil servants were retrenched, no general salary increase was granted, and defense expenditures were cut by 2 percent of GDP" (International Monetary Fund 1998). Such measures seemed to be felt immediately; word of a few vacancies in the Royal Oman Police ended, according to "rumors" in Bahla, in a small but rare riot outside the recruiting headquarters.

Oil is also present, of course, through the experiences of those working in the oil industry and through discussions, official and otherwise, about Oman's relatively small and limited supplies. Population estimates for Oman vary, as do employment figures and the percentage of Omanis working at Petroleum Development of Oman (PDO), Oman's semiprivate national oil company. After the government, PDO is the second largest employer of Omanis in the country and holds 90 percent of the country's oil reserves (Alexander's Gas and Oil Connection 2003). According to PDO's 2003 annual report, it had a "net total" of 3,648 Omanis on its payroll, making up about 80 percent of the entire staff.[25] Considering Oman's population of about 2.5 million people, however, 3,648 is not a large number to be on the national oil company's payroll.[26] Other "downstream" oil-related work, including jobs in gas stations, is dominated in Oman, as elsewhere in the Gulf, not by "nationals" but by people from the Indian subcontinent.

Rather than through personal experience in the oil industry or even remittances from family members in the oil industry, many Omanis experience oil in other ways—that is, not so much through direct connection with the oil industry as through government jobs that the rentier state produces and through emblems of wealth and glamorous infrastructure, sometimes within reach and often beyond. Indeed, oil fields are located in the desert, far from villages and towns. Oil is transported to the capital through underground (and sometimes sleek overland) pipes, with signs along the way indicating potential danger. At the port in Muscat, a clean white container holds oil to be shipped abroad. A second refinery is being built, but until now there has been only one refinery in Oman, in the Muscat harbor and limited to domestic consumption. Oil, in other words, provides few tactile reminders of its presence and is often experienced instead as wealth: as the gold doors of a bank, roads, schools, and shopping malls.

In addition to histories of war, uncertainties produced by price fluctuations, and the ephemeral quality of oil, Oman's limited reserves and supplies, in particular, and official and personal discussions about them have helped shape the complex sensibilities about oil and about the future. Oman produced approximately 365,000 barrels per day (bpd) between 1967 and 1980. With the discovery of new fields in the 1980s, production rose to about 700,000 bpd by 1990. By 2000 production reached 940,000 bpd, but it returned to 743,000 bpd in 2006. Compared with Kuwait's 2.5 million bpd and the UAE's 2.4 million bpd, not to mention Saudi Arabia's 9.5 million bpd, Oman's oil production is relatively minor (Platts 2007). Oman is also struggling to maintain this output because, as an article from *Middle East Economic Survey* recently noted, "the major fields reached plateau production prematurely and other fields did not compensate for the loss" (*Middle East Economic Survey* 2002). Similarly, with "proven reserves" at about 5.5 billion barrels, a quick calculation of a 700,000-bpd projection provides for twenty years of oil, a number that has continued to be employed in discussions of Oman's future prospects.

From my first trip to Oman in 1995 to the present, acceptance of the finite nature of oil has been commonplace; after recognition of the great strides the sultan made in transforming Oman, many of my conversations with government officials began with the acknowledgment of Oman's limited supplies. Indeed, although making headlines in the *New York Times* as a scandal, it was no surprise to many Omanis when, in April 2004, Royal Dutch/Shell, the largest private shareholder of PDO (with 34 percent), announced that "the figure for proven oil reserves in Oman was mistakenly increased in 2000, resulting in a 40 percent overstatement" (*New York Times*, April 8, 2004). When I asked a friend who works in PDO about the news report, he responded, "Yes, we know. We've all known for a long time. This is nothing new." This "knowledge" became widespread common sense not simply because of distrust of the government's discourse about "progress" but because of the state's own feats of "preparation" and statements in local newspapers and radio programs about uncertainties and limited supplies.

The tensions between oil's absence and presence, its visibility and invisibility, and between dreams and realities, past and present, help shape some of the uncertainties and expectations of the future as they become evident in people's personal comments and actions. These understandings about the finitude of oil combine further with uncertainties about rule and about the contingent or the possibly cyclical nature of historical processes. The living memory of pre-oil and pre–Sultan Qabus days, as well as acknowledgment of and continued pronouncements about limited supplies, provides a complex ground, not only on which different engines of state produce national sentiments of shared progress and simultaneously its foreclosure, but also on which people interpret and understand the nature of their personal and national futures.

PALM-FROND HUTS

On my first visit to Oman, in 1995, I had the occasion to meet, through an especially helpful military historian living and conducting research in Muscat, an outspoken, engaged, and distinguished businessman, Kamal Abdulredha Sultan. The military historian directed me to him because Mr. Sultan was a thoughtful, unofficial spokesman for an important Shi'ite community in the capital and might be able to arrange for me to visit the community's walled and self-regulated neighborhood. Also, he was particularly interested in Oman's history. Although Mr. Sultan did not question the official representations of Oman's "renaissance," he was very much interested in drawing attention to Oman's "true" history—a history that could not ignore the three wars of the second half of the twentieth century that had accompanied, but did not parallel, transformations in rule and that were, to varying degrees, about establishing national boundaries and control over oil territory. For Mr. Sultan, however, "history" was less concerned with exploring these turbulent pasts than with tracing more distant dynasties, as well as the migrations, economic endeavors, and social lives of Oman's cosmopolitan communities.

When I returned to Oman to conduct fieldwork for my dissertation in 1996 and 1997, I went to visit Mr. Sultan again. This time, we had a longer conversation. As we sat in one of the beautifully and elaborately decorated rooms of the wood-engraved, silently air-conditioned, and marble-laden mansion (of a style that one might associate more with India than with the Arabian Peninsula) that overlooked a lush back garden, a servant brought us piles of fresh fruit. We began talking. Mr. Sultan hailed from a family of merchants who had made their fortune in a trading firm in the nineteenth century. The firm's partners had included an American, a Scot, and an Indian Omani. The firm imported kerosene to Oman and exported dates to the United States, as well as dried fish and pomegranates to India. At the beginning of the twentieth century, the Omani partner inherited and bought his partners' shares. As Oman's fortunes declined in comparison with other Persian Gulf states, Mr. Sultan's family—like other merchant families—solidified its businesses in Kuwait. Drawing on family connections throughout the region, in the pattern of successful merchant families throughout the Gulf, his family took advantage of shortages and surpluses to build the firm into one of the most important in Oman. The family, although not wealthy by today's standards, was certainly well-off with respect to the rest of the Gulf and especially Oman. The family lived in the walled Shi'ite neighborhood of the commercial capital, in coral and gypsum buildings, and had maintained its position since at least the nineteenth century as one of the most important business families in Oman.

In our conversation, as I continued to try to obtain his family history—at the time, I believed it to be the most interesting aspect of our meeting—Mr. Sultan insisted on returning our conversation to the problems of the country's young people, their ignorance about the past, and the country's dangerous lack of economic diversification. This discussion was one I had become familiar with during visits to Oman and seemed to be a repetition of commonly held notions. Since my first visit to Oman in 1995, I had engaged in many conversations about Oman's youth, their disrespect for and ignorance of the difficulties of the past, and their inability to grasp the threats of the future. I therefore attempted to change the course of our discussion back to his family's history. Besides some basic facts about his family and the history of his business, however, Mr. Sultan would not give way and again returned our conversation to Oman's youths and uncertainties about the future. With no choice but to give in to his insistence on returning to these questions, I soon came to understand the degree to which the past and these questions were intensely resonant for Mr. Sultan, as well as the ways in which they spoke to a complicated relationship with "development" and "progress."

Indeed, as we continued talking, Mr. Sultan's commitment to the legacies and fate of his country became more evident. As president of the Omani Historical Association, he was certainly interested in Oman's past and believed that an understanding of it was critical. Catering primarily to English-speaking expatriates (with a nostalgic love for Oman's austere beauty) and "Zanzibaris" (Oman's Swahili-speaking, cosmopolitan intelligentsia with historic connections to East Africa), the association brings together visiting scholars, local history buffs, and, less often, university professors. Similarly, Mr. Sultan had written a number of editorials for both English- and Arabic-language newspapers about problems he saw with the national education system, students' lack of knowledge about their past, and the possibility of mass tourism eroding Oman's unique and pristine historic sites. Because public expression of discontent in Oman is often either subtle or subdued, these editorials were especially strong statements of doubt. As I left his house that day, he handed me copies of these editorials, with pages of the deleted or censored portions of the articles stapled to the back, another small act of defiance.

In addition to his interest in the past and his outspoken, editorialized concerns about the future, Mr. Sultan made a direct and symbolic statement about Oman's fate: he had a palm-frond hut, known as a *barasti*, in his lush back garden. Barastis, which thirty years previously were found all over coastal Oman, were by then relatively rare. If not rejected as happily forgotten signs of Oman's past poverty, they were beginning to become incorporated into Oman's growing heritage industry. What struck me about this rebuilt barasti, however, was not so much Mr. Sultan's attention to national traditions, for he had already demonstrated his keen interest in history, but his conscious claim about the future and his own family's place within it. He had the structure built because, he said, "That is where we came from and where we will be returning."

Within the confines of the marble- wood- and bougainvillea-laden mansion, this past form of dwelling stood in stark contrast to contemporary luxuries. The past ("That is where we came from") was simple, earthy, and rugged; the present appeared luxurious and opulent. This stark contrast between the barasti and the marble mansion, however, was not only one of before and after. It was also, as Mr. Sultan explained, one of now and after, conforming to a logic of return. The *now* in this construction is the temporary and anomalous state of wealth between the eras of poverty, reminding me of the representations of sleeping and waking evident in the soap opera and reversing the language of rebirth, renaissance.

Also evident in Mr. Sultan's presentation of the barasti as both past and future for Oman was an effacing of class in favor of an essentialized vision of Omaniness. Certainly, what qualified as "we" in such a context was ambiguous. Mr. Sultan's family had never lived in a barasti and was extremely unlikely to do so in the future. With the suggestion that "we" all came from and will return to the same poverty and simplicity, today's *supposed* equality—that is, that Omanis are all wealthy—was being projected into an image of a future equality of a "simple" life, a life without oil wealth. Mr. Sultan was equating his family's prospects with the nation's. Unlike other personal and national quests for connections with Oman's past, this was not simply a nostalgic rendering that kept the past at a comfortable, even if tenuous, distance. Rather, this hut was constructed precisely in anticipation of the future. As an anticipatory project, it was also pedagogic, mostly for the youth and probably for Mr. Sultan's own children, who would not remember the general (or their own family's) hardships of the preceding era and yet could or should expect to be "poor" again. Seen another way, this businessman was constructing not so much a "space of hope"—unless religious salvation and redemption necessarily come with a return to a poor and simple life (some in Oman who tend to advocate the return of the imamate argue that they do)—but rather a space of doom. He was placing the constructions of the spaces of hope and doom into a cyclical historical timeline, not a teleology of progress.

PERHAPS HE HAS A SON

While Mr. Sultan was making a statement about his expectations about Oman's future prosperity, other national uncertainties—about Sultan Qabus's mortality—were being addressed officially and locally. In September 1995, just after my first trip to Oman, Sultan Qabus was in a serious car accident. One of his closest advisers, Qays Zawawi, died in the accident. Another British companion, Air Marshal Sir Erik Bennett, was slightly injured (*Sunday Times*, September 17, 1995). As was his custom at the time and in a publicly acknowledged act of self-reliance reminiscent of King Hussein of Jordan's propensity to fly jets, Sultan Qabus drove his own car rather than rely on a driver. Sultan Qabus's survival sparked some demonstrations in his support (and, it was rumored, in "celebration" of the adviser's demise). The near-fatal car accident, however, was also an all-too-real reminder of the sultan's mortality and, it is generally assumed, lack of an heir. As a result of this accident, in November 1996 the government, in a surprise move, issued a constitution providing measures for the period after the sultan's demise.

I had just moved to Bahla several months before and was living with my hosts in their large new cement house on a plot that a decade earlier had primarily been agricultural land belonging to the husband's family. Such shifts in the structural conditions of personal living spaces and the unevenness with which these shifts took place were constant reminders of the speed and inequalities of Oman and Bahla's transformations. I was in my upstairs room one afternoon, taking notes from my morning conversations and waiting for everyone to conclude their afternoon prayers, when there was a furious knock at my door. Knocks at my door were generally much more tentative and much lower on the door frame, usually from one of the children coming to call me downstairs to join the family. But as the knock was somewhat more forceful and much higher on the door frame, I instinctively threw on a head scarf, which I had been asked to wear during my time in Bahla, and went to the door. To my surprise, one of the older sons of my landlord was standing there. In this religiously conservative household, it was extremely unusual for an adult male to come to my door. We were both suddenly very uncomfortable.

Agitated, Majid suddenly and without the perfunctory salutations said, "Have you heard? There has been a coup, the government has changed!" Like most people in Bahla at the time, my hosts did not have satellite television or access to the Internet. Their (and my) main source of "news" was national television, radio, and newspapers, as well as rumors that flew all over the country, from the town of Salalah in the south to Muscat and the Jebel Akhdar Mountains, through family, mosques, the local market, and women's neighborly visiting groups. International radio news supplemented national news. Because Oman is hardly the focus of much international coverage, local and national events had to be gleaned from other sources. Apparently, the afternoon programming of cartoons had been abruptly cut short. An official newscaster made a statement that a very important message was to be announced by the government. In a country where "nothing happens," this kind of announcement probably fueled thousands of instant stories. Indeed, the announcement was so unusual that it propelled Majid to jump in his car, drive from his own house in one of the new suburbs of Bahla to his father's house, over horribly rutted dirt roads within the old walls of the town, and knock on my door. We hurried downstairs, where everyone was gathered solemnly and seriously around

the television, which had suddenly transformed from a source of back-
ground noise and entertainment for children into a source of serious information that might determine their collective fates. My landlord, also in
unusual fashion, stood almost directly in front of the television with his
hands clasped behind his back, waiting for new information.

It soon became clear that there was no coup. Majid had been so
excited about "any news" that this unusual interruption had clearly fed his
imagination about the implications of the announcement. Indeed, it seems
that Majid had so anticipated some sort of end that he had preempted it.
Instead, the television newscaster announced that the government was
propagating a constitution, the first in the nation's history, and that this
constitution was going to provide, among other things, provisions for the
eventuality of the sultan's demise.[27] The constitution was going to be
called, according to the newscaster, the "White Book" and was going to be
made available to the public the next day. When the national newspapers
printed articles about "the White Book" the next day, the mystery of the
future was only partially solved. Although the constitution consists of
eighty-one articles in seven chapters, covering topics from "Principles
Guiding State Policy" and "Public Rights and Duties" to the Oman Council
and the judiciary, it was on the particular question of succession—article
5—that many conversations in Bahla focused. According to the constitution, the future sultan had to be a male descendant of Sayyid Turki bin
Sa'id (r. 1871–1888), effectively disqualifying the descendants of both the
Zanzibari branch and any imamate past of the al-Bu Saidi dynasty. At the
same time, it was announced that the sultan had written the name of his
intended successor in a sealed and secret envelope and that the envelope
would be opened at his death. The successor would have to be approved by
the Council of Ministers, an appointed body of advisers to the sultan. If an
agreement could not be reached, the military would take control of the
government until a decision was made. Thus, on the one hand and at least
in theory, the line of succession was clarified. On the other hand, the name
of the future sultan, hidden in a sealed and secret envelope, fueled further
mysteries and, not surprisingly, conversations.

One evening, a week after the constitution was made public, as I was
sitting in the family room with my hosts after dinner, we began discussing
the provisions for the future as laid out by the new constitution. Usually
limiting his references to the sultan to unadulterated praise, my landlord
added, "Only God knows what will happen. Maybe Qabus has a son. We did
not know that his father, Sultan Said bin Taimur, had a son. So perhaps
Qabus bin Said also has a son, too." On the one hand, this comment was

one of the more hopeful suggestions I had heard during the week of speculation. The words were geared at continuity and made in the face of no evidence that the sultan did in fact have an heir. On the other hand, the comment rested on the acceptance of mystery, surprise, and uncertainty. Omanis had not known that Sultan Said bin Taimur had a son, so it was likely that they did not know whether Sultan Qabus bin Said had a son— the continuity of mystery. Rather than rejecting the state's production of mystery in its secret-envelope succession policy, my landlord was creating his own new mystery: a secret son.

At the same time, it should be noted that my landlord, although extremely loyal to and supportive of Sultan Qabus, was also rumored to have been supportive, like most people in Bahla, of the theocratic administration during the imamate (as opposed to one of his brothers, who enjoyed telling me how he fought, unlike the vast majority of Bahlawis, on the side of Sultan Said bin Taimur). Although the majority of Bahlawis would not necessarily actively support a returned imamate in the near future, depending on conditions, they and other Omanis know that it is a possibility. My landlord's comment, therefore, instead of signaling an actual belief in the possibility of a hidden son, suggested not only that God alone knows the future but further that teleologies of progress (or their reversals) cannot be predicted. Although Mr. Sultan had suggested a cyclical history, my landlord suggested that surprise, if not exactly an acceptable foundation of rule (he had opposed Said bin Taimur's approach), was integral to its particular formation in Oman.

AFRICA

While the businessman was preparing his children for future poverty and while the circulation of the white book both quelled and fueled questions about the future of political rule in Oman, Fatima, an elderly woman who lived across the street from me in Bahla, made explicit her understanding of the contingent nature of wealth and history. One day in June 1997, I went to visit her. I enjoyed visiting Fatima, and after our greetings, as always, we sat down on the plastic floor mats in her sparsely decorated cement room. We began, also in customary fashion, to drink our coffee and eat our dates from a tray in the corner of the room prepared for such visits. Quite unlike Mr. Sultan's marble mansion and my hosts' larger, carpeted, and enclosed house, Fatima's house was an example of some of the more common post-1970 forms of dwelling in Bahla, with plastic mats covering the cement floor and external access to the various rooms. Fatima, like many Bahlawis, had lived in East Africa as a child. However, unlike other Bahlawis with connections to East Africa, Fatima had been born on the East African mainland (rather than on the island of Zanzibar) and continued to speak Arabic with an accent discernable and generically recognized as "African." Unlike my hosts, who were understood to be Arabs, Fatima was from a servant caste (*akhdâm*); her father, who was from Bahla, was a descendant of slaves from East Africa. Omanis had been traveling to East Africa for centuries. In the nineteenth century, not only did Oman establish direct rule over Zanzibar, but also the Omani sultan moved his entire court there, temporarily making Zanzibar the capital of the Omani Empire. Earlier and nineteenth-century migrants from the Arabian Peninsula to Zanzibar tended to be from the coast, becoming part of the "Creole," Swahili-speaking elite. In the early twentieth century, thousands of poorer Omanis from interior regions such as Bahla migrated, looking for seasonal work, trading opportunities, and fertile land. In the early twentieth century, members of both groups, Arabs and servants, traveled from Bahla to East Africa, to Zanzibar in particular. Not surprisingly, many of the men married other Arabs, Creole Omani Zanzibaris, and Omani descendants of slaves. Some people, like Fatima, were the children of unions between Omani men and mainland African women. This connection with East Africa, however, came to an abrupt end in 1964, when, during a revolution in Zanzibar, thousands of Omanis—both Arabs and servants and mostly living in rural areas of Zanzibar—were killed or forced to flee.

Although I knew that Fatima had some East African connection, as many people in Bahla did, I did not know much more. I was curious. So on this visit, I asked Fatima to describe her childhood and what she remembered about her arrival in Oman. She began by explaining that she was the daughter of a Sudaniya, or black woman, and a Bahlawi man who had traveled to East Africa as a trader and had married her mother. "This was before the war, when parts of the East African mainland were German," she added. She did not mention that her father was *khâdim* (servant) but signaled this status through her description of the neighborhood from which he hailed; at the time, neighborhoods in Bahla were segregated along caste lines. "When my father died, my mother couldn't take care of us," Fatima said. "She was by herself, and her family didn't want her children, children of an Omani." Fatima's mother, she explained, then gave her children to an Omani family to raise. When Fatima reached puberty, in the 1940s, she was married, also to a Bahlawi man. Her husband, Fatima explained, wanted to return to Bahla and asked her whether she would be willing to go. Fatima described her thoughts as she tried to decide whether or not to go with him to Oman: "I talked to the women in the house, and they didn't think I should go. They thought I was crazy to go. They kept saying, 'Why would you agree to go to Oman? There was nothing there. Life will be very difficult. You will spend all your time carrying wood. There is no rain there.'" This, of course, was before oil was discovered in Oman and when the east coast of Africa provided work and money to Omanis; Oman at this time was considered the place to leave.

Fatima explained that after hearing all the opposition to her departure, she decided in the end to follow her husband to Oman, where she was, admittedly, miserable. By this time, other women from the household had joined us for coffee, dates, and conversation. Fatima described her trip to Bahla—how several people died on the way, how hot it was, how she did not know how to ride the camel that served as their transportation, and generally how uncomfortable she was. The other women shook their heads in agreement and understanding, saying, "Poor things." When she arrived in Bahla, because she did not speak Arabic, her neighbors did not respect her. She said that Bahla itself was quite awful: hot, dusty, and dangerous. Africa, in contrast, was a place where it rained, where fruit and food were everywhere, where the earth was fertile. It was, after all, the place to which Omanis had migrated from their drought-ridden and fly-infested towns. But, she said, eventually Bahla became her home.

I then asked her whether she ever returned to Africa to visit her family. Wasn't it difficult, I asked, to leave everyone? Her two brothers had remained there. Her mother was there. Her adoptive father and family were there as well. Fatima said that of course it was difficult but she had also asked herself what she would have done if she had remained in East Africa. She would have had to find someone else to support her. Besides, she was already pregnant with her first child. She then explained that she had returned once to East Africa several years before. But by then, most people she had known as a child had died. She did, however, see her brothers. Made by car and airplane rather than camel and boat, this trip was much easier. When I asked her what it had been like to go back, she said that she would not go back again: "It was good to see my brothers, but it was not my home. The lights would go out; it was dangerous; it was dirty. I was scared." Fatima then paused and said, "Who would have guessed that one day Oman would be rich and Africa would be poor?"

The surprise at the historical turn of fortunes was provoked not only by the outcome but also by the suddenness of the turn. She and most people she knew, she suggested, would never have imagined that Zanzibar and what became Tanzania would appear so poor and that Oman, which had been a place of poverty her entire youth and much of her adult life, would become prosperous. It was the suddenness of this transformation that was especially shocking and surprising. In ten years, roughly between 1965 and 1975, the paths of Tanzania and Oman seemed to move in opposite directions. With her comment, Fatima was expressing a sentiment common among many people over thirty-five years of age: one cannot predict historical processes. Just as one could not have known that Oman would one day be rich, we cannot know what Oman will be in the future.[28]

CONCLUSIONS: THE GLORIFICATION OF THE PRESENT

Although asphalt roads, luxury goods, schools, piped water, and wealth are recurrent themes of modern Oman, Omani discourses of development and resources in which these themes are placed reveal a paradox: their finiteness. Further, this finiteness is not something that the state hides in promises of infinite progress. Rather, it is something that continually reappears, in a continually forward-pushed twenty years. Twenty years, that ever-pushed-forward date for the end of oil, is significant. It suggests that this potentially bleak or redemptive future will come soon—but not too soon, not tomorrow. Although this future will arrive in the lifetime of today's children, its repercussions may not necessarily be devastating for those who have had the full benefit of living during the "renaissance." Thus one should be aware, and might even prepare, but perhaps need not worry so much as to hamper the pleasures of today.

In light of this expectation in Oman, as perhaps elsewhere in the Gulf and the Arabian Peninsula, it often seems, to me at least, as though much of the construction of monuments, much of the language and many of the images in school textbooks, in newspapers, and on television—that is, the official structures and discourses about change—do not have so much, or not *only* so much, to do with attempts to produce a national sentiment about the past for the present or even for pride of progress. These constructions are also entangled in expectations of the future. In fact, I believe that in Oman much is built for the future, a future that is expected to be without oil. Of course, appeals to tradition are always to some extent a way of securing a future, but such appeals are usually done to contain a future of progress, not a future in which the past could return. In other development states, appeals to a traditional past often seek to contain progress and modernity. Here, however, it is not that a future is contained through these invocations of the past but rather that the past is resurgent and the future appears as a return. Therefore, the experiences of today should also be understood through the eyes of the future. In Oman, that future memory will attribute this age to the figure of a sultan who miraculously produced oil wealth without the oil but at the same time cannot be blamed for a future in which this natural resource no longer exists.

When a wealthy businessman in the capital region builds a palm-frond hut in the backyard of his mansion, saying that it is there to remind him where he came from and where he will one day return, when an elderly man suggests that the sultan might have a mysterious son, and when an elderly woman in Bahla is continually amazed at the strange twist of fate that suddenly made Oman rich and Africa poor, it certainly seems that uncertainty and pessimism, rather than continued development and progress, form the starting point for people's understandings of the present and expectations for the future.

Notes

1. It seems to me that this "twenty-year" deferral is precisely the kind of forecasting that might be considered a "near future," a temporal frame that Jane Guyer (2007) has suggested has been evacuated in recent years. The near future, Guyer argues, has been replaced by a focus in macroeconomic and evangelical discourse, as well as in anthropology and public rhetoric, on either the "immediate" or the long term.

2. For some English-language studies of Ibadism, see Ennami 1972; Hoffman 2004; Lewicki 1971; al-Maamiry 1980; and Wilkinson 1987.

3. Although the thirty-one people arrested were found guilty and sentenced to prison terms ranging from ten to thirty years, the sultan pardoned them, and they were freed.

4. See Anderson 2003a for his reflections on what would happen to nationalism with a shift from optimism to pessimism.

5. This year, often given in the Gregorian calendar rather than the Hijri Islamic calendar of 1390, is the beginning of the new era. The Gregorian calendar, popularly called the English calendar, has become an increasingly standard way of marking the passage of time, especially particular national events.

6. This particular naming was not immediate. In the first years after the coup, Sultan Qabus used the term *new era*. He first referred to the post-coup era as al-nahda in a speech given on the fourth National Day, November 18, 1974.

7. The Salafiya revival movements emerged in the nineteenth century, particularly in Egypt and Saudi Arabia. The name derives from the word *salaf*, meaning "ancestors of Islam."

8. The Zanzibar Press of Sultan Barghash (1870–1888) helped this synthesizing and explaining. Scholars began publishing commentaries, in particular on "classic" Ibadi texts, as well as encyclopedia-type compendiums, the most famous of which is the

Kitâb al-Nîl by the North African scholar 'Abd al-Aziz bin Ibrahim al-Thamini (d. 1808). The *Kitâb al-Nîl* continues to be popular in Oman.

9. This renaissance is not only a time of awakened industriousness; it is also a time of progress and development (tatawwur). As Ferguson (1990) has illustrated, development is an "anti-politics machine." In Oman, discourses of development are antipolitical, in the sense that changes are simply part of the reawakening of a sleeping spirit of industriousness and hard work and therefore are nothing new or threatening. But with the de-emphasizing of oil's place in the production of the unified state, the history of war and the imamate tends to fade away from the history of the emergence of modern Oman.

10. For a general discussion of a similar rhetoric of light and dark in Indonesian nationalist writings, see, for example, Anderson 1990:241–270.

11. This is not to argue that the sole and intentional purpose of changing National Day celebrations to November was to personalize the role of the sultan as the unified state. I suspect that a large motivating force was the extreme July heat and the departure of many of the Omani elite, the diplomatic corps, and many foreign managers for the summer. Nevertheless, the point here is to suggest that one of the *effects* of this move was to consolidate the image of the state into the figure of the sultan, mystifying both the dependence on oil (and the productive labor necessary to extract and export it) and the various and complex aspects of the state.

12. This percentage is of course variable because it is tied to the price of oil, among other things. In the 1980s, oil accounted for about 95 percent of total revenue; in the 1990s, about 80 percent of total revenue; and in 2006, according to the *Kuwait Times*, about 65 percent of total revenue.

13. The question of the boundaries of Muscat was raised with regard to possible oil exploration in 1934. In a message from Major C. E. U. Bremner, political agent in Muscat, to the British resident in Bushire (Iran), Bremner expressed concern about oil concessions and therefore where to draw boundaries between states and tribal areas. In 1936 British diplomats disagreed over which towns were included in Muscat territory. The political agent in Muscat, Major R. P. Watts, stated that the territory included the area between Musandam at the Straits of Hormuz and Sohar on the coast, 240 km north of Muscat—that is, Khor Fakkan and Fujairah, two towns in what has become the United Arab Emirates. Tom Hickinbotham (British Consul to Muscat) disagreed and drew the boundaries as they are today.

14. These British officials clearly did not expect that taking control of the interior would require much weaponry.

15. Organizing the arms subsidies was an important feature of British relations with Oman. On this occasion, the following was decided: "List price of this equipment is

roughly Rs. 120,000 but we consider that as in case military stores recently supplied to Afghanistan list price should be reduced by 50%, difference of approximately Rs. 60,000 being shared by His Majesty's Government and Government of India in same proportion as Muscat War Subsidy, namely 45:55. We propose subject to concurrence of London Munitions Assignment Board to release equipment from stocks held in India." This file also makes clear that British officials in London were anxious that the requests for arms and personnel support appear to come from the sultan and, further, nothing that all military advisers had to be British be written: "With regard to question of obtaining an undertaking from Sultan to obtain advisers in future solely from British sources, His Majesty's Government are anxious that no written agreement should be made which might later be used against His Majesty's Government as an example of interference in sovereignty of an independent State." (India Office Records Archive, R/15/6/242)

16. For a fascinating account of the sultan's campaign to take control of the interior region, see Morris 1957.

17. A "cell of terrorists" arrested in Oman in 2005 was not, as first announced, tied to al-Qaeda. Rather, members were predominantly local scholars from interior Oman who had allegedly formed a group aimed at fomenting unrest and the reestablishing of the Ibadi imamate,

18. In 1967 Oman exported 57,000 barrels per day, with the average price of oil in 1967 about two dollars a barrel. From 1967 to 1970, oil production increased annually, reaching 332,000 barrels a day. In 1971, however, oil production declined. According to Hughes (1987), it was uncertain how much more oil would be discovered. A new field was discovered in 1972, however, and with prices rising with the OPEC oil embargo in 1973 (although Oman is not part of OPEC), Omani GNP increased from OMR 81,800,800 in 1970 to OMR 445,700,700 in 1974. See United Nations Statistics Division 2007.

19. Oil exploration provided ripe fodder for Marxist rebels, who could denounce the labor policies of the multinational corporations that organized oil exploration on behalf of Sultan Said bin Taimur and then Sultan Qabus bin Said. For leftist accounts of the reasons for the continuation of the Dhofar War after 1970, see the 9th June Studies booklets of the Gulf Solidarity Committee, such as "Oman: A Class Analysis," "Oil and Investment in Oman," and "Documents of the National Struggle in Oman and the Arabian Gulf," as well as the committee's quarterly publication, *Gulf Solidarity*. These supporters of the Dhofar rebellion argued that the coup d'état resulted in the formation of a working class that was in the service of the oil companies, as well as under the control of "traditional" tribal rulers who could perpetuate feudalistic control over the population. For another account of the Dhofar War, also from a Marxist perspective, see Halliday 1974.

20. See Peterson 1978:202.

21. Halliday states that "the outbreak of guerrilla war in the Omani interior on 12

June, 1970 spurred the Shell oil company to urge action on the part of the British" (Halliday 1974:288).

22. I would not want to speculate on whether it is simply coincidence that the Omani coup was on July 23, the same date of the Nasserist coup in Egypt earlier in the century. For an account of the coup, see Peterson 1978:201–204.

23. In fact, in his first public statement after the coup d'état, Sultan Qabus announced that the first thing he would focus on would be the establishment of "modern government."

24. For a detailed analysis of the relationship between oil economy and shifting forms of state bureaucracy, see Chaudhury's 1997 analysis of Saudi Arabia. Chaudhury argues that "the oil revenues of the 1970s created new channels through which resources circulated within the bureaucracy, rendering extractive and regulatory agencies obsolete and reorienting bureaus toward the distributive branches of government" (1997:141). My point here is not so much about the form of the bureaucracy, whether emphasizing extractive, regulatory, or distributive branches, or the relationship between this form and new and old social classes, but rather to highlight how the formation of the modern Omani state is imbricated in the history of oil exploration and exportation. For a study of state formation and oil in two other Persian Gulf states, see Crystal 1990. Jill Crystal, a political scientist, examines the ways in which oil allowed for the continuation of monarchic political systems in Kuwait and Qatar, even though merchants, a once powerful group, were no longer part of the ruling coalition. Crystal argues that with oil, rulers were no longer dependent on local power structures for support. According to Crystal, revenues coming from oil and through the exigencies of multinational corporations freed rulers from local political obligations and thus from merchants. The "state" in this formulation is composed of a "ruling family." My interest in state formation and oil centers instead on the effects of oil's simultaneous omnipresence and discursive disappearance.

Furthermore, although the "ruling family" is important in Oman, as it is in Qatar and Kuwait, Oman has a more extensive and expansive bureaucratic structure. John Davis's (1987) work on the combination of oil economy and leadership cult in Libya provides a nice parallel to the Omani case.

25. Instead of hiring Omanis or non-Omanis, PDO has increasingly relied on contracts with private labor companies. According to PDO, in 2003 it "provided work for an additional 12,000 contracted staff, of whom more than half are Omani" (Petroleum Development of Oman 2003).

26. Dale Eickelman makes a similar point in his essay "Omani Village: The Meaning of Oil" (1983).

27. For an analysis of the constitution, or Basic Law, see Siegreied 2000.

28. I wish to thank Christine Walley for her insights on this aspect of this project.

3

Rocks of Ages

Temporal Trajectories of Mexican Mined Substances

Elizabeth Emma Ferry

Guanajuato is a small central Mexican city, capital of the state of Guanajuato. One substance mined in Guanajuato—silver—is generally considered a "nonrenewable natural resource." Other substances, mineral specimens—the rocks one sees at gem fairs, at new age boutiques, and in the collections of the Smithsonian and other museums—are also mined in Guanajuato. These rocks are made up of similar, although not necessarily the same, mineral compounds as ore-bearing rock, occur side by side with it, and are extracted at the same moment and by the same people. Yet mineral specimens are rarely talked about as "nonrenewable natural resources." What are the effects of this difference? What happens when one calls something a resource?

In this chapter, I look at what it means that these very similar kinds of objects participate in different social and cultural processes that value one as a resource but not the other. I am especially interested in how different experiences and perceptions of time are associated with each substance and how these temporal frames affect their status as resources or as something else. This perspective helps us explore how the concept of "resources" emerges within a particular political and social context that entails certain consequences for the experience and structuring of time. I also examine how acts of resource-making (and unmaking) produce certain temporal effects. By examining the emergence and divergent paths of two types of mined substances from Guanajuato, Mexico, and the temporalities associated with each, I hope to shed light on some of the conditioning factors and consequences of the concept of resources.

The very notion of "resource" and what it presupposes may entail certain kinds of temporalities. In a speculative vein, let me propose that to call something a resource is to (1) imagine ways of profiting from it—that is, to see it as a repository of potential use-values (and often also exchange-values);[1] (2) "objectify" it—that is, to make even intangible, ephemeral, or virtual resources into objects that can be measured and transacted (see Handler 1991 for a discussion of "objectification" in the context of languages of property); (3) view it as at least potentially "scarce"; (4) presuppose a particular relation between humans as exploiters of resources and "nature" as the ground from which resources are exploited; and (5) thus imagine a fundamental separation between humans, "nature," and the resources that emerge in an encounter between the two. These entailments of the idea of resources tend to suggest a certain kind of temporality, one that is linear, continuous, measurable, and finite.

The particular paths taken by objects classified as resources engage particular temporal and spatial understandings: these objects make spatial and temporal "paths" (Giddens 1995) or "maps" (Gell 1992) as they move. Of course, as Nancy Munn and others have pointed out, "in a lived world, spatial and temporal dimensions cannot be disentangled, and the two commingle in various ways" (Munn 1992:94). However, in this chapter I focus especially on *temporal* dimensions by examining the emergence and divergence of these paths.

TEMPORAL WORLDS AND VALUE-MAKING

Anthropological studies of temporality have drawn especially on Durkheim's revised Kantian rationalism, which emphasizes the social origin of temporal understandings, and on Bergson's (via Schutz's) distinction between time as lived duration and time as abstract, periodic system. In some cases, they have argued that the distinction between "primitive" and "civilized" cultures lies in the absence or presence of abstract forms of time reckoning and/or temporality.[2]

Some anthropologists have focused on temporality as a defining feature of a particular cultural worldview (Farriss 1987; Geertz 1973; Whorf 1956). Others have described the interaction of multiple forms of temporality in different contexts, such as Evans-Pritchard's counterpoint between structural time and ecological time (1940), Maurice Bloch's 1977 critique of Geertz's essay "Person, Time and Conduct in Bali" (1973) on the grounds of a separation between ritual and nonritual communication, Kevin Birth's discussion of the political uses of multiple temporalities in Trinidad (1999), and Sharon Traweek's ethnography of the competing temporal frames within which high-energy physicists conduct their careers (1988).

We also find, especially within those areas of anthropology influenced by Karl Marx, an emphasis on the rootedness of temporal understandings in particular material-social relations of production, of which a prime example is E. P. Thompson's 1967 article on time, space, and industrial work-discipline (see also Bloch 1977; Bourdieu 1963; Giddens 1995; Rigby 1983). These studies tend to focus especially on time reckoning, sequence, and techniques of historical narrative-making rather than on the relation between the past, present, and future that I focus on here (although Pierre Bourdieu's discussion of peasant temporalities is a notable exception).

In many cases, as Giddens has pointed out, they also rely on assumptions of evolutionism, on the one hand (that successive historical ages are characterized by particular temporalities rooted in relations of production), and functionalism, on the other (that aspects of particular societies, including temporality, are best examined in light of the social functions they fulfill) (Giddens 1995:14–25). My analysis of the temporalities associated with the extraction and circulation of mineral substances seeks to recapture the materialism of these approaches while avoiding the foregone conclusions associated with both evolutionary and functionalist perspectives.

Questions of memory and the production of history have been a central concern for anthropologists over the past two decades, but the future and related concepts and categories have been relatively ignored. Munn's remark that "anthropologists have viewed the future 'in shreds and patches,' in contrast to the close attention given to the 'past in the present' (a title evoking a whole field of study)" (1992:115–116) still holds true, at least in part. In the 2000s, in reaction to increasing attention to global movements of capital, labor, commodities, and so on, several anthropologists have begun to examine the role of the future, especially in market capitalism (Guyer 2007; Maurer 2002; Miyazaki 2003b; Miyazaki and Riles 2005; Zaloom 2004). These scholars have found an ethnographic arena from which to critique still-taken-for-granted understandings of the market as a virtual meeting place of "rational actors" and to examine hope, failure, risk, and other future-oriented concepts. Building on these recent discussions, I address the circulation of commodities on which markets are at least partially based, thus reintroducing a material perspective with the aim of unpacking the cultural construct of "the future" in different contexts. I argue that the material conditions and qualities of minerals and ore make certain temporal constructions and experiences more likely and thus reinforce certain social and political consequences. I am not making a determinist or even, strictly speaking, causal argument; rather, I attempt to take seriously the idea that the material and the social are produced together or that, as Webb Keane has recently put it, "signs are not the garb of meaning" (Keane 2005:182).

MINING AND TIME

The mines of Guanajuato, Mexico, some of Mexico's most spectacularly productive in the colonial period (Brading 1971; Villalba 1999), have produced both ore (especially silver, but also gold, copper, zinc, lead, and antimony) and mineral specimens. How do the different trajectories of ore and mineral specimens affect the understandings of time, its passage, and the links between the past, present, and future of those who come into contact with them (producers, distributors, and consumers)? What can examining these temporal frameworks tell us about resources and value-making? To begin with, let me lay out the counterpoint between these two substances— silver ore and mineral specimens. By tracing the paths taken by these substances, we can begin to see how they articulate with different temporal understandings.

My fieldwork among members of the Sociedad Cooperativa Minero-Metalúrgica Santa Fe de Guanajuato, or Santa Fe Cooperative, and among miners, merchants, collectors, and curators in Mexico and the United States underlies these considerations of mining and temporality. The cooperative controlled seven of the most famous and productive mines of the Guanajuato district from 1939 to 2005, when it sold its holdings to a Mexican subsidiary of a Canadian mining company. For much of its life (including the time of my longest period of fieldwork from 1996 to 1998), the cooperative had around one thousand members and was one of the largest employers in the city. In July 2005 its membership numbered just over three hundred.

Silver ore from the cooperative mines was sold to a foundry in San Luis Potosí at a set price for each of the metals contained within it (the presence of some metals is also debited from the payment). The prices of these metals are determined daily on the world market. The ore was then melted down into ingots that were transported across the US–Mexico border to Amarillo, Texas.

And then what happens? The website of the Silver Institute, a "worldwide association of silver miners, refiners, fabricators and manufacturers," states that

FIGURE 3.1

Image from the Silver Institute website (courtesy Silver Institute).

sparkling tableware, shining jewelry, and living spaces bright-
ened by silvered mirrors are the obvious contributions of silver
to our daily lives. It is, however, the silver behind the scenes that
makes our modern world function efficiently. Inside switches, silver contacts efficiently and safely turn on and off the powerful
electric current that flows into our homes, our lamps and our
appliances. It is silver under the keys of computer keyboards,
behind automobile dashboards, and behind the control panels
of washing machines or microwave ovens that switch on or off at
the touch of the finger. And inside the 220-volt line circuit
breaker boxes in our homes or inside the 75,000-volt circuit
breakers in power stations, silver performs a safe and steady task
of switching on or off our most dependable servant, electric
power, throughout our lives. (Silver Institute 2007b)

This statement, disseminated by the association that dedicates itself to
improving demand for silver, neatly expresses the dual associations of silver
as decorous and elegant substance and as material of modernity, glinting
behind electrical transformers and computer keyboards. Figure 3.1 shows
an image from the Silver Institute website to give a sense of how these associations are deployed.

In 2004, 42 percent of silver fabrication went to industrial uses, 28 percent to jewelry and silverware, 21 percent to photography, and less than 1
percent to coins and medals (Silver Institute 2007a).[3] Some people also use
silver as a safe investment strategy on account of its so-called intrinsic value,
which makes silver (and even more so gold) an effective hedge against
unstable markets. The thinking is that in the event of a crash, investors
will gravitate toward precious metals, which will thus become "magnets"
of value.

We can also make some general statements concerning silver supply. In 2004, 72 percent of silver supply came from primary mining (the other main sources were silver scrap and net government bullion sales). Mine production registered a 4 percent increase from 2003, to 634.4 millions of ounces (Moz.). Total supply in 2004 reached 879.2 Moz., compared with 768.6 Moz. in 1995. The five top silver-producing countries in 2004 were Mexico, Peru, Australia, China, and Poland (Silver Institute 2007a).

Once silver leaves the mine and foundry and enters the market, it becomes subject to new regimes of temporality, formed in and through the price-setting markets of the world. A few words about how this market works serve to give a sense of the sociality, and temporality, of the market. Silver is traded as a commodity in Zurich, London, New York, Chicago, and Hong Kong. Its most important market is London, where there is a daily "fix" price.[4] Silver can be traded in spot prices and as futures, for which the biggest markets are the New York and Zurich commodities exchanges.

Naturally, how the price of silver gets determined at any moment is extremely complicated. To give a few salient points, there are several categories of silver supply and also several categories of demand. Supply sources are generally divided into underground (primary mining) and aboveground (recycled) sources. Demand takes the form of fabrication (including jewelry, coins, and industrial inputs) and investment demand. These two sources are especially important for silver because it is considered both a commodity for luxury and industrial uses and also a "store of value."

The silver market since the 1970s has been volatile because of silver speculation, as well as shifts in fabrication demand.[5] Attempts to corner the silver market in the early 1980s, which drove the price from five to fifty dollars in less than a month, gave way to steadily declining prices in the late 1980s and early 1990s (figures 3.2 and 3.3). The price rose somewhat in the mid-1990s and then declined from 1997 through 2004. In part, this decline was due to the replacement of film and photography by video and digital media.

However, silver as an investment (both as asset and in futures trading) has grown in the 2000s. The price rose from $4.85 in 2003 to $11.57 in 2007 (London fix price). In May 2007, the monthly average price was $13.15. The April 2006 establishment of Barclays' Global Investors iShares Silver Trust Exchange Traded Fund (ETF), which has purchased nearly 138 million ounces to date, seems to have fueled this trend.

All of this happens on a very different scale than the activities of workers drilling, crushing, and smelting silver, and it seems to emerge not only

FIGURE 3.2

Annual silver prices, 1990–1999. (Silver Institute).

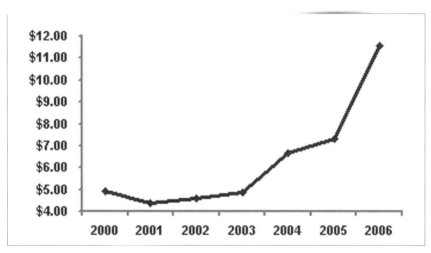

FIGURE 3.3

Annual silver prices, 2000–2006. (Silver Institute).

from a completely different space but also from a completely different time. The time of the market seems an endless blank path into the future, as suggested by the x axis in figures 3.2 and 3.3. Miyazaki's discussion of the temporalities of the market represented through futures trading provides a good example of this version of time in which there is always a future, commensurate with and comparable to the present, through the translating medium of price. Traders make their money on exploiting the gap between present and future prices, but they are able to make those calculations based on the idea that these are simply points on an ongoing x axis running off the right edge of the page.

This linear, ongoing temporality playing out on a global scale and crystallized through daily prices nevertheless intersects continuously with the lived experiences of mining companies and their workers. For instance, during the last fifteen years of the Santa Fe Cooperative's existence (1990–2005), there were periods of social and political unrest among members in 1990–1992, 1997, and 2001–2003.[6] These years correspond to the lowest points in the price of silver during that period. The line of silver prices running through the "homogenous empty time" of the Silver Institute graph touches down into the life spans of mines and the lifetimes of miners.

At the same time, although these things (and many more) can be said about the social constitution of temporal experience through the marketing of silver bullion, the substance from any particular mine is almost impossible to trace—mostly because silver ore is melted down with ore from other mines and then broken down for its ultimate uses. In fact, as I have discussed elsewhere, silver ore is valuable only to the extent that it can be melted down and mixed with ore from other sources. Its value derives at least partly from its ability to shed its own history (Ferry 2005a). In the case of silver, it is hard to apprehend the consumption phase, except through generalities.

Because mineral resources, as everyone knows, are nonrenewable, mines have finite spans of production. Every mining enterprise must calculate the amount of reserves left in the mine, based on current information about the amount of ore; cost of extraction, processing, and transport; and commodity price. These reserves are usually calculated in terms of time; a company might say that a given mine can continue at current levels of production for two years or twenty years, for example.

Of course, it is often in the interest of companies to estimate reserves generously (and sometimes in their interest to estimate them stingily, as in negotiations with unions). Also, estimates change with changes in technology, price, or transport costs. Monetary fluctuations also play a role; the strong dollar in the 1990s helped Mexican mining because mining companies were able to pay labor and other costs in pesos while receiving dollars for the sale of their product. Thus these estimates can be largely rhetorical, but they are still relied upon in production, labor, and purchasing decisions.

The finiteness of "in-the-ground" supply, technological change, and the ongoing fluctuations of demand are three of the main factors driving the silver market. The awareness that silver can run out drives silver prices, and, in fact, the successful management of scarcity is an essential part of a price-making market. As David Harvey has pointed out, "Scarcity is in fact necessary to the survival of the capitalist mode of production, and it has to be carefully managed, otherwise the self-regulating aspect to the price mechanism will break down" (Harvey 1974:272). So the experience of scarcity with respect to individual mines is carried over into the global silver market.

The combination of finiteness and fluctuation makes the life of the mine comparable to some aspects of a human life. A person has a finite life span, although that span is not known in advance and can be affected by many factors. But it is confidently asserted that no person lives forever. Indeed, in many contexts, people liken the "life" of the mine to the life of a human being, as they liken the "body" and "veins" of ore to a human body and veins.

To liken the mine to a physical, living body is to raise the question of its aging and ultimate mortality. One miner said to me, to indicate how depleted the Valenciana mine had become in his time, "When I first started working here, the mine was a little girl." The statement was spoken in a wistful, even regretful tone, recalling the mine's past rich promise and implying its current state of depletion. This sense of decline and exhaustion, coupled with a memory of past (relative) prosperity, is typical among miners in Guanajuato and among Guanajuatenses more generally. And I would venture to say that in this respect, Guanajuato is like many mining centers. From the perspective of the production site, the extraction of silver depletes the mine and hastens its demise.

One day, several months after I began fieldwork, I accompanied the Industrial Safety Team on a trip through the drainage tunnels of the tailings dump. It was late spring, and the rains were beginning. The sludgy mud of the tailings nearly reached the tops of our boots. Suddenly I fell, becoming nearly submerged and whacking my knee and wrist against a rock. My companions mocked and comforted me; this turned out to be one of the turning points in my fieldwork, as the ice was broken along with my wristwatch and (nearly) my knee. Martín, who ended up as my good friend and key informant, solemnly informed me that they should take a picture and I could use it as a frontispiece to my thesis, with the caption "The Fall of Mining in Guanajuato" (*La caída de la minería en Guanajuato*).

The specter of the "ghost town" looms over the future of many mining towns, and there are many strategies to avoid this fate, such as economic diversification, heritage tourism, migration, and so on. These strategies become necessary because mining tends to overwhelm a regional economy, ineluctably drawing subsidiary economic activity into its orbit and thus fortifying the tendency toward a particular end. The source of mineral resources is fixed and nonrenewable, so it appears that there can be only one end, which can be put off but never completely avoided. The sense of predestination, a kind of nostalgia in the future perfect tense, can lend romance and poignancy to mining centers, even in times of bonanza.

It can also appear as a threatening horizon. Mandana Limbert describes how even as oil as a source of wealth is downplayed, the sense that this wealth is fickle, transitory, and even unreal seems to pervade the consciousness of many Omanis (Limbert, chapter 2). This particular expectation of the future hinges, as Limbert suggests, on the recognition of oil as a finite resource.

Miners and others involved in mining economies deal with the inevitable depletion of the mines in various ways, by deploying metaphors of agricultural production (Harris 1988; Nash 1979) or sexual reproduction and birth (Eliade 1978; Ferry 2005a; Finn 1998), by attempting to arrange "sustainable mining" practices, or by assuming that mining will provide the impetus for a "takeoff" into modernization that will survive the loss of the mines or collapse of the market (Rostow 1960; see Ferguson 1999 for a critique of modernization theory in the context of the Zambian Copperbelt). In spite of these various reassurances, many who dwell in mining areas or depend on mining-centered economies live in the shadow of future depletion and emiseration.

Guanajuatenses also engage in these sorts of strategies. Elsewhere I have described in detail attempts by Guanajuatenses to replace *silver* with the *memory of silver* as a source of jobs and economic prosperity—that is, turning the mines and the city built by silver into a tourist destination for those who wish to see the material remains of this past (Ferry 2006). This is a common strategy for former mines, factories, and other industrial sites. Indeed, a whole sector of the tourist industry focuses on "industrial heritage tourism." A 1998 article in *Episodes*, the journal of the International Union of Geological Sciences, reviews heritage museums in Potosí, Bolivia; Almadén, Spain; and Blaenafon, Wales. The authors conclude:

> For declining historical mining areas the preparation of in-mine
> visits and mineralogical-mining museums can palliate, and in
> some favorable cases (accessibility, technologically advanced cul-
> tures, and so forth), can solve a declining mining district's eco-

nomic problems. However, taking this possibility into account ahead of time would be expedient. We therefore propose changes in the environmental mining laws in historical districts to include these new points: to include a space in-mine which will be safe for visitors and to store a good collection of historical objects. These previsions could help the future development of tertiary sectors (hotels, shops, and so forth) in often impoverished areas. (García-Guinea, Harffy, and Bateman 1998:35)

These observations were published not in a journal of museum studies, cultural resource management, or tourism but in one aimed at "the global earth-science community." They suggest a high awareness of the risks of economic devastation in the wake of mining depletion. In effect, the authors advocate preserving objects in the present in anticipation of the present becoming "history." These remarks also extend the notion of "tertiary" sectors into the future, so ancillary economic activities are seen to depend not only on current production but also on the memory of that production later on. These strategies seek to turn the past as "immanent" in the mines and other industrial sites into present and future economic security (Birth 2006).

In Guanajuato, tourism projects aimed at *patrimonio minero* (mining heritage) are often joint university–business–governmental projects. At the same time, such projects often spark bitter debates among these groups and factions within them, usually over who has legitimate claims over the past and legitimate expectations for future benefit. In the summer of 2003, when the mining cooperative I was studying seemed to be veering ever more closely to bankruptcy, both cooperative members and outside observers described how the government was "circling like vultures" in hopes of developing luxury tourism on the monumental grounds of the Rayas mine, controlled by the cooperative. In the summer of 2005, I spoke to a cooperative member, the captain of the Valenciana mine, on the phone. He told me that the government did not want to help the cooperative survive; it wanted to take over the cooperative's holdings and develop them for tourism.

In July 2005, a Mexican subsidiary of the Canadian mining company Great Panther approached the cooperative with an offer to purchase the holdings for $7.25 million. After several weeks of conflict, the general assembly voted to accept the offer, thus bringing to a close the history of Mexican mining cooperativism, at least for now. When I spoke to a historian from the University of Guanajuato who has been very involved in documenting the oral history of cooperative members, she said that members felt they had to sell in order to keep the cooperative out of the hands of the state government, which hoped to purchase the lands for tourist development at the bargain-basement price of twenty million pesos (1.87 million dollars).[7] This resentment by cooperative members of the government's interest in heritage tourism is only one of many vectors of tension over these questions.

Silver extraction in Guanajuato tends to reinforce some temporal understandings over others—a sense of the past as glorious and the future as unknowable and possibly bleak, of history as a sine curve of booms and busts written against a backdrop of linear time (as exemplified by the x axis of historical silver price graphs), and of notions of the past as a potentially valuable resource for the future, one that seems to belong to all yet is always in danger of being captured by and for particular groups. These temporalities tend to follow from the extraction of a nonrenewable resource whose profitability is governed mostly by factors external to it, such as the world price of silver, the exchange rate, and the cost and efficiency of technology.

MINERAL COLLECTIONS AND TIME

My examination of the journeys and the temporal dimensions of mineral specimens comes from a further research project on mineral extraction and circulation in Mexico and the United States. Both archival and ethnographic, this project focuses on miners, dealers, collectors, and curators on both sides of the border. Informants include miners, dealers, curators, collectors, mineral photographers, earth science teachers, mineralogists, and others.

As I discuss below, mineral specimens are much easier to trace than silver. Furthermore, specimen extraction is often both clandestine and seen as trivial in comparison with silver mining. For these reasons, in the case of silver it is hard to examine consumption, except in the aggregate.[8] With minerals, it is the moment of production that is often obscured. Individual mineral specimens can be traced to their production locales, but the details of production are hard to see clearly; the labor of production is obscured even as the labor of consumption is accentuated (indeed, fetishized; see Ferry 2005b). As we shall see, this shift from production to consumption also highlights aspects of temporal experience and its relation to power.

In Guanajuato, mineral specimens are extracted by mining engineers, foremen, and miners (usually drillers) more or less furtively because most mining companies do not allow the removal of specimens and some punish infringements with dismissal. Miners then give specimens away, keep them for their own use, offer them on altars to saints and virgins, or sell them to tourists and itinerant dealers and collectors. In the Santa Fe Cooperative, as I have noted elsewhere (Ferry 2005b), members were more freely (though tacitly) allowed to extract mineral specimens, and they often made considerably more than their wages by selling minerals. They often sold to intermediary dealers, who in the past sold by catalog and the cultivation of social and business connections. These days, dealers increasingly use the many local, national, and international mineral shows. Even more recently, they use the Internet and eBay.

Where do these stones end up? There are specimens from Guanajuato in every major mineralogical collection (although Guanajuato is by no means the most famous or spectacular producer of mineral specimens—only one of several important sites). Some of these collections are in private hands; others are in museums. Often, private collectors give or bequeath their collections to local, university, or national museums. Some of the most famous and important museum mineralogical collections are those of the National Museum of Natural History in Washington, DC (the Smithsonian), the British Museum of Natural History, the Harvard University Mineralogical Museum, the American Museum of Natural History in New York, the Los Angeles County Museum of Natural History, the Houston Museum of Natural Science, the Sorbonne, the Naturhis-torische Museum of Vienna, the Freiberg School of Mines Museum, and the Seaman Mineral Museum at Michigan Technological University.

Mexican mineral specimens surged in availability and popularity in the 1960s and 1970s. The growth of the Tucson Gem and Mineral Show, with the strong ties between Arizona and Mexico, undoubtedly fueled this trend. Mexican specimens were plentiful and cheap in this period, allowing some collectors to jump-start their collections by buying in bulk and then selling or trading for specimens from other places. Thus the investment of the Mexican state in mining helped fuel the mineral collecting market in the United States and particularly the rise of Tucson as a central place for mineral dealing and collecting.

As they travel along their several paths, mineral specimens tend to acquire complex pedigrees, trailing behind them like comets' tails. First, they should carry with them the name of the mineral locality (and preferably the mine) from which they emerged. A specimen without known locality is nearly worthless from the perspective of scientists, curators, and collectors alike. Some specimens also pass through the hands of famous dealers, such as A. E. Foote or George English, or through famous collections, such as those of Richard Rashleigh or Clarence Bement. As with works of art, these narratives of the specimen's journey (its provenance) can greatly enhance its price. Thus, unlike silver, it is often possible to trace a particular specimen's source, no matter how long it has been traveling. Mineral specimens follow different paths than mined ore, with different temporal orientations. Unlike ore, the value of mineral specimens depends largely on their uniqueness and the degree to which they can be traced to particular localities and even mines. Indeed, a mystique attaches to the distinctiveness and fragility of mineral specimens. A story from Edward Henderson, who helped curate the mineral collections of the National Museum of Natural History for many years, illustrates this point:

> I knew of a man who had a high appreciation for minerals. He was in a foreign country at a mine one day, when they were bringing out beautiful minerals, they [had] just struck a lead with some beautiful minerals. They showed him the specimens on a table, and he was admiring them—and also hoping that he would be able to buy one or get one in some way—when the boss of the mine said, "Now you're through with these, are you?" "Yes." He took them out and threw them in the ore bin. They went in as ore!…If it was melted down, they recovered a little copper metal, I guess, but that was all. The mineral specimens were unique, but to a mine boss—what the heck—ore is important! (Smithsonian Institution Oral History Project, interviews with Edward P. Henderson, 1984–1985)

The regret expressed in this story depends on the idea that these unique and irreplaceable objects should be subjected to the homogenizing and dehistoricizing logic of copper ore mining. This idea has two implications for minerals and temporality. First, mineral specimens are not "used up" the way ore is; they tend to persist as identifiable objects. Second, mineral specimens acquire histories, and the longer and more complete their accompanying historical narratives, the more valuable they can be.

The fact that minerals thus persist as identifiable objects and accrue multiple sources helps solve the problem of scarcity that we encounter with respect to silver. Because any ingot of silver is like another (provided that it meets the same specifications), scarcity (and therefore a viable market) must be managed at a higher level of generality. But minerals emerge as distinctive objects, and they may become more and more distinctive (and thus less and less equivalent to other minerals) as they travel.[9] Thus they are—potentially—almost infinitely scarce because each one potentially comes to have its own uniquely constituted value.

Now, from the perspective of the production site, this situation may not make much difference. As a rule, specimens accrue these value-making histories only if they leave their original locality. In fact, they often seem to have multiple sources: specimens "come from" a particular mine but often also "come from" particular collections or dealers. It is almost as if the specimen is reborn from a new source once it enters a famous collection. A Guanajuato specimen might also become a Rashleigh Collection specimen, for instance, or a US National Museum specimen, and so on. Like Kula valuables, the mineral specimen becomes more valuable as it comes into contact with famous and powerful persons (as with Kula, these are usually men). This rule seems to be even truer these days than in the nineteenth and early twentieth centuries. At the Denver mineral shows in September 2005, I heard dozens of conversations between collectors concerning the movement of specimens from hand to hand, peppered with phrases like "That rhodochrosite was Bill's and then he traded it for the blue topaz, and now I have it." A poster (figure 3.4) in the gallery of Stuart Wilensky, a successful mineral dealer and collector, shows a magnificent blue topaz. The poster is signed by the five people who are known to have owned the topaz and by the photographer.

Mineral specimens have the capacity to endure through time and even to acquire new life in their travels. They do not seem to be "nonrenewable resources" in the same sense as ore, although they are certainly finite, and the closing of particular localities can add to their value considerably by closing down the possibility of further supply (rather like a painting that gains value after the painter's death). It is as if they renew themselves in their journeys.

Sometimes people use their own bodies to move minerals along their paths. The image for the tattoo in figure 3.5 shows a group of tourmalines in a pocket discovered on Good Friday 1978 in the Jonas mine in Minas Gerais, Brazil. The pocket no longer exists, but the minerals do; they are traveling from collector to collector. One specimen was originally sold for $1.3 million to a collector in the United States and subsequently sold for more.

Minerals, if they are not damaged or lost en route, usually become part of mineral *collections*, either in private hands or in museums. In some cases, the collection (especially if it is venerable or otherwise noted) then becomes the recognized source of the mineral. Collections, as has often

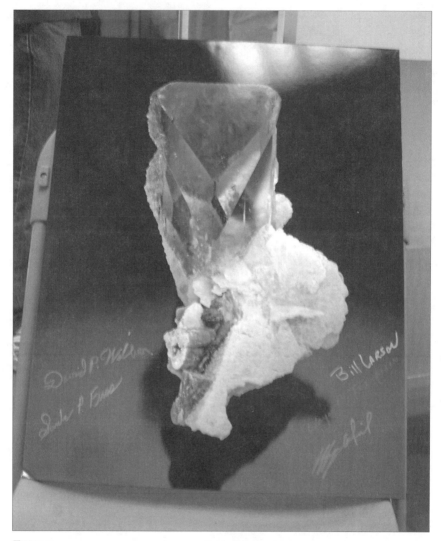

FIGURE 3.4

Topaz poster in a mineral dealer's gallery (courtesy Elizabeth Ferry).

been noted, impose new forms of order and understanding upon objects. They have the capacity to transcend, bracket, or otherwise erase both history and geography. They can also "revalue" objects by subjecting them to new forms of classification that become new sources, partially replacing the mine as original locality and regenerating the value of the specimen itself.

Krsysztof Pomian defines collections as "sets of artificial and natural

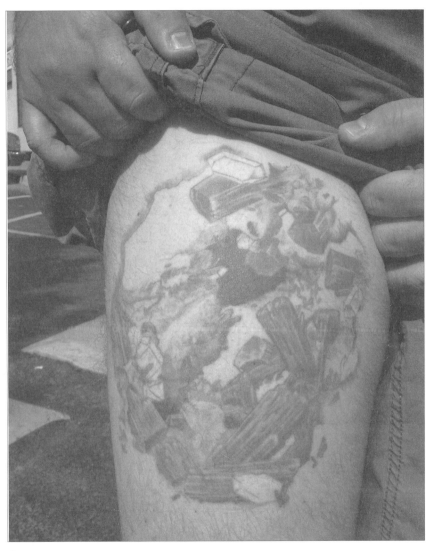

FIGURE 3.5
Tattoo of a Brazilian mine pocket (courtesy Elizabeth Ferry).

objects kept out of the sphere of economic circulation and placed on display" (Pomian 1996:11). This definition has a certain resonance but does not always hold true. As much as possible, museum curators do not promise to maintain collections donated to them intact. As Henderson states, "No museum should *promise* to do that, because they can't." This rule is even truer for private mineralogical collections, which are sometimes

67

spoken of approvingly as "fluid." I asked seven high-end mineral collectors (those willing and able to pay $50,000 or more for a single specimen) if they cared whether their collection was intact or dispersed in fifty years. Only two said yes (and one of these had already sold his collection).

These data suggest that the power of collections derives not from (or not only from) the fact that they are removed from economic exchange but from the fact that the idea and system of the collection are sufficiently strong that even if some items are exchanged, the whole still maintains its character as a collection. The collection encompasses the items that make it up, imposes a system on them, and in doing so establishes precedence over them.

When I was a child, I was told that the molecules in our bodies are continually changing, so over time, the body's substance is completely replaced. Yet in most circumstances, people experience their bodies as "the same" throughout life.[10] The same can be true of other "corporate" entities, such as a church, club, or political party. Few collections change to this degree, but the corporate quality is comparable. And this quality allows collections to renew themselves in a way that mines, for instance, never can.[11]

So we have two kinds of bodies: the organic, corporeal body of the mine and the man-made (and I use the term advisedly), corporate body of the collection. At the risk of pushing things too far, these are strikingly reminiscent of the "king's two bodies" in medieval political theology (Kantorowicz 1997[1957]). And in that case, as here, the "corporate" body seeks to solve the problem of the "corporeal" body's mortality.

This distinction between the corporeal life of the mine and the corporate life of mineral specimens can also be seen in terms of the different kinds of labor that produce these different kinds of life. The productive labor of miners is limited by the mortal bodies of those miners, as well as by the exigencies of workers' compensation, social security payments, and pensions, all costs predicated on the entropic nature of the human body. This labor is displaced by the labor of consumption (R. Foster 2005; Miller 1987), which is dispersed among multiple bodies and thus appears to be almost infinitely reproducible.

An example from the National Museum of Natural History further makes the point.[12] One of the major components of the national mineral collections is the collection of Washington A. Roebling, donated to the museum in 1926 by his son, John Roebling. Along with the collection, John Roebling established a fund for further field trips and purchases. The new specimens become part of the Roebling Collection. I asked Dr. Jeffrey Post, curator of the National Collections, whether it was possible to distinguish between the original Roebling Collection specimens and more recent acquisitions. He responded:

> Well, you can always go back to the records, and even by looking at the accession number—the original Roebling specimens cover a certain range, [of numbers], so you know if it's outside that range it's a more recent acquisition. But in a sense, we don't want to make that distinction. The argument that it's not a dead collection but it's acquiring more and more pieces every year that are labeled as Roebling specimens is a powerful one. *The collection is the thing*—and it's continuing to grow. All collectors face the fact that they can't take it with them, and they want to know that the collection will continue to live after they are gone. (Author interview, August 9, 2005; emphasis added)

This statement, with its distinction between living and dead collections, nicely expresses the degree to which, by asserting a greater value to the collection as a whole, collections can confer new temporalities on specimens.

Indeed, some pieces in the original Roebling Collection have been exchanged for other, "better" specimens. This process is allowed in the Roebling bequest, which states that specimens can be exchanged for the "improvement" of the collection itself. As Henderson said, "the word 'improvement' gives a little latitude in there, because in the present curator's eyes, maybe 'improvement' would go along this road, and the next time something else." Some collections donated to museums such as the Smithsonian have conditions, for example, that the collection should remain intact, but in many cases individual items can leave the collection, for instance through trades for other specimens. The collection itself endures and continues to bestow value upon the specimens in it. As Dr. Post nicely puts it, "the collection is the thing."

Mineral specimens seem able to extend their temporal horizons nearly indefinitely. They are able to do this for several reasons: they are not used up; they can acquire histories; and they gravitate toward collections. In these journeys, the focus shifts from the depleting source in "nature" (the mine) to the enduring and even regenerating source of collections. As one collector of Mexican agates told me, in justifying his decision to sell his collection, "I've got all the best ones now. So it's not a collection any more, it's a static, dead thing." Like living beings, collections can grow and can slough off parts without losing their essential character. Unlike living beings, they do not appear to have finite life spans. Collections aspire to life without mortality. Mines cannot reach so high; they can only get as far as life defined through its mortality.

Remarking that "the problematic of temporality is fundamental to the collecting process," Jean Baudrillard (1994:15) describes how collections displace time as a unidirectional, irreversible process. This process has the effect, he argues, of allowing the collector to move past the trap of temporality, to "*live out his life uninterruptedly and in a cyclical mode, and thereby symbolically transcend the realities of an existence before whose irreversibility and contingency he remains powerless*" (1994:17; emphasis in original).

Susan Stewart also points out the degree to which systematicity in collecting displaces temporality:

> The collection seeks a form of self-enclosure which is possible because of its ahistoricism. The collection replaces history with *classification*, with order beyond the realm of temporality. In the collection, time is not something to be restored to an origin; rather, all time is made simultaneous or synchronous within the collector's world. (Stewart 1993:151; emphasis in original)

In the essay "Unpacking My Library," Walter Benjamin describes collecting as a more complex process, manifesting "a dialectical tension between the poles of order and disorder" (1999:487). The classification that Stewart points out is in tension with the chaotic piling up of memories triggered by the objects collected. In this sense, it is perhaps better to say that a new, ordered form of temporality is superimposed on (without entirely erasing) the hurtling pace of the past. This new ordering of temporality, always juxtaposed with and pulling against the "real time" outside the collection, allows the objects and by extension their collectors to be renewed. As Benjamin says, "To a true collector the acquisition of an old book is its rebirth....To renew the old world, this is the collector's deepest desire when he is driven to acquire new things" (1991:487).

Benjamin thus sees the collection and its special form of temporality in dynamic—indeed, dialectical—tension with the world outside the collection. It is for this reason, I suspect, that he pays such attention to the ways in which objects are acquired in the first place. This view gives a richer understanding of collections as they exist in the real world of museums and private collections, where collections endure and retain authority even as their constituent items come and go. It is, at least in part, the movable source of specimens that allows collections to transcend finite temporalities and confers upon them a sense of immortality. As Dr. Post pointed out, "This is a powerful argument" for potential donors who hope to live on in their collections as living, growing (but not dying) entities.

The image of the enduring minerals tattooed on the collector's thigh in figure 3.5 nicely captures the tension between the mortal flesh and the seemingly immortal stones. The pleasure he and his companions got from my photographic documentation of his thigh is a further expression of this tension. What do the photo and the tattoo do to the temporal horizons of mine, pocket, drawing, and thigh?

At a dinner for wealthy private mineral collectors in Boulder, Colorado, the host brought his guests to see his small but spectacular collection in the "Rock Room," a cherrywood-lined tower on the grounds of his house. He took the opportunity to make a plea that mineral collectors should donate or bequeath minerals to museums. He said:

> Anyone who studies the rocks knows that the earth wasn't created in ten thousand years. Minerals make us aware of our own mortality. So then the question is, What is going to be your legacy? How are you going to make your mark so that someone can see a label in a museum and say, "Dan was here. He was a part of this"?

The issue of geological time and its observable traces in enduring minerals also affects temporal understandings for collectors. Perhaps the enduring and monumental quality of geological time seems more evident, more insistent, when its rocky instances also endure.

Several guests disagreed with their host's suggestion that they had an obligation to donate their collections to museums. One said, "In my opinion, the market is the best caretaker of minerals because people who will pay for them will take care of them." But even though these collectors disagreed on the best strategy to care for minerals, they concurred on the potential for and desirability of minerals' endurance through time (and perhaps in the process the possibility that their own names might endure).

The intersection of the enduring quality of geological time and the individual lifetimes of collectors echoes a similar counterpoint described by Sharon Traweek with respect to high-energy physicists (1988). In Traweek's account, the fleeting present and the threat of obsolescence contrast with the unchanging timeless quality of the natural laws that physicists seek to uncover (and for which they long). The case is slightly different with mineral collectors, for they do not see geological nature as unchanging but rather as changing in a way that is analogous to human time, but very much slower. Geology is not outside time; rather, it participates in an awesome, inexorable temporal narrative that leaves its traces in the mineral specimens.

ELIZABETH EMMA FERRY

CONCLUSION

This regenerative capacity of mineral specimens, the ability to create new sources and new extensions of life as they travel, may mean little to producers. Often this value through the extension of life does not return to the original locality of production. In fact, this type of market in part depends on extracting value from the original source.[13] Mineral specimens from Guanajuato fetch a lot more in Tucson than they do in Guanajuato. True, if we see Guanajuato as a place for which, at least in part, "its face is its fortune," then the endurance and transmission of the name and fame of Guanajuato may be of some value to Guanajuatenses as well. This is certainly the strategy advocated by the authors of the article on establishing museums in former mining localities. However, the fact that the temporalities associated with collections are more regenerative and rejuvenating than those associated with mines is itself, among other things, a sign of the greater wealth and power of those who consume minerals compared with those who produce them.

Of course, the concept of resources is contextually defined: things may be more strongly or weakly defined as "resources" at different phases of their production, distribution, and consumption and by different actors. Mineral specimens, for instance, used to be meaningful to collectors primarily for their ability to represent other things—a system of mineralogy, or the "mineral resources" of a particular region. They were the illustrations to accompany mineralogy or economic geology. In the past forty years or so, mineral specimens have come to be valued as aesthetic objects, comparable to fine art and obliged to represent only themselves.

Because they regenerate their sources (through collections especially) and because they are generally not used to make something else or to represent something else, they do not pose the kinds of problems that so-called resources like silver do—they do not raise anxieties about the proper relationship between humans and nature and the more or less enduring or mortal character of each. Indeed, the pleasure of collecting minerals may partly stem from their ability to avoid and thus seem to resolve such problems. The counterpoint between minerals and silver and their attendant temporalities works to illuminate the politics of resources and thus the relationship between nature, economy, and society.

Notes

1. Debates over anthropocentric versus ecocentric views of nature, including ecosocialist and ecofeminist perspectives, are deeply concerned with this question (Dobson 1990; Eckersley 1992; O'Connor 1998; Plumwood 1986).

2. For a cogent discussion of these themes within anthropology and a critique of this distinction on both philosophical and ethnographic grounds, see Gell 1992.

3. The total does not equal 100 percent because of rounding.

4. According to Barclay's Global Investors International, the London fix is the price per ounce of silver set by three market-making members of the London Bullion Market Association at noon (GMT) on each market day.

5. Until the 1970s, the US government played a central role in the regulation of silver prices, because of the presence of silver in the US dollar (the US government was a major silver purchaser) and because the US Treasury maintained a policy of guaranteed purchasing and sale of silver. This meant that the Treasury helped bridge the gap between supply and demand at least part of the time, keeping the price of silver both stable and relatively low.

6. The crisis in the cooperative that began in 2001 continued until its sale in 2005, even though the price of silver had begun to rise (but it rose dramatically only after the sale had already gone through).

7. Although the cooperative was sold in December 2005, the sale of surface properties did not take place until the summer of 2007.

8. Except in the case of minted silver in silverware, coins, and so forth.

9. Although the Hope Diamond is a gem (a cut stone) and not a mineral specimen, it gives a good example of the accretion of sources and the implications for increasing scarcity. The contemporary fascination with the Hope Diamond has as much to do with its multiple histories as a social object as with its size and beauty. It has achieved the status of a person in its own right (Kurin 2006).

10. In this example, I remain agnostic about the universality of this sense. I am using it as an analogy rather than as an inquiry into the cognitive category of "person."

11. See also Marshall Sahlins's example of an Amazonian forest in *Waiting for Foucault, Still* (2002).

12. The case of the Smithsonian, which holds the National Collections of the United States, may be one of the few where the concept of "resources" is applied to mineral specimens—which are often seen as the resources of the nation. Given that natural resources are often also linked to nation-states, as evidenced by their frequent appearance on stamps, money, and so forth, there is certainly more to say about the link between nationhood, the concept of resources, and temporality. I reserve these lines of inquiry for another discussion.

13. However, mineral localities construct entire economies around mineral specimen production and sale and are acutely sensitive to the fluctuations in price of specimens from their mines. Examples of these localities are Mapimí, Mexico; Tsumeb, Namibia; and the state of Minas Gerais, Brazil.

4

Wildlife as Renewable Resource

Competing Conceptions of Wildlife,
Time, and Management in the Yukon

Paul E. Nadasdy

Over the past fifteen years, the majority of Yukon First Nations have signed and ratified land-claim and self-government agreements with the governments of Canada and the Yukon[1]. Among other things, these modern-day treaties establish a new regime for the cooperative management of land and resources throughout the territory. In the process of laying out the various parties' roles and responsibilities in this regard, the agreements classify fish and wildlife (along with trees and other wild flora) as *renewable resources*. This is in contrast to *nonrenewable resources*, such as oil, gas, and gold. The very notion of resources as renewable implies a particular sense of time—one that is distinct from that implied by the notion of nonrenewable resources (see chapters 2 and 3 by Limbert and Ferry respectively). The phrase *renewable resource* conjures up an image of temporal cycles, of periods of renewal and regrowth punctuated by episodes of exploitation. Indeed, this image of cyclical growth and renewal resonates with Euro-American wildlife managers and Yukon First Nation people alike; both are apt to think about animals in relation to temporal cycles,[2] although, as we shall see, there are important differences between them.

Anthropologists have described notions of cyclical time among various peoples the world over. They have long argued that a sense of time as cyclical arises naturally from the cycling of days, tides, and seasons and the ways in which these natural cycles structure human activities (for example, Evans-Pritchard 1940; Hallowell 1937; Thompson 1967). Agriculture is among the most important domains of human activity to be shaped by these natural cycles, and the agricultural cycle features prominently in anthropological analyses of how people conceive of time. At first blush, it seems that these anthropological insights should be directly applicable to a study of renewable-resource management, a set of practices clearly rooted in an agricultural worldview. Indeed, forest managers quite explicitly see themselves as engaged in a kind of long-term farming; the planting, care, and cultivation of trees are as important (at least in theory) as harvesting in the silvicultural cycle. The agricultural roots of wildlife management are also quite apparent. In 1933 Aldo Leopold, widely regarded as the father of scientific wildlife management in North America, wrote *Game Management*, the first textbook in the newly emerging field. In it, he defined wildlife management in explicitly agricultural terms:

> Game management is the art of making land produce sustained annual crops of wild game for recreational use. Its nature is best understood by comparing it with the other land-cropping arts.... Like the other agricultural arts, game management produces a crop by controlling the environmental factors which hold down the natural increase, or productivity, of the seed stock. (Leopold 1933:3)

Since Leopold's time, the agricultural metaphor has continued to play an important role in structuring the knowledge and practice of wildlife management.[3] Wildlife biologists and government hunting regulations regularly substitute the verb *harvest* for the less metaphorical *shoot* or *kill* when talking about what hunters do to animals, and they refer to the overall number of animals within a species killed by hunters in a given territory each year as the *annual harvest*. Similarly, Yukon biologists studying Dall sheep populations are keenly interested in obtaining an estimate of the annual *lamb crop*, or the number of lambs born into a population in any given year.

All of this suggests that Euro-American wildlife managers view what they do as somehow analogous to the production of crops and domesticated animals. They see fish and wildlife populations as renewable in much the same way as, say, a wheat crop is renewable. Like domestic species, fish and wildlife have natural life cycles; they are born, grow, reproduce, and die. Each cycle is similar to those that have gone before, although the individual organisms themselves are continually replaced. Humans can exert a degree of control over those cycles by "harvesting" animals, killing predators, rearing fish in hatcheries, and so on, but they must be very careful about these interventions. Like farmers, they need to limit the overall harvest in any year to allow for the survival of sufficient "seed" for the propagation of future generations. Through their intervention and control, wildlife managers are expected to *ensure* the continued renewal of wildlife populations. From this perspective, humans do not merely adapt to the "natural" cycles of animal populations; rather, humans are critical to their maintenance. Indeed, we have already seen that the notion of human *control* over other species is central to wildlife management.

The situation is quite different, however, for Yukon First Nation people, who are not—nor have their ancestors ever been—farmers. Indeed, Yukon First Nation people, like hunting peoples elsewhere, are often quite explicit in their rejection of the agricultural metaphors of wildlife management. At a wildlife management meeting I attended in 1995, for example, one member of Kluane First Nation objected to the use of the term *harvest*. Kluane people, she maintained, are hunters, not farmers: "We don't 'harvest' animals; we kill them." She objected to the term *harvest* in particular because its use implies ownership and control; people harvest crops that they themselves plant, so they are entitled to harvest them all. Indeed, farmers replant annually, so they expect to harvest their entire crop every year. She argued that this mindset is very dangerous when it comes to wildlife management and urged all meeting participants to use words like *hunt* and *kill* rather than *harvest* (see Stevenson 2006:170).[4]

Although Yukon First Nation people generally reject the agricultural metaphors of wildlife management, there is nonetheless something compelling to them about the cyclical temporality implied by the idea of a renewable resource. They are, of course, very knowledgeable about animal life cycles and seasonal patterns of animal behavior. Scholars have written extensively about northern hunters' annual subsistence round, their strategy for adapting to those seasonal patterns (for example, McClellan 1975: 95–105). However, they understand the temporality of these cycles very differently than do biologists. I suggest that this difference has to do with what Alfred Gell (1992:30–36) referred to as the "topology" of time. Gell noted that two very different senses of time—each with its own distinct topology—have been confused with each other because both are "cyclical." He argued that we need to distinguish between *cyclical* time, characterized by the periodic recurrence of events of the same type (as one summer follows another), and *circular* time, in which the *same event* recurs over and over again.

Like other northern hunting peoples, many Yukon First Nation people conceive of hunting as a reciprocal relationship between humans and animals. In this view, fish and animals are other-than-human persons who give themselves to hunters in exchange for the hunters' performance of certain ritual practices. These practices vary across the North—as well as by animal—but they commonly include the observance of food taboos, ritual feasts, and prescribed methods for disposing of animal remains, as well as injunctions against overhunting and talking badly about or playing with animals. Hunting in such societies should not be viewed as a violent process whereby hunters take the lives of animals by force, but rather as a long-term social relationship between animal-people and the humans who hunt them.[5]

Central to any understanding of the temporal dimensions of such a relationship is northern hunters' belief in the reincarnation of both human- and animal-people. As long as a hunter follows the prescribed ritual procedures, the animals he or she kills do not really die but will instead be reborn to give themselves to the hunter again in the future (see Brightman 1993). Thus many Yukon First Nation people view hunting as part of an ongoing social relationship between human- and animal-people that transcends the lifetime of any individual hunter or prey animal. The complex nature of these human–animal relations is expressed in a large body of "Long Time Ago" stories. These stories concern events that occurred in the distant past, such as the creation of the world, and explain how animals and people came to assume their current forms and roles. Although most non–First Nation people regard these stories as mythical, many First Nation people maintain that they are not "just stories" but that they are true. Indeed, although the events they recount occurred "a long time ago," there is another sense in which they are quite contemporary. Indeed, the ritual practices in which First Nation hunters engage and that continue to structure reciprocal relations between humans and animals *presuppose* the contemporary and real-life existence of animal-people as they appear in Long Time Ago stories (Tanner 1979; see also Nelson 1983).

There is, in fact, an important sense in which all the people from Long Time Ago—animal and human alike—are still alive today. When First Nation hunters kill a moose, say, they do not merely participate in an event that is similar to those in which they have participated in the past. Rather, they take part in yet another iteration of the same event, an event they have participated in over and over again since the relationship between human- and moose-people was first forged in the distant past of the Long Time Ago stories. The hunt is the instantiation of an ongoing social relationship between *the same* human- and animal-people across multiple lifetimes. This means that the temporality of First Nation hunting is not *cyclical*, as it is for farmers who harvest the same crop (but different individual plants) every year; rather, it is *circular*. This distinction has important implications for how First Nation people understand the role of human agency in relation to animal populations.

Like scientific wildlife managers, First Nation people see themselves as intimately involved in animal cycles and as able to affect those cycles in important ways. Through the observation of certain ritual practices and the maintenance of proper social relations, First Nation hunters play an important role in the renewal of animal populations. (For example, proper disposal of animal remains is critical if the animals are to be reborn.) Although First Nation hunters may resort to trickery and even a degree of coercion in their conduct of social relations with animals (Nadasdy 2007), they do not generally subscribe to the view that humans *control* animals, who may abandon hunters at any time if they decide that their human partners are not living up to their social obligations. This view stands in sharp contrast to that of Euro-American wildlife managers, who attempt to control animal cycles in much the same way that a farmer seeks to control the agricultural cycle. Indeed, many Yukon First Nation people find the assumption of control inherent in wildlife management at best ludicrous, possibly even offensive. As one Kluane First Nation hunter regularly noted at wildlife management meetings, the term *wildlife management* itself is a misnomer. Humans cannot "manage" wildlife populations, he said. Animals are quite capable of taking care of themselves; they make their own decisions about when to reproduce and where to go—decisions that are quite independent of any desires on the part of humans. Wildlife management, he said, is not about managing animals; it is about managing people.

Thus Euro-American wildlife managers and First Nation hunters can agree that wildlife is a renewable resource and that humans play an important role in the maintenance of the temporal cycles in which they, along with animals, are enmeshed. But the term *renewable resource* here is *fundamentally contested*, an appellation I use to describe a situation in which all parties to a conversation agree on a term's importance and centrality but at the same time understand it to mean very different things.[6] Those employing such terms often assume that these "reflect a shared universe of meaning" when in fact they "actually represent non-congruent realities" (Morrow and Hensel 1992:42). In such cases, participants in the discussion are seldom aware of the semantic discrepancy, and talk takes place *as if* they all shared an understanding of the term's meaning. This situation can lead to serious misunderstandings—often without the parties to the conversation even being aware of it. And these misunderstandings can have significant political consequences, especially in contexts of social inequality, because it tends to be the meanings ascribed to fundamentally contested terms by parties with access to power that are acted upon in broader sociopolitical contexts.

In this chapter, I build on the work of Morrow and Hensel (1992), who demonstrated the analytic value of attending to fundamentally contested terms in cross-cultural negotiations over wildlife management in Alaska, and that of Michael Asch (1989; see also Usher 1986:81–83), who focused on the contested nature of the term *wildlife* itself in northern Canadian land-claim negotiations. I focus in particular on the fundamentally contested notion that fish and wildlife are *renewable resources*. In the next two sections, I examine in somewhat more detail the different spatiotemporal topologies underlying each conception of renewability: the circular and the cyclical. After dealing with each in turn, I consider the political consequences of this spatiotemporal heterogeneity.

THE CIRCULAR SPACE-TIME OF FIRST NATION HUNTING

As suggested above, hunting enmeshes Yukon First Nation people in a temporal order that resembles what Walter Benjamin (1968) called messianic time. Following Benjamin, Benedict Anderson notes that messianic time is characterized by "a simultaneity of past and future in an instantaneous present. In such a view of things, the word 'meanwhile' cannot be of real significance" (Anderson 1991:24). Similarly, Gurvitch describes a sense of time that he refers to as enduring time, in which "the past is relatively remote, yet it is dominant and projected into the present and future" (Gurvitch 1964:31). Such a conception of time was prominent in—among other places—medieval Europe (but see Le Goff 1980 for a description of temporal heterogeneity even then), and it implies a disjunction between concepts of time and space. In Lewis Mumford's analysis of the medieval worldview, for example, he notes that time and space were relatively independent systems:

> The medieval artist introduced other times within his own spatial world, as when he projected the events of Christ's life within a contemporary Italian city, without the slightest feeling that the passage of time has made a difference.... When a medieval chronicler mentions the King...it is often a little difficult to find out whether he is talking about Caesar or Alexander the Great

or his own monarch: each is equally near to him. Indeed, the word anachronism is meaningless in medieval art: it is only when one related events to a coordinated frame of time and space that being out of time or being untrue to time became disconcerting.... The connecting link between events was the cosmic and religious order. The true order of space was Heaven, even as the true order of time was Eternity. (Mumford 1962[1934]:19)

Although there are many significant differences between medieval Christianity and the beliefs and values surrounding Yukon First Nation hunting, they seem to share a similar spatiotemporal orientation. Because of beliefs about reincarnation and human–animal reciprocity, there is a very important sense in which the animals encountered by Yukon First Nation hunters out in the bush in 2006 are *the same animals* (just as the hunters are *the same hunters*) as those in the Long Time Ago stories that teach Yukon First Nation people how to relate properly to animal-people. This situation is possible only if time and space are disarticulated in the manner described by Mumford.

For those who subscribe to such a view, animals are very different sorts of "resources" than they are for most Euro-American hunters and biologists. In an analysis of Rock Cree hunting in northern Manitoba, for example, Robert Brightman (1987, 1993) concluded that hunters historically did not believe that humans could affect animal populations through overhunting. Because animals do not die forever when hunters kill them (so long as the hunters observe all the necessary rituals), overhunting of the sort warned against by wildlife biologists is not possible. As a result, Brightman argues, there was no indigenous conservation ethic among the Cree. Still today, he notes, Euro-American notions about wildlife conservation coexist uneasily alongside aboriginal ideas about reincarnation and proper human–animal relations. Similarly, Ann Fienup-Riordan (1990) reports that many Yup'ik Eskimos of western Alaska continue to doubt that overhunting is possible, which leads at times to serious tensions between Yup'ik villagers and state wildlife managers.

Yukon First Nation people subscribe to many of the same beliefs and practices described by Brightman and others. Although the historical record is unclear on whether Yukon First Nation people ever regularly engaged in practices of overhunting and meat wastage like those described by Brightman and Fienup-Riordan, most contemporary Yukon First Nation people now believe that human hunting can affect the size of animal populations and have incorporated prohibitions against overhunting and waste into the set of obligations that hunters incur toward animals through the act of hunting. This does not mean, however, that they have abandoned beliefs about animal reincarnation and human–animal relations. Indeed, one of the main First Nation objections to the controversial (in the Yukon) practice of catch-and-release fishing is that it is a repudiation of the reciprocal act at the very heart of the relationship between human- and animal-people: "The fish comes to you as a gift. It's offering its life to you. And if you don't accept it, that's an insult. Sooner or later, the fish will stop coming to you" (Mark Wedge, quoted in Yukon Department of Renewable Resources 1997:21).

Although Yukon First Nation people and biologists agree that over-hunting can reduce the number of animals, they differ fundamentally in their interpretation of *why*. At least some Yukon First Nation people now believe that overhunting and waste affect the animals not because they reduce the number of animals in the total population, as biologists would have it, but because such practices offend the animals, making it less likely that hunters will be able to kill them in the future. For them, animals are still a potentially unlimited resource, their availability dependent on the maintenance of social relations between animal- and human-persons in accordance with the principles laid out in Long Time Ago stories. Indeed, it is through the reciprocal relations of hunting that humans and animals each contribute to the others' renewal.

None of this is to say that Yukon First Nation people live out their lives in the enduring space-time of the Long Time Ago stories. Indeed, we will see that First Nation people also engage with human- and animal-people in social contexts that are structured by very different senses of space and time. Yet Long Time Ago stories and the spatiotemporality associated with them continue to inform many First Nation people's understanding of their interactions with animals and with other people in relation to animals.

THE CYCLICAL SPACE-TIME OF SCIENTIFIC WILDLIFE MANAGEMENT

Euro-Canadian wildlife managers conceive of the renewability of fish and wildlife very differently than do many First Nation people. For them, space and time are linked such that a given hunter can kill a given animal only once. Following Benedict Anderson (1991), I refer to this second spatiotemporal framework, within which the management of animal cycles takes place, as homogeneous empty space-time. Homogeneous empty space-time is characteristic of (and, indeed, essential to the administration of) the large and complex bureaucracies that govern corporations, as well as nation-states, under contemporary capitalism.[7] According to Anderson, the development of a conception of homogeneous empty time was a necessary prerequisite for the emergence of the "imagined community" that is a nation:

> The idea of a sociological organism moving calendrically through homogeneous, empty time is a precise analogue of the idea of the nation, which is also conceived of as a solid community moving steadily down (or up) history. An American will never meet or even know the names of more than a handful of his 240,000,000-odd fellow-Americans. He has no idea what they are up to at any one time. But he has complete confidence in their steady, anonymous, *simultaneous* activity. (Anderson 1991:26; emphasis added)

Drawing an explicit contrast to messianic time, Anderson notes that in homogeneous empty time, "simultaneity is, as it were, transverse, cross-time, marked not by prefiguring and fulfillment, but by temporal coincidence, and measured by clock and calendar" (Anderson 1991:24). It is only in relation to such a notion of simultaneity, he notes, that the concept "meanwhile" can have any meaning, and it is only by means of measurements made with devices such as clocks and calendars that the concept of simultaneity as temporal coincidence makes any sense.

Although there is not necessarily a single spatiotemporal framework associated with clocks and calendars, both are generally associated with notions of cyclical—as opposed to circular—time. Tributary states and capitalists alike have long used them as tools for controlling agricultural production, collecting taxes, regulating the length of the working day, and managing a host of other similarly cyclical processes, including those related to wildlife. As administrative tools, calendars and clocks help produce a sense of time as homogeneous and empty. Of the calendar, Bourdieu notes:

> Just as a map replaces the discontinuous, patchy space of practical paths by the homogeneous, continuous space of geometry, so a calendar substitutes a linear, homogeneous, continuous time for practical time, which is made up of incommensurable islands of duration, each with its own rhythm, the time that flies by or drags, depending on what one is doing. (Bourdieu 1977:105)

Although of more recent vintage than the calendar, the mechanical clock has been in existence since at least the fourteen century. Its invention facilitated dramatic changes in people's perception of time. "The clock," according to Lewis Mumford, "is a piece of power-machinery whose 'product' is seconds and minutes: by its essential nature it disassociated time from human events and helped create the beliefs of an independent world of mathematically measurable sequences" (Mumford1962[1934]:15). He noted that there is little foundation in everyday human experience for belief in such an abstraction,[8] but that once such a conceptual leap has been made, it has profound consequences: "When one thinks of time, not as a sequence of experiences, but as a collection of hours, minutes, and seconds, the habits of adding time and saving time come into existence. Time took on the character of an enclosed space: it could be divided, it could be filled up, it could even be expanded" (Mumford 1962[1934]:17).

It is no accident that Mumford—like Anderson—uses spatial terms to describe this notion of abstract time (that is, as an empty space that people "move through"). Homogeneous empty time and the concept of simultaneity with which it is associated (that is, as temporal coincidence) *necessarily* imply a spatial dimension (for example, *meanwhile* "x" is happening *somewhere* else). Indeed, Mumford notes that the emergence of abstract time coincided with similar developments in the conceptualization of space. At the same time that the mechanical clock was spreading across Europe, artists were discovering the rules of perspective, and mapmakers were developing modern cartographic methods. Just as the mechanical clock coincided with dramatic changes in the way people could think about time, so the rules of perspective and proportional mapping both reflected and helped bring about a fundamental shift in the way people conceptualized space: "Space as a hierarchy of values was replaced by space as a system of magnitudes" (Mumford 1962[1934]:20; see also Harvey 1990: 240–259). Indeed, Renaissance paintings and maps implied and facilitated movement through space (imagined or real) in a way that older medieval paintings and maps had never done, and it was movement that linked the concept of abstract empty space inextricably to that of abstract empty time: "Within this new ideal network of space and time all events now took place; and the most satisfactory event within this system was uniform motion in a straight line, for such motion led itself to accurate representation within the system of spatial and temporal coordinates" (Mumford 1962[1934]: 20–21). Thus, "the categories of time and space, once practically disassociated, had become united: and the abstractions of measured time and measured space undermined the earlier conceptions of infinity and eternity" (1962[1934]:22).[9]

The concept of abstract, homogeneous, and empty space-time forms the basis for modern scientific inquiry; indeed, it was a necessary precondition for the development of Newtonian mechanics. It also underlies the development of capitalism. David Harvey (1990:252) observed that a concept of "homogeneous universal time" is implicit in "conceptions of the rate of profit...the rate of interest, the hourly wage, and other magnitudes fundamental to capitalist decision-making" (see also Landes 2000 on time and value). Marx himself made it clear in his discussions of surplus value and the length of the working day that capitalism depended in large part upon the institutionalization of a new way of thinking about time. It is by now well accepted that the rise of the capitalist labor process—along with the concept of value to which it was linked—led to new ways of thinking about time.[10] In this chapter, however, I would like to suggest and explore another aspect of the spatiotemporal order wrought by capitalism. This has to do with the imperatives of bureaucratic administration.

Under capitalism—especially industrial capitalism—production, distribution, and consumption become ever more complex processes linking far-flung peoples and places to one another. The activities of all these people must be coordinated if the whole system is to work (parts and raw materials must arrive at the factory on time; finished products must be transported to markets; payments must be sent, received, and processed on time). As the whole process speeds up (because of improvements in transportation and communication), coordination becomes all the more crucial. The calendar, no doubt invented at least in part to coordinate activities in the tributary state (Rotenberg 1992), becomes more crowded with events that require coordination. The clock, which can subdivide the calendar day into smaller and ever more precise units, becomes a critical tool for the fine-grained scheduling and coordination necessary for administration, as well as production.[11]

There are few if any social forms as well suited as bureaucracy to the task of coordinating events in a complex capitalist society. Max Weber noted that although bureaucracy predates the rise of capitalism, the particular demands of the capitalist economy are what led to the perfection of the bureaucratic form:

> Today, it is primarily the capitalist market economy which demands that the official business of the administration be discharged precisely, unambiguously, continuously, and with as much speed as possible. Normally, the very large, modern capitalist enterprises are themselves unequaled models of strict bureaucratic organization. (Weber 1946:215)

Although Weber was well aware of the many deficiencies of the bureaucratic form, he nevertheless argued that bureaucracy is by far the most
effective means for administering large and complex social systems, such as
corporations and modern industrialized states:

> The decisive reason for the advance of bureaucratic organiza-
> tion has always been its purely technical superiority over any
> other form of organization. The fully developed bureaucratic
> mechanism compares with other organizations exactly as does
> the machine with the non-mechanical modes of production.
> (Weber 1946:214; see also 228–229)

Bureaucracies are "machinelike" in that they are complex hierarchical
organizations characterized by an elaborate internal division of labor.
Their various components are highly integrated with one another and
replaceable (in theory at least) so that although each attends to only a
small part of the overall problem of administration, their combined efforts
enable the bureaucratic apparatus as a whole to administer the extraordinarily complex affairs of an industrialized state or corporation. Such activity is necessarily based on a notion of homogeneous empty space-time. To
see why, consider what bureaucrats actually do.

Government bureaucrats in industrial states (for example) are faced
with the daunting task of administering very large and complex systems of
people, institutions, land, and resources. To accomplish this, they must,
among many other things, keep track of and collect a multitude of different forms of revenue. They must schedule and execute the distribution of
funds both internally and externally. They must plan and administer social
programs throughout the territory. They must implement and enforce all
laws and regulations—including those governing resource use—throughout their jurisdiction. They must plan, oversee the construction of, and
maintain public infrastructure. They must negotiate and oversee political,
economic, and social relations with their counterparts in the bureaucracies
of other states, as well as those in the bureaucracies of corporations
and other levels of government. To invoke Anderson in a new context, it is
clear that all these administrative functions demand—indeed are premised
upon—the conception of a "sociological organism [composed not only
of the bureaucracy itself but also of the entire society] moving calendrically through homogeneous empty time" (Anderson 1991:26) While
one bureaucrat is making sure that sufficient funds are transferred to a
government-sponsored health care program, for example, he or she has

confidence that another bureaucrat somewhere else—whom he or she has probably never met—is tending to the collection of oil and gas revenues.

It is not enough, however, simply to assert that the administrative functions of bureaucracy are premised upon a conception of homogeneous empty space-time. Although homogeneous empty space-time may be a conceptual prerequisite for the administration of large and complex social systems, in practice the spatiotemporal framework of bureaucratic administration remains neither "empty" nor "homogeneous" for long. Indeed, imparting order and structure to the imagined abstraction of homogeneous empty space-time is a critical part of bureaucratic practice; it is a large part of what bureaucrats actually do on a day-to-day basis. Consider again the task of bureaucratic administration. Bureaucrats must accomplish all the diverse goals described above with the finite resources (time, money, personnel) at their disposal. For bureaucrats administering a complex social system, there is always more to do than can be accomplished in any given period of time. As a result, they must prioritize. They do so by engaging in elaborate processes of planning and evaluation that include, among other things, the preparation and approval of work plans and budgets (which are continually being revised), the negotiation of (inter- and intragovernmental) funding agreements, and the preparation, evaluation, and auditing of interim and annual reports. Work plans, budgets, reports, audits, and similar administrative tools bring structure to the homogeneity and emptiness of abstract space-time. While bureaucrats plan and carry out the construction of a new road somewhere, they know of other roads and bridges elsewhere that, because of budgetary constraints, are not scheduled for construction until next year or the year after. And there are other bureaucrats who prepare, review, and approve (or reject) year-end reports and audits to make sure that government employees or contractors building the road adhere to proper timetables and budgets (so that there will be sufficient resources to construct those other roads and bridges in the future). It is precisely through the use of plans, budgets, reports, accounting techniques, and the other "soft technologies" of administration that bureaucrats seek to impose a particular spatiotemporal structure upon the abstract field of homogeneous empty space-time.

In 1900 the government of Canada devolved jurisdiction over fish and wildlife to the Yukon territorial government. The twentieth century witnessed the gradual development of an elaborate administrative apparatus for the management of fish and wildlife.[12] The development of a modern transportation and communication infrastructure in mid-century enabled bureaucratic managers to enforce an ever-more-complex set of management policies and regulations across hitherto largely inaccessible parts of the territory (see Nadasdy 2003:38–41). The hiring of staff biologists (beginning in the 1970s) ushered in an era of scientific management with the aim of controlling the natural population cycles of fish and wildlife for the maximum benefit of humans. The growing management bureaucracy increasingly made use of the administrative technologies discussed above, thus enmeshing the people and animals of the territory within a single spatiotemporal framework, a framework structured by bureaucrats wielding budgets, work plans, accounts, and reports.

Having examined the two different spatiotemporal perspectives from which Yukon people view animals and human–animal relations, we are now in a position to consider the political consequences of this spatiotemporal heterogeneity.

THE POLITICS OF SPACE-TIME AND HUMAN–ANIMAL RELATIONS IN THE YUKON

Since the influential works of Durkheim (1915), Evans-Pritchard (1940:100–104), Hallowell (1937), Leach (1961:114–136), and others, anthro-pologists have accepted it as a given that conceptions of time are socially constructed and vary considerably across cultures. Although those early scholars recognized that cultures are not necessarily characterized by a single, totalizing notion of time,[13] it was only relatively recently that anthropologists began to focus in a systematic way on the multiplicity of temporal orders within any given society. This multiplicity inevitably raises questions of power (for example, Greenhouse 1996; Rutz 1992). Among the first to attempt a systematic exploration of the multiple forms of social time, Georges Gurvitch (1964) was also among the first to conceptualize time in explicitly political terms: "Each society, each social class, each particular group, each micro-social element—indeed every social activity…has a tendency to operate in a time proper to itself…no society, no social class, no structured group…can live without trying to control these times" (Gurvitch 1963, cited in Rutz 1992:15). In this view, the temporal order of any society is not a cultural given but rather the product of struggles among social actors to determine which of the multiple possible forms of social time should constitute the basis for any particular social interaction or process. For this reason, "the social construction of time must be seen as a political process" (Verdery 1992:37). Henry Rutz notes that "a *politics* of time is concerned with the *appropriation* of the time of others, the *institutionalization* of a dominant time, and the *legitimation* of power by means of the control over time" (1992:7; emphasis in original). All these dimensions are evident in the politics of wildlife management in the Yukon.

Environmental historians and anthropologists agree that the development of bureaucratic wildlife management at the beginning of the twentieth century was inextricably bound up with the expansion of state power (Feit 1998; Jacoby 2001; Marks 1984). In many parts of the world, including North America, the imposition of state wildlife management and conservation programs first brought not only land and wildlife under the effective control of central governments, but local and aboriginal people as well. This certainly describes the situation in the Yukon throughout much of the twentieth century (Nadasdy 2003).

Recently ratified Yukon First Nation land-claim and self-government agreements, however, have altered this dynamic, although to what extent is not yet clear. On one hand, these agreements have dramatically increased the complexity of wildlife management in the Yukon and have given First Nation and other village Yukoners a genuine role in the management process. As a result, First Nation people now possess the political means— at least in theory—to challenge the spatiotemporal assumptions underlying scientific wildlife management and to advocate management strategies based on their own very different perspectives. On the other hand, however, I will argue that the structure of these new land-claim agreements in some ways actually makes it more difficult to mount such challenges. As I have shown elsewhere (Nadasdy 2003), these agreements are extremely bureaucratizing. First Nation people had to construct bureaucratic structures of their own that mirror those of the federal and territorial governments as a prerequisite for even sitting down to negotiate with them. The agreements themselves are extremely complex legal documents that define First Nations as a "third order of government" (the federal government and the provinces/territories being the other two) and lay out the relationship among these orders of government. Because the federal and territorial governments are themselves large bureaucracies, the formal mechanisms for intergovernmental relations are necessarily bureaucratic in form. In other words, it is primarily at the bureaucratic level that these complex agreements are implemented. Federal, territorial, and First Nation bureaucrats must work closely together to implement these agreements, and their relations with one another are mediated (and in large part instantiated) by the administrative practices and technologies discussed above: budgets, work plans, financial reports, and audits. Wildlife management is no exception. The provisions governing rights to the use and management of fish and wildlife create a formal space within the existing management bureaucracy for First Nation people and governments (Nadasdy 2005a). To assume their role within this bureaucracy, however, First Nation people have no choice but to wield the administrative technologies discussed above, technologies that presuppose a bureaucratic notion of space-time as homogeneous and empty. This process effectively institutionalizes the spatiotemporal assumptions of bureaucratic management, making it very difficult for First Nation people to challenge them and the power relations they support.

In the remainder of this chapter, I examine the spatiotemporal politics of wildlife management in the Yukon. As we shall see, however, it is not simply a matter of different actors invoking different spatiotemporal orders depending upon their particular interests and/or cultural backgrounds. Rather, the spatiotemporality of wildlife resources is context dependent; certain social contexts are predicated upon particular spatiotemporal orders (which structure them). Actors who would engage with wildlife (or with one another in relation to wildlife) in such a context—whatever their individual interests or cultural backgrounds—often have little choice but to do so from that particular spatiotemporal perspective. One can reject that perspective as inappropriate, as some First Nation people do, but only by rejecting the whole bureaucratic context of wildlife management. Other social contexts, however, allow more latitude for struggles over the spatiotemporality of wildlife. Either way, such struggles are deeply political.

Because wildlife management in the territory is now occurring within the larger context of land-claim agreements, I necessarily begin with a brief discussion of these agreements, particularly the provisions dealing with wildlife management.

THE YUKON LAND-CLAIM AGREEMENTS AND THE BUREAUCRATIZATION OF WILDLIFE MANAGEMENT

In 1993 representatives of Canada, the Yukon Territory, and the Council for Yukon Indians signed the Yukon Umbrella Final Agreement (UFA). Although the UFA is not in itself a land-claim agreement, it serves as a framework for the negotiation of specific final agreements between each of the Yukon First Nations (there are fourteen) and the federal and territorial governments (Council for Yukon Indians 1993). The UFA contains many general provisions that apply to the entire Yukon and others that identify areas in which individual First Nations may negotiate provisions specific to their own needs. Eleven of the fourteen First Nations in the Yukon have now signed and ratified final agreements based upon the UFA. These final agreements are extremely complex documents consisting of twenty-eight chapters that deal not only with land but also with financial compensation, heritage, taxation, renewable and nonrenewable resources, economic development, and more. Of particular relevance here is chapter 16, which establishes a new regime for the co-management of fish and wildlife. One of the primary objectives of the chapter is "to enhance and promote the full participation of Yukon Indian People in Renewable Resource management" (Council for Yukon Indians 1993:153). To this end, the agreement provides for the establishment of the Yukon Fish and Wildlife Management Board (FWMB), a territory-wide body, and fourteen Renewable Resources Councils (RRCs), one for each of the fourteen Yukon First Nations. The UFA establishes the FWMB as the "primary instrument" for fish and wildlife management throughout the Yukon (Council for Yukon Indians 1993:166) and each RRC as the "primary instrument" for renewable-resources management within each First Nation's traditional territory (for example, Kluane First Nation 2003a:241).[14] The FWMB and RRCs are considered co-management bodies because half the members of each are nominated by the Yukon government and half by the Council of Yukon First Nations (or the relevant First Nation government in the case of RRCs). These bodies are charged with the responsibility of carrying out public consultations on management issues (on either a Yukon-wide or traditional territorial basis) and making recommendations to the relevant government in any particular case.[15] Board and council appointees are not government officials and are not expected to act as representatives for the governments that appointed them. Rather, they are "ordinary citizens" chosen on the basis of their interest in and knowledge about wildlife.[16] In other words, the board and councils are supposed to be external to the bureaucratic structures of government; their role is to consult with the wider public and provide government bureaucrats (both territorial and First Nation) with recommendations based on those consultations. In fact, board and council members do come from all walks of life; very few of them are government officials or have any experience working in a bureaucratic setting.

Despite the requirement that co-management bodies such as RRCs stand at "arm's length" from government and the fact that, for the most part, appointees to these bodies are not themselves professional bureaucrats, co-management of this sort does not represent as radical a break from centralized state management as is often supposed. Indeed, I have argued elsewhere (Nadasdy 2005a) that far from representing an *alternative* to bureaucratic state management, co-management bodies like those created by chapter 16 of the Yukon UFA are firmly *embedded within* that bureaucracy. Their establishment was accompanied by the creation of a set of administrative rules and procedures regulating not only how they function internally but also how they relate to external bureaucratic institutions in the territorial and First Nation governments (although, as we shall see below, those rules and procedures have been subject to fairly intense struggle). Such rules enable co-management boards to interface with existing offices and institutions of state management, and this process is absolutely essential if they are to play their appointed roles. In this important sense, co-management boards are inherently bureaucratic. Rather than liberate First Nation people from government bureaucracy, then, the creation of such boards has simply given First Nation people their own "slot" in the bureaucratic system.

RENEWABLE RESOURCES COUNCILS AND BUREAUCRATIC TIME

As we saw above, the administration of a large and complex state such as Canada is necessarily premised on the conception of a "social organism moving calendrically through homogeneous empty time." The bureaucratic administrators of such a social system must have faith in the "steady, anonymous, simultaneous, activity" not only of other officials but also of all those people and processes they administer. Co-management bodies, such as the RRCs, being bureaucratic entities themselves, are necessarily part of all this steady, anonymous, simultaneous activity. As noted above, however, it is not enough simply to note that RRC members function in the homogeneous empty space-time of bureaucratic practice. Rather, they are necessarily caught up in the ongoing struggle and negotiation among bureaucrats wielding administrative technologies to structure the abstract expanse of homogeneous empty space-time.

Stephen Lukes (1977) argues that structure implies power. If this is so, then the use of any administrative techniques to impose a particular structure upon the spatiotemporal order necessarily has a political dimension. And indeed, as John Sweetman (1984:3) notes, "administration is the means by which power is exercised," an observation borne out by recent work on the political dimensions of accounting, audits, and other modern administrative practices (Neu 2000; Power 1997; Strathern 2000). This idea suggests that some understanding of these administrative technologies—and their histories—is crucial to any study of the contemporary politics of space-time in the Yukon.

Chapter 16 of each First Nation final agreement describes in broad strokes the roles, powers, and responsibilities of the Renewable Resources Councils (see, for example, Kluane First Nation 2003a:241–246). First Nation final agreement implementation plans, which are attached to each agreement, provide a bit more information, including statements of each RRC's total annual operating budget for the year it is established and a multiyear financial forecast (see, for example, Kluane First Nation 2003b: 432–436). Aside from these broad guidelines, however, the agreements provide relatively little detail about day-to-day operations of the RRCs or about the administrative context in which they are to operate. As a result, RRC members, along with the First Nation and territorial officials responsible for dealing with them, have had to work out many of these practical details for themselves. The result has been ongoing negotiation and struggle both within individual RRCs and between RRCs and territorial and First Nation bureaucrats. One of the most important areas of contestation during the ten years since the first agreements were put in place has been how to structure the homogeneous empty space-time within which the RRCs are to function. Much of this negotiation and struggle has taken place in the realms of planning, budgeting, reporting, and other forms of administrative practice.

The final agreements state that "each Council shall prepare an annual budget, subject to review and approval by Government. The budget shall be in accordance with Government guidelines" (for example, Kluane First Nation 2003a:243). The agreements further specify that these budgets may include (1) "remuneration and travel expenses" for RRC members to attend meetings; (2) "the cost of public hearings and meetings"; (3) "research review, public information and other activities"; and (4) "other items as the Council and Government agree on" (for example, Kluane First Nation 2003a:243). The implementation plans lay out each RRC's annual operating budget and also provide a recommended budget for its first year of operation, with spending broken down into only three major categories: administration, meetings, and support. They further stipulate that "annual budgets prepared by the [RRC] in subsequent years will provide greater detail than that provided in the Year 1 Budget to better reflect the operational requirements of the [RRC]" (for example, Kluane First Nation 2003b: 436). The government's role in approving RRC budgets and line items gives territorial administrators a potentially important role in defining and regulating the activities in which RRC members can engage.

The federal government ultimately bears the costs associated with the operation of the RRCs, but because the Yukon government has jurisdiction over fish and wildlife in the territory, the federal government transfers the appropriate funds to the territorial government on an annual basis. So it is largely the territorial government that is charged with reviewing and approving RRC budgets, negotiating contribution agreements with RRCs, distributing payments, and otherwise administering these funds. As we shall see, its control over the budgeting process enables it to exert direct influence over RRC activities.

In 2003–2004 I served as the Kluane First Nation's representative to the Yukon Implementation Review Group (IRG), an intergovernmental body charged with conducting a formal nine-year review of the Yukon Umbrella Final Agreement and those First Nation final and self-government agreements that had been in effect for at least five years.[17] The object of the review was to assess how well the parties had implemented the agreements and to identify problems or obstacles to their implementation—with an eye to possibly renegotiating problematic sections of the agreements. As part of the review process, the IRG invited written statements from each of the RRCs and invited members to appear before the IRG in person to present their concerns and answer questions. Territorial officials were also invited to appear before the IRG to express concerns and answer questions about government–RRC relations.

Disagreements over reporting requirements and other aspects of administration have been a source of tension between RRCs and the Yukon government since the first RRCs were established in 1995. For the first few years, the projected annual budgets prepared by most RRCs were not much more detailed than those spelled out in the implementation plans. This should not be too surprising; as we have already seen, few RRC members were themselves bureaucrats or had any experience in preparing budgets, work plans, or other administrative documents of this sort. What is more, each RRC prepared its own budget, so there was considerable variation in the detail and quality of the budgets submitted. Each RRC also used its own spending categories and budget format. The lack of standardized budgets made it difficult for Yukon officials to deal with the RRCs in a coordinated fashion and forced them to spend a great deal of time (at public expense) on the phone with RRCs clarifying what was going on. Yukon officials noted that during the first few years, they even had trouble getting year-end audited financial statements from some of the RRCs and that several RRCs continue to this day to submit them late.[18] Gradually, Yukon officials introduced a series of new reporting requirements. Some of these, such as requiring RRCs to use a standard budget form, were calculated to reduce the variation among individual RRCs and to rationalize the overall process and were seen by RRC members as generally helpful. Other changes, however, were resisted by RRCs, who viewed them as onerous or as attempts by territorial officials to exert inappropriate influence over RRC activities.

Nearly all the RRCs—either in their written submissions to the IRG or in their oral testimony—expressed concerns over reporting requirements imposed by territorial officials. Several complained that nearly every year territorial officials changed the format of the required reports and that they were constantly returning documents to the RRCs to be revised to meet the current guidelines. RRCs complained that these requirements were becoming more and more onerous, using up excessive amounts of the RRCs' scarce time and resources on what they viewed as pointless paperwork. Yukon government officials, for their part, saw changes in the reporting requirements as part of an effort to fine-tune the administrative process. They maintained that such changes were not arbitrary, as they seemed to the RRCs, but were instead always in response to particular issues; and they argued that in the aggregate such changes were leading to an increasingly rational and streamlined process. They did admit that in at least one case, changes to the reporting requirements had *not* been primarily about increasing administrative efficiency. That case, however, had been the result of "political" (that is, extrabureaucratic) pressures over which they had had no control.[19] Yukon officials also denied that the RRCs' reporting requirements were particularly onerous. On the contrary, they asserted that appropriate reporting was necessary to ensure that RRCs remained accountable to Canadian taxpayers, whose money they were spending, and officials described several incidents of inappropriate spending by RRCs to back up their position.

One particularly contested issue had to do with the production of annual work plans. Several years before my tenure on the IRG, that body (as part of a formal five-year review of the agreements) had agreed that the RRCs were underfunded and had recommended that the federal government provide an additional $20,000 per year to each council. The federal government agreed to increase RRC funding, but in return RRCs were compelled to produce detailed annual work plans laying out how they would spend the extra money. Because it would have made very little sense for RRCs to plan only how they would spend the *extra* $20,000 (and not do the same for the rest of their budgets), territorial officials were soon requiring that RRCs submit work plans detailing how they intended to spend their entire projected budgets. Some RRC members conceded that putting together an annual work plan was a potentially useful exercise (because it might help them set priorities for the coming year), but most found the process at best irrelevant; many feared that it was actually undermining the RRCs' autonomy.

Because of their small budgets, RRCs are severely limited in the number of staff they can hire and the other resources at their disposal. At the same time, they are widely viewed as key institutions of the land-claim agreements; territorial and First Nation governments must (and do) consult with them on all manner of issues related to renewable resources, from the granting of water licenses and land-use permits, to proposed changes in hunting regulations, to plans for development anywhere in their traditional territories. In addition, new federal and territorial legislation can increase the roles and responsibilities of Yukon co-management boards, sometimes without corresponding increases in their funding levels.[20] Many RRC members complained that, as a result of all this, it was impossible for them to be proactive. Rather, all they could hope to do was to respond to the many demands placed on them by governments. Thus, although in theory the RRCs had the power to structure their time as they saw fit, in practice they could often do little more than react to outside pressures, and any planning they may have done at the start of the year was largely irrelevant.

Worse yet, the RRCs felt that to the extent they *did* have the time and resources to pursue their own agendas, their ability to do so was being undermined by officials in the territorial government. Nearly all the RRCs complained that territorial officials were using the required work plans to interfere with council activities. Although RRC mandates are spelled out in the final agreements, there is considerable room for disagreement over how these mandates should be interpreted. RRC members felt that territorial officials were inappropriately using their power to approve or reject work plans to enforce their own particular (and, members felt, excessively restricted) interpretation of RRC mandates. Yukon government officials, for their part, denied that they were interfering inappropriately. They did, however, feel that on behalf of the parties, it was their role to make sure that RRCs stuck to their mandates. One of the most contentious areas of dispute in this regard was whether RRCs should be allowed to fund wildlife research. Yukon government officials felt that funding and carrying out wildlife research was the sole responsibility of the territorial government. They maintained that if RRC members decided that some particular wildlife study was necessary, they should make a recommendation to the territorial government that it be carried out. Several of the RRCs vehemently disagreed, arguing that the territorial government had its own research agenda, which often did not correspond well with the interests of First Nations and RRCs. They argued instead that identifying significant gaps in existing knowledge about wildlife and devising ways to fill those gaps was a critical part of their mandate and this might well include funding wildlife studies. In fact, the official RRC mandates—as spelled out in the agreements—are unclear on the issue of research. But because

Yukon officials controlled the RRCs' budgets and steadfastly refused to approve budgets and work plans that funded wildlife research, they were effectively able to enforce their own interpretation of the mandate.[21] In this way, they were able to exert considerable influence over the ordering and structuring of events within the homogeneous empty space-time of wildlife management.

Yukon officials' control over the situation, however, was far from complete. The RRCs did not submit passively to what they saw as Yukon officials' efforts to dictate to them the terms of their own mandates. In some cases, they simply funded research that was outside their approved budgets and work plans, knowing full well that at year end they would face the ire of territorial officials. Having been presented with a fait accompli, however, these officials could do little more than scold RRC members retroactively for having exceeded their authority. Another important means utilized by RRCs in their efforts to regain control over their mandates was to raise their own funds from nongovernmental organizations, such as the Gordon Foundation. They could then use these funds to carry out research and other activities that territorial officials would not have approved.[22] "Resistance" of this sort has its own temporal implications, however. Proposal writing is extremely time-consuming, and there is no guarantee that proposals will be successful. Given the time pressures faced by RRC members and staff, the choice to pursue nongovernmental funding is a risky one; even when RRCs are successful at it, those that choose this route necessarily put off—or forsake entirely—engaging in other important activities.[23]

We have seen that government officials, RRC members, and others caught up in the wildlife management bureaucracy wield administrative technologies as they vie with one another to structure the empty homogeneous expanse of bureaucratic space-time. To the extent that they do so, however, they necessarily take for granted the spatiotemporal framework upon which those administrative tools are based. They take for granted the "steady, anonymous, simultaneous, activity" not only of humans but also of the animals they would manage. This process effectively enmeshes First Nation people in a set of practices rooted in a spatiotemporal order that is in many ways incompatible with their notions of what constitutes proper human–animal relations. The fact that these practices have become entrenched within new institutions of governance and management created by land-claim and self-government agreements, however, makes it very difficult for First Nation people to question them. As we shall see, the only option for those who would challenge the dominant spatiotemporal framework is to reject the land-claim agreements themselves, along with the assumptions of bureaucratic management upon which they have been built.

COMPETING SPATIOTEMPORAL FRAMEWORKS AND CATCH-AND-RELEASE FISHING

As noted earlier, many Yukon First Nation people do not regard human–animal interactions as occurring within homogeneous empty space-time. The simultaneity that connects a contemporary Yukon First Nation hunter with the animal-people of Long Time Ago stories is of a very different order than the simultaneity that structures practices of bureaucratic wildlife management. Similarly, although First Nation hunters and Euro-American wildlife managers can agree that wildlife is a renewable resource, they have very different ideas about the role humans play in the maintenance of animal cycles. As a result, many First Nation people regard the basic assumptions and practices of bureaucratic wildlife management with suspicion. It is well known, for example, that many First Nation people object to standard management practices such as the radio-collaring of animals by wildlife biologists, because they see such treatment as insulting to animal-people. But the insult does not lie merely in the fact that such practices subject animals to the indignities of being drugged, handled, and forced to wear radio collars. Equally problematic is the fact that through such practices, wildlife biologists impose upon animals their own time schedules, budgets, and research agendas. Rather than try to understand animals on their own terms, biologists force them into the context of bureaucratic space-time in an attempt to wrest knowledge from them by force. This work is completely at odds with Kluane people's notions about what constitutes respectful behavior toward all persons, whether human or nonhuman (see Nadasdy 2003:108–111).

Thus many standard wildlife-management practices are insulting to animal-people, not merely because these practices subject them to physical indignities but also because they impose on human–animal relations a new spatiotemporal framework, one that is geared specifically toward asserting what many First Nation people see as an inappropriate degree of control over animals. No amount of wrangling over budgets and work plans can address the concerns of First Nation people who object to such practices on these grounds. For them, the only option is to reject the spatiotemporal assumptions of bureaucratic wildlife management, an option that is becoming increasingly difficult because of the entrenchment of such assumptions in the provisions of Yukon land-claim agreements. The struggle over catch-and-release fishing is a case in point.

In the late 1990s, the Fish and Wildlife Management Board, aware of First Nation concerns about catch-and-release fishing, commissioned several studies to investigate whether voluntary catch and release was an appropriate technique for the management of fish stocks. As Easton (2002) notes, knowledge that the board was investigating the practice of catch and release generated a contentious public debate. Yukon government fisheries managers and most Euro-American sports fishermen and tourism operators supported catch and release because it enables fishermen to be selective about the fish they kill, allowing them to release the large spawners that are critical for the reproduction of fish populations. Clearly underlying this perspective on the practice are assumptions about the cyclical temporality of fish as a resource and the notion that humans can and should control their natural population cycles through the regulation of "harvest" levels (among other things).

In contrast, the vast majority of Yukon First Nation people oppose the practice of catch-and-release fishing (Muckenheim 1998). They do so both because it subjects fish-people to the indignities of insulting treatment at human hands and because releasing fish is a repudiation of the act of reciprocal exchange that lies at the heart of the relationship between human- and animal-people (see Easton 2002; Nadasdy 2003:81–83; Natcher, Davis, and Hickey 2005:246). First Nation stories such as "The Boy Who Stayed with Fish," a well-known tale about a boy who spoke disrespectfully about a piece of fish, make clear the dangers of such behavior. As a result of his disrespectful behavior, the boy was transformed into a fish, and he lived among the fish-people for several years. Eventually, he regained his human form and taught people the proper way to treat fish.[24] In one of the reports prepared by the board, a First Nation person objected to catch-and-release fishing because it "goes against the fundamental beliefs of the First Nations people....They consider [it] to be 'playing with the fish' which is very disrespectful." They believe that "you only fish for food...and that you never, never play with the animals. You must respect them or they won't come back" (cited in Muckenheim 1998; see also Easton 2002:17). This phrasing suggests that if one treats a fish properly (that is, one kills and eats it rather than releases it), it *will* "come back" to be caught again. Indeed, because both humans and fish are reborn, there is an important sense in which everyone in "The Boy Who Stayed with Fish"—human and fish alike—is still alive today and continues to enact this age-old relationship of reciprocal exchange in the manner prescribed by the fish-people themselves and relayed to humans via that boy.[25] In contrast to the perspective of biologists and sport fishers, then, the First Nation perspective on catch-and-release fishing is based on the assumption that fish populations are *circularly*, rather than *cyclically*, renewable and therefore fish management should be about maintaining social relationships rather than controlling biological cycles.

Despite a great deal of talk about the need to find "common ground" on the issue, in 2000 the Fish and Wildlife Management Board recommended that voluntary catch and release continue to be used and promoted in the Yukon, although the board did recommend that only barbless fishhooks be used in an effort to reduce the mortality of released fish. They also created the Fish Think Tank, a working group charged with educating the public about catch-and-release fishing and promoting it as a management practice (Fish and Wildlife Management Board 2000:20; see also Easton 2002:16). Easton is highly critical of the way in which the board disregarded First Nation interests and values. He attributes this situation to a discursive strategy by proponents of catch and release to frame First Nation concerns as "ethical" in nature (and thus not an appropriate basis for policy making), in contrast to their own concerns, which they portray as rooted in biological and economic realities (the proper bases for the regulation of fisheries) (Easton 2002:19–21). Easton views as disingenuous proponents' self-proclaimed desire to "keep ethical decisions out of the fishing regulations," noting that "the law and its regulations are precisely the codification of ethics within a statutory frame by which they can be legitimately enforced by the State" (2002:20).

I would add that it is possible—indeed *necessary*—to dismiss First Nation concerns as "merely ethical" because First Nation conceptions of animals and the *circular* spatiotemporality of human–animal relations are fundamentally incompatible with assumptions of scientific and bureaucratic fisheries management. Because of this incompatibility, there is *no way* to make fisheries policy that is consistent with *both* First Nation and biological ideas about management. To truly accept First Nation concerns as the basis for making management decisions, one would first have to *reject* the cyclical spatiotemporality that underlies biological conceptions of fish and fishing. Indeed, at least one wildlife biologist has recognized this point explicitly. He believes that most members of the board and various RRCs take First Nation beliefs and values seriously in their deliberations. Difficulties arise, he said, when board members try to "operationalize" these beliefs in the realm of management, and the problem is especially evident when First Nation beliefs and values *contradict* those of biologists. A good example of this, he told me, was the debate over catch-and-release fishing, because it was impossible to act on the beliefs and values of First Nation people in relation to this issue without *denying* the insights of biologists (see Povinelli 1995 for a similar dilemma in the Australian context).

So why did First Nation members of the Fish and Wildlife Management Board go along with recommendations to continue and even promote catch-and-release fishing? One First Nation board member told me that he had done so reluctantly and for pragmatic political reasons. He noted that First Nation people make up less than a third of the Yukon population and that "we all have to live together." He told me that he would never practice catch-and-release fishing himself but, he did not feel right dictating to non–First Nation people how they should behave. Like all members of the board, he was also acutely aware that any recommendation to prohibit catch-and-release fishing would have ignited a political firestorm.[26] Although such a position is certainly understandable from a pragmatic standpoint, it is worth considering its full social and political implications. In the first place, when First Nation people acquiesce to Euro-Canadian desires to practice catch and release, they are making a huge sacrifice. Because improper behavior by Euro-Canadians can destroy the delicate social relationship between fish and *all* humans, First Nation people consciously risk their children's futures in the name of social harmony.[27]

Second, and perhaps more important, in acquiescing to catch and release, First Nation people implicitly accept the biological assumptions about fish that underlie the practice. In so doing, they tacitly agree to use the framework of bureaucratic space-time as the only legitimate basis upon which to make—and contest—fisheries management decisions. They are still free to vie with others in the attempt to bring structure to homogeneous empty bureaucratic space-time (in the ways described above), but it becomes increasingly difficult for them to question the conceptual bases of bureaucratic management.

CONCLUSION

Anthropologists and others have noted that the social construction of time is an inherently political process. In the second half of this chapter, I explored the political dimensions of wildlife management in the Yukon, which can be seen at least in part as a struggle between First Nation people and bureaucratic wildlife managers to impose their own particular spatiotemporal perspectives on human–animal relations in the territory. Although First Nation people can and do assert some degree of control over space and time within the new bureaucratic context of wildlife management in the territory, that very context takes for granted the cyclical topology of bureaucratic space-time and so is incompatible with their view of proper human–animal relations. To some extent, then, First Nation people's participation in the bureaucratic co-management process (and acquiescence to the spatiotemporal assumptions underlying it) makes it increasingly difficult for them to challenge dominant Euro-Canadian views of wildlife management and human–animal relations.

In this chapter, I used Gell's concept of temporal topology to analyze the idea that fish and wildlife are *renewable resources*. Although everyone in the Yukon agrees that fish and wildlife populations are renewable, there is a fundamental disagreement over the concept of *renewability* itself and the spatiotemporal order it implies. Wildlife biologists view animal populations and human–animal relations as embedded in cyclical time, characterized by the periodic recurrence of similar events of the same type. First Nation people, by contrast, are more likely to view them as embedded in *circular* time, a temporal framework within which the *same event* recurs over and over again. This difference has significant implications for how each group conceives of the animal resource. Many First Nation people, for example, view animals as a potentially unlimited resource, their availability dependent only on the maintenance of social relations between animal- and human-persons, whereas non–First Nation hunters and biologists tend to view animals as a finite resource vulnerable to overexploitation. This view, in turn, leads them to subscribe to different notions about the proper role of human agency vis-à-vis animals and about what constitutes appropriate management.

Notes

This chapter could not have been written without the help of many people. To begin with, I would like to thank Elizabeth Ferry and Mandana Limbert for organizing the advanced seminar at SAR in Santa Fe that spawned this volume and for all their hard work editing the manuscript. I would also like to thank all of those who participated in the seminar; this chapter benefited immensely from our discussions there (particularly from Karen Strassler's insightful comments). I also received helpful comments on this chapter from Norman Easton, Marina Welker, and two anonymous reviewers. As always, I gratefully acknowledge the help and friendship of the people of Burwash Landing, Yukon Territory, without whom I could never have written this chapter. I also thank all the members of the Implementation Review Group, especially Cathy Constable, who provided me with extensive comments on the middle sections of the chapter; any errors that might remain there are mine alone. Finally, this chapter could not have been written without generous funding from the National Science

Foundation (grants 9614319 and 0233914) and the Wenner Gren Foundation for Anthropological Research.

1. For those not familiar with the Canadian context, *First Nation* is the accepted term for referring to aboriginal peoples and their governments.

2. Some scholars (for example, Notzke 1994:1–2) argue that the resource concept is firmly rooted in Euro-American notions about human superiority over nature and so is incompatible with aboriginal worldviews. The concept certainly implies a view of the world that foregrounds utility to humans. But for reasons I elucidate elsewhere (Nadasdy 2005b), I am not convinced that all such perspectives *necessarily* imply human superiority over nature or that they are necessarily incompatible with aboriginal views of the world. Be that as it may, First Nation people in the Yukon do regularly talk about fish and wildlife as renewable resources.

3. See Nadasdy (in press) for more on the central structuring role of the agricultural metaphor and its continued importance in the discipline of wildlife management.

4. For the rest of the day, everyone at the meeting attempted to follow this woman's advice, but it proved to be quite difficult to do so because of the frequency with which the term is used in such contexts. Over and over again throughout the day, biologists—and First Nation people as well—caught and corrected themselves. The effort did not seem to make a lasting impression on meeting participants, however. At subsequent meetings (and I attended many with the same people over the next three years), they all lapsed back into old habits. I never again heard anyone explicitly object to the term in a meeting.

5. For the classic description of animals as other-than-human persons and hunting as a part of the reciprocal relationship between human- and animal-people, see Hallowell 1960; see also Brightman 1993. For more on the specifics of the Yukon case, see Nadasdy 2003:ch. 2, and for reflections on the theoretical and political significance of such accounts, see Nadasdy 2007.

6. This is similar to what Lawrence Rosen (1984:185–186) has referred to as "essentially negotiable concepts." See also Fujimura 1992 for use of a similar idea in a very different context.

7. This is not to say that homogeneous empty space-time is exclusive to capitalism. Indeed, some conception of time as empty and homogeneous is probably essential to the administration of any large state or enterprise. Nor would I assert that homogeneous empty space-time is the only conception of time and space associated with large late-capitalist bureaucracies. Indeed, Michael Herzfeld (1992) identifies another important form of temporality (or, perhaps more accurately, atemporality) produced and reinforced by modern state bureaucracies. Although it would be interesting (and

fully in keeping with the development of a politics of time) to explore alternative temporal orders and struggles over their use *within* bureaucracies, such an inquiry unfortunately lies outside the scope of the present study.

8. He does, however, suggest that it may have been the rhythms of labor (spiritual as well as physical) in the monasteries of medieval Europe that led to the invention of the mechanical clock in the first place (Mumford 1962[1934]:12–14).

9. Henri Bergson (1910) argued that "abstract time," the homogeneous medium of physics, is entirely reducible to space. He contrasted abstract time with "duration," the experience of which he viewed as purely qualitative and unmeasurable. Although I disagree with the implication that abstract space is a more fundamental category than abstract time, I agree that the two are wholly implicated in each other. Thus I refer throughout this chapter to "space-time" rather than "time" or "space" alone.

10. Culturally minded Marxist scholars (Le Goff 1980; Thompson 1967) built upon Marx's insights by examining how European conceptions of time (as well as technologies for keeping it) changed in association with the rise of the capitalist labor process. Thompson, for example, citing Evans-Pritchard, characterized this change as a shift away from the irregular work rhythms of a "task-oriented" society—in which there is very little demarcation between "work" and "life" and in which people conform to the natural rhythms (seasons, tides, and so forth) that govern their subsistence—to a labor process that is strictly governed by the clock, where for the first time it becomes meaningful to speak of "spending" and "wasting" time. Significantly, however, he does not argue that the capitalist conception of time replaced the preexisting task-oriented conception. Rather, he points out that both continue to exist and that struggles over these alternate conceptions were intense and continue into the present.

11. It is not always possible to draw a clear distinction between administration and production. Indeed, although some scholars (for example, Piore and Sabel 1984) heralded the introduction of just-in-time production in the 1980s as a revolution in the nature of capitalist production, it was in large part a set of administrative innovations made possible by technological advances in transportation and communication.

12. Today, the Fish and Wildlife Branch of the Yukon Department of Environment has forty-eight employees, and Conservation Officer Services employs another thirty-two people territory-wide.

13. Evans-Pritchard distinguished, for example, between "oecological" and "structural" time among the Nuer, and Hallowell considered what happened when people enmeshed in "non-Western" time came into contact with the temporal order of capitalism.

14. The traditional territory of each First Nation is a geographical area, defined in the UFA, within which specific provisions of that First Nation's final agreement are

valid. The traditional territory defines the region of jurisdiction for each final agreement's RRC.

15. The question of jurisdiction can be fairly complex. In general, the Yukon government retains jurisdiction over fish and wildlife throughout the territory. First Nations, however, have jurisdiction over fish and wildlife on "settlement lands" retained under the agreements (subject to the limitation spelled out in section 16.5.1.8 of the agreements), and the federal Department of Fisheries and Oceans retains jurisdiction over the management of anadromous fish, such as salmon, throughout the territory.

16. The UFA has a provision requiring that RRC appointees be permanent residents of the traditional territory.

17. This review is called for in the agreements themselves.

18. Yukon government officials are themselves required to report to the federal government on the use of RRC funds. At one point, Canada redefined the Yukon's reporting requirements to include copies of each board or council's annual report and audited statement. At the same time, federal officials insisted that until they had received all those documents, no funds for any Yukon board would flow to the territorial government. As a result of this pressure, territorial officials in at least one case had to threaten to cut off the flow of funds to force an RRC to produce an audited statement.

19. In that case, certain new reporting requirements had been imposed at the request of federal bureaucrats by order of a federal minister whose government was under public pressure to increase the "accountability" of First Nations.

20. At the IRG review, for example, members of the Fish and Wildlife Management Board complained that the new federal Species at Risk legislation created a number of new roles and responsibilities for the board yet the federal government steadfastly refused to consider a corresponding increase in its funding.

21. Because of the uncertainties about board mandates, members of the IRG ended up recommending that the parties "communicat[e] and clarify...to RRCs and the FWMB the different mandates, responsibilities and roles of RRCs, the FWMB, Ministers and YFNs with regard to managing local, regional and territorial renewable resources, including fish and wildlife populations" (IRG 2007:recommendation 8.3.4).

22. It should be noted that fund-raising of this sort was more than just a response to perceived "meddling" by territorial officials. In fact, the Fish and Wildlife Management Board and RRCs began seeking nongovernmental funds almost immediately after they were established, in an effort to augment what they saw as insufficient government funding. Nevertheless, they maintain that government officials have no right to tell them how to spend money they have obtained through outside grants— which in any case must usually be spent according to the terms under which the grant

has been awarded. During IRG meetings, federal and territorial representatives challenged this practice, questioning whether it was appropriate for public co-management bodies to seek outside funding—because then they would be beholden to private foundations that have their own agendas. First Nation representatives asserted that unless the federal government would commit to providing these boards with sufficient funds to achieve their mandates, First Nations would not support any recommendation restricting their ability to look elsewhere for the funds they need to operate.

23. All members of the IRG acknowledged that fund-raising by these boards was not an ideal solution to the problem of inadequate funding. In the end, they recommended that "the Parties establish a base for the funding of each Board that eliminates the need for Boards to engage in fundraising activities to meet the financial requirements of their mandate. Boards should be advised that this is the approach that the Parties are taking and instructed to curtail fundraising activity that is disruptive to mandated work" (IRG 2007:recommendation 8.2.8). Of course, it remains to be seen whether this recommendation will actually lead to adequate board funding levels.

24. For complete versions of this story, see Cruikshank 1990:75–78, 208–213. See also McClellan 1975:185.

25. For another example of a Yukon First Nation person evaluating catch-and-release fishing in precisely this light, see Julie Cruikshank's (1998:57–58) account of an interaction between a biologist and a First Nation elder. The biologist explained the usefulness of catch and release as a management tool. In response, the elder told him the story of the boy who stayed with fish.

26. Indeed, as Easton points out, the controversy over catch and release was intense enough that the board felt compelled to announce—more than a year before it had completed its own study of the issue—that it did not intend to prohibit the practice (Easton 2002:16–17).

27. That improper behavior by Euro-Canadians can have a negative impact not only on their own relationship with fish but also on First Nation people's is evident in the following. In the summer of 2006, some First Nation people attributed low salmon numbers at Klukshu, a historically important fishing spot in the southern Yukon, not to overfishing but to the fact that Euro-Canadians had insulted the fish by bathing in the creek. As a result of this behavior, not only Euro-Canadian but also First Nation people were unable to catch fish.

5

Extinction Is Forever

Temporalities of Science, Nation, and State in Indonesia

Celia Lowe

This conception of life as the mobilization of maximal difference links these abstract metaphysical questions to the concerns of contemporary politics, that is, to the productive destabilization of present social and cultural arrangements. Rethinking time and matter may help transform how we understand politics and political struggle.

—*Elizabeth Grosz*, The Nick of Time

The evolutionary sciences, such as paleontology or conservation biology, inhabit a sphere of vital politics. Unlike studies of the body, the most extensively explored site of vitalism (Canguilhem 1991; Rose 2006), evolutionary sciences extend the politics of life to geographical sites of discovery and preservation. Scientists wish to conserve and preserve evolutionary histories and the objects that reveal them, and discovery and preservation must often occur in situ within the nations and localities where they are found. In this way, evolutionary science can be understood as social without any need to frame society as "evolving" or to reduce the social to such boiled-down terms as *survival* or *fitness*. Species and specimens are discovered within the confines of nations by scientists with national identities and commitments. From within these national confines, new species or fossilized remains enter into the realm of vital ethics, and evolutionary science becomes a focus of situated forms of governmentality, expertise, and subjectification.

Evolutionary science, however, proposes an unmarked scientific temporality with its origins in nature, not culture. The scientific temporality of biological evolution is putatively determined by the internal workings of life itself. Grosz writes:

> Operating at a different, a faster or slower rate of speed than much of the material universe, life is always challenged to overcome itself, to invent new methods, regions, tactics, and goals, to differ from itself, to continually invent solutions to the problems of survival its universe poses to it, using the resources the universe offers it, for its own self-overcoming. (Grosz 2004:9)

Evolutionary science explores continual change in forms of life—how life continually differs from itself—and speculates on how these changes have come about. Scientists give social value to evidence of morphological and functional change. Practices of valuation are always social, however; value implies a human agent who values.

Evolutionary scientists are particularly interested in preserving the evidence of and the capacity for biological change. The science of conservation biology, for example, concerns itself with three time scales that transform fatality into continuity: (1) the short-term maintenance of viable populations; (2) the maintenance of the ability to continue to evolve; and (3) the continued capacity to speciate (Groom, Meffee, and Carroll 2005:394). Preserving the ability to change means preserving "natural" transformations, not human-induced ones. Extinction is forever, and humans can destroy the capacity of life to preserve itself through adaptation.

The possibility of extinction, or the loss of scientific evidence for past forms of existence, lends urgency and moral value to the evolutionary sciences. From the perspective of conservation biology, for example, the finitude of extinction motivates the need to preserve biodiversity. From the perspective of paleontology as well, the fragility of the paleontological record and the irreplaceability of paleontological evidence give value to bone fragments and their sites of discovery. From a Buddhist perspective, in contrast, a museum full of paleontological specimens would not have this value because such a collection would imply grasping at permanence. For natural scientists, the value of evolution's products and artifacts comes from the temporality of evolutionary change and is inherent in nature, not culture. The history of biological evolution is so much deeper than human history as to appear to make human history irrelevant.

In this chapter, I explore how relative values and human histories make their way into the evolutionary sciences in Indonesia, despite the presumption within paleontology or conservation biology that only the natural temporality of evolutionary change is salient or meaningful. Specifically, I explore how bone fragments and species can become a resource for making and defending the Indonesian nation-state through efforts to conserve them. When species and specimens emerge as "Indonesian," the histories of nation and state become intensely relevant to the practices of science. Science becomes a resource for making and maintaining the nation-state, similar to the waterfalls, forests, mines, and native peoples that Ferry and Limbert mention in the introduction to this volume. For this reason, I explore the opportunities and also the considerable limitations that "nations" and "states" offer scientists in their study of evolutionary processes.

The overlapping contributions of scientific, national, and state temporalities come to light most clearly in controversies over preservation and conservation. For the science of conservation biology, inventory and the discovery of new species go hand in hand with the desire to integrate into conservation efforts those (usually rural and politically marginal) peoples who live near the natures illuminated by scientific inventories. As scientists engage with preserving biodiversity, it becomes important to know what they will make of those people who live in proximity to biodiversity. How will scientists represent them? As threatening to nature, or as owning helpful local knowledge? Do people who live near biodiverse resources possess special rights as resource users, as residents, as citizens of the nation? In answering these questions, evolutionary scientists become producers of the "social," as well as the "natural."

The scientific value of species and specimens is also in dialogue with the use-value of nature as a resource for the nation-state. Scientists are forced to confront the question of whom the products of biological evolution will be saved for. Are they for the well-being of Indonesia as a whole, for the people who live near biodiverse natures, for wealthy elites in the nation's capital, or for foreign tourists? This is a point of contention for scientists, whether they are citizens of the nation or foreign explorers. Conserving entails complex political, economic, and semiotic negotiations, in which the "absolute" temporality of evolutionary science inevitably rubs up against other agendas with their own paces.

While Indonesian scientists make scientific claims in the name of the nation, the state facilitates access to field sites, specimens, and species that Indonesian scientists would not otherwise have. In fact, it is possible to argue that the condition of possibility for Indonesian science is the nation-state. In this way, science in Indonesia is made permeable to the human historical temporality of both nation and state. For this reason, it is important to understand how histories of the nation-state are made and at what points and in what manner they enter into the natural sciences.

In this chapter, I explore how temporalities of science, nation, and state are made in Indonesia to claim that, despite the universalist dreams of scientific discovery as a value- and context-free enterprise, human history ultimately does play an important role in the way we understand the history of nonhuman life, past and present.

THE HOBBIT AND THE COELACANTH

In 2002 Indonesia's most prominent paleoanthropologist, Professor Teuku Jacob of Gajah Mada University, found himself embroiled in scientific controversy when an Australian-led team of foreign and Indonesian scientists discovered a series of new hominid fossils in a cave on Flores Island in eastern Indonesia (see Culotta 2005; Dalton 2005a, 2005b). According to Professor Jacob, the Australians had appropriated the work of Indonesian paleontologists who had been working intensively at the site since the 1970s. When the foreign scientists announced their find to the public, declaring *Homo floresiensis* (whom they nicknamed the Hobbit) a new species of hominid, they did it without the presence of their Indonesian colleagues. The discovery was presented to the international scientific community as the work of the foreign scientists alone.

Professor Jacob set to work to rectify the situation. He had the specimens transferred from Jakarta to his lab in Yogyakarta, and he sent a slice of femur to Germany for DNA analysis. From his personal inspection of the fossils, he concluded that the Hobbit was a diseased, microencephalitic form of *Homo sapiens* rather than a new species of smaller-skulled hominid. Professor Jacob took the petite size of some contemporary Flores peoples as further evidence supporting his analysis. In making these new claims, Jacob was also making a claim on behalf of the Indonesian nation. The nation-ideal inspired him to make internationally recognized truth claims in its name and to view the Australian intervention as a familiar form of colonial hegemony.

From the point of view of the Australian scientists, however, Professor Jacob had broken the rules of scientific collegiality by appropriating and analyzing the remains without the permission of their original discoverers. Further, Jacob had mishandled the specimens, unnecessarily damaging them in the process, and he had violated international treaties on fossil remains to which Indonesia, Australia, and Germany were all signatories. From the perspective of the Australians, this was a case of national pride mistakenly prevailing over the epistemologically neutral science of paleontology, and important materials from the fossil record of human evolution were now lost for good.

Although we could say that the nation-ideal played a prominent role in Professor Jacob's intervention on behalf of Indonesian paleontology, the Indonesian state also has been instrumental in creating a space for Indonesians' science. The discovery of the coelacanth, which took place a few years earlier, is but one example. The coelacanth is called the dinosaur fish because the fossil record of the fish is 350 million years old. At one time, the fish was believed to have gone extinct 65 million years ago. Since 1938, however, the coelacanth has been known to inhabit the Comoro Islands off the east coast of Africa. In 1998 the wife of American biologist Mark Erdmann observed the fish in a Sulawesi (Indonesia) market. It took several months for the pair to realize the importance of the find. Once they did, the couple began to look throughout North Sulawesi for another speci-men. When Om Lameh Senathan, a fisher from Manado Tua Island, pulled a coelacanth out of his shark net, Erdmann was able to transform Om Lameh's catch, his wife's observations, and his own biological knowledge into a moment of scientific discovery (Weinberg 2000:167–181).

While Erdmann was in the midst of his analysis of the coelacanth, how-ever, the Indonesian Institute of Science (LIPI) confiscated the fish. A team of Indonesian and French scientists then began to study it under the aus-pices of this state scientific institute. They assigned it a Latinate name before Erdmann was able to, and they claimed the discovery for Indonesia. As described in the journal *Nature*,

> The whole issue is already shrouded in controversy. After analyz-ing the specimen that Erdmann had given to the Indonesian authorities, Pouyaud and his colleagues at the Indonesian Institute of Science named it as a distinct species, *Latimeria mena-doensis*—to the chagrin of Erdmann, who had been analyzing tis-sue samples independently. (McCabe and Wright 2000)

In the case of the coelacanth, the state played a critical role in facilitating the work of Indonesian scientists. The power of the state scientific institute was behind their ability to gain access to the specimen and to name the fish after Manado, the capital of North Sulawesi.

Although Indonesian scientists could take pride in their work with the coelacanth, Erdmann was dismayed at the controversy surrounding the discovery of the fish. In his opinion, the state had played an inappro-priate role, and the nationalistic reaction of the Indonesian biologists was not rel-evant to the science of evolutionary biology. He wrote:

> Much has been made of the nationalistic animosity that has
> tainted the saga of the Coelacanth. In our opinion, nationalism
> plays no role in good science, and is irrelevant in chance discov-
> eries such as that of the Indonesian Coelacanth. As scientists it is
> our responsibility to study and conserve. The Indonesians and
> Comorans are rightfully proud of efforts in their two countries
> to preserve these rare and very special fish. What pride can we in
> the western scientific community take in this affair? (Erdmann
> and Caldwell 2000)

For the Australian scientists who claimed Flores Man as their discovery
and for Mark Erdmann, who saw the discovery of the coelacanth as a contribution of "Western" science, the value of their discoveries lay in the temporality of evolutionary processes, not in the historical specificity of the
Indonesian nation-state. The importance of *Latimeria menadoensis* to evolutionary biology or *Homo floresiensis* to paleontology is said to lie in each
creature's ability to open a window upon the evolutionary record of life on
earth. For Indonesian scientists such as Teuku Jacob, on the other hand,
the Hobbit and the coelacanth were each part of the specificity of
Indonesian history, as well as evolutionary time, and were resources for the
nation. For the scientists at LIPI, it was important that new species and discoveries enter into the scientific record *as* Indonesian. Their postcolonial
refiguration of scientific practice was an antidote to the normative and hidden practices that cause scientific discovery to enter into circulation as
"Western" without noting the historical and spatial specificity of the "West"
as a concept.

SCIENCE AND THE INDONESIAN NATION-STATE

> Man is a species-being, not only because he practically and theoretically makes
> the species—both his own and those of other things—his object, but also—and
> this is simply another way of saying the same thing—because he looks upon
> himself as the present, living species, because he looks upon himself as a uni-
> versal and therefore free being.
>
> —*Karl Marx, "Economic and Philosophic Manuscripts"*

Using the past to give meaning to the present, paleontologists and conservation biologists seek to preserve the record of biological evolution.
Althhough extinction is forever, evolutionary scientists can secure a future,

transcend finitude, even guarantee an afterlife, we might say, by ensuring the preservation of their specimens and species. From the perspective of the evolutionary sciences, the study of evolution precludes reference to recent social history. The future of humankind appears not to be in question, while other species are the ones vulnerable to extinction and disappearance. From a different vantage point, however, at the very heart of overcoming finitude and extinction is the ability to conserve man's own species-being, what Marx describes as the human ability to sustain a universal and free self. In the examples I have described above, science helps the nation-state secure a universal subjectivity for postcolonial Indonesians. In examples I will describe below, however, science plays another role—one of subverting utopian national ideas on behalf of the instrumental developmental state.

In Benedict Anderson's (1983) model of the nation, the nation assumes from the enchanted domain of religion the tasks of securing a future, transcending finitude, and guaranteeing an afterlife. He argues that whereas the great contribution of world religions had been their concern with "man-in-the-cosmos, man as species being, and the contingency of life" (Anderson 1983:10), the cultural significance of the nation is to provide for that concern in an enlightened secular world. Nation and science overlap in both the process of making species (through identifying, classifying, naming, preserving) and the process of preserving man's species-being (by guaranteeing Indonesians' full humanity as knowledge producers). The affective nation as a source of hope makes it possible for Indonesian scientists to imagine that they have something unique and valuable to contribute to the process of scientific discovery. The bureaucratic state, on the other hand, makes it technically possible for Indonesian scientists to safeguard the field sites, specimens, and naming rights that are necessary for producing scientific observations.

Separately and together, affective nation and bureaucratic state each produce in Indonesian evolutionary studies something other than a value- and context-free science. Both affective nation and bureaucratic state provide a temporality to the practice of science in Indonesia that gives science a social history. Anderson (1983) parses different temporalities for "nation" and "state" through his well-known rubrics of "popular" and "official" nationalism.[1] The temporality of the popular nation is utopian and revolutionary, he says, fortuitous and unpredictable. The popular nation's relevance comes from its ever-receding "over the rainbow" quality (Anderson 2003b:240). In contrast to the ever-receding nation of the people is the ever-proceeding nation of official nationalism. The state-time of official nationalism is planned, teleological, and technocratic. Rather than by the "angel of history" of the utopian popular nation, the state's official nationalism is best characterized by the "engine of progress." The rational bureaucratic state frequently comes into conflict with the utopian nation. When this happens, the nation-state is no longer a protector of its citizens and becomes the target of resistance and struggle.

The commitment to enduring differentiation within evolutionary science suggests a politics of difference shared in common with the popular nation. Yet, as fascistic states have made clear, a passion for heterogeneity is not a consistent hallmark of nation-states. Although the nation-ideal inspires Indonesian contributions to transnational evolutionary science and the bureaucratic state saves research sites and specimens for Indonesian scientists, the question of how diverse Indonesian peoples fit within the ideal nation, or how difference is manipulated by the bureaucratic state, is more unsettled. The lived reality of difference within Indonesia is more complex and contested than the aspirations of the popular nation-ideal would indicate.

Indonesia is a country with hundreds of ethnic groups and tremendous regional cultural differences. It also has five national religions and countless forms of local beliefs and practices. During the thirty-three-year rule of Indonesia's President Suharto,[2] the state used a limited and limiting formula to shape religious, ethnic, and other social difference. Aesthetic forms of difference that could be viewed as merely superficial, such as weddings, regional languages, and the performing arts, were acceptable. Political mobilization on behalf of ethnic or sectarian identity was not. A rhetoric of "primitivism" helped to authenticate and naturalize this social formation. Agrarian people, those dependent on forest and coastal resources, or anyone not yet converted to one of the five state religions were all viewed as still primitive or "left behind" in the project of national development. The term terasing, meaning "foreign" or "alien," was applied to Indonesia's marginalized peoples, literally signifying that they were outside the boundaries of the idealized nation.

Issues of national and natural diversity have intersected at various points in Indonesian history. During the long Suharto dictatorship, heritage-based land claims were overridden for the sake of national economic development. National parks were given precedence over local people's natural resource access. And the state was known to claim village lands through eminent domain for golf course construction and other elite development projects. In the name of the nation, the state dispossessed marginalized Indonesian peoples of their lands and resources. This is quite a different picture from the nation-state that protects and enables science and scientists. Although the Suharto state was exclusionary, limitations on national belonging began to unravel at the end of the Suharto period. New questions were asked: Would acceptable cultural difference continue to be narrowly defined by the bureaucratic state, or might new forms of identity be folded into the nation's understanding of itself?[3] Might the populist ideals of the Indonesian Revolution be recovered?

Indonesian science would have its own role to play in these debates over social and natural heterogeneity. Indonesian scientists were defended by the state, yet they also could be found acting as its agents. The prestige and "neutral objectivity" of science made Indonesian scientists allies of the state and induced them to support state projects, even when these went against their scientific objectives of species or specimen conservation. Despite the sense that Indonesian science contributed to the achievement of a universal and free self among scientists, it also carried the capacity to subordinate and dispossess others within the nation. In the sections that follow, I explore Indonesians' science as a form of practice imbricated with the temporalities of both utopian nation and developmental state to show how the human temporalities of the nation-state are an active force within natural science in Indonesia.

STATE-TIME IN THE INTEGRATED CONSERVATION AND DEVELOPMENT PROJECT

> Everything was known as far and as well as it was mapped…the number of people killed by lightening, tigers, crocodiles, snakes, wild boars, "other animals," the number of victims of tuberculosis, the number of rat holes even. Yet, and the government itself made no secret about it, all the data made only a very particular sense of knowing.…The numbers, the maps, and all the other gadgets of the watching technology were applied so that the matter is not touched.
>
> —*Rudolph Mrazek*, Engineers of Happyland

In Suharto-era Indonesia, the state was deeply invested in natural resource extraction, including the economic utilization of minerals, timber, and oil. State interests were facilitated ideologically through the concept of "development" reinforced by modernization theory. Scientists who were interested in preserving specimens, species, land, or marinescapes found themselves in an awkward relationship with the state. The state had cleared a space for Indonesian science, but it also required something in return. The state asked that knowledge be produced in the name of national economic development and that scientists work to facilitate state projects of rule and order. We can see this situation clearly in the relationship between the science of conservation biology and applied projects to conserve land and marinescapes.

Biologists concerned with the evolution of species need to conserve land and marinescapes where rare and unusual plants and animals live. This work entails both social changes on the part of people who live near these species and specimens, and control over the spaces where people, plants, and animals reside. Practices of social change and control over space both bring scientists into the territory of the state. State and conservation interests were brought together during the 1990s through integrated conservation and development projects (ICDP). ICDPs propose that people who live in or near conservation areas have a right to make a living from their surrounding land and marinescapes but that this income should come from nonconsumptive uses of nature. "Ecotourism" was the most common solution to emerge out of the ICDP concept and was designed to align biodiversity conservation with state and transnational projects of liberal economic development. Development activities allowed scientists to pursue their conservation agendas without coming into conflict with states.

What "development" would mean in Indonesia was interpreted through the Indonesian state's understandings of national progress and advancement. Development (*pembangunan*) in 1990s Indonesia possessed a certain "structure of feeling," a specific discursive and interactive modality predicated on the intervention of the state in cultivating modern Indonesian subjects. Both the state's instrumental appropriation of national modernist sentiment for its own economic well-being and its cultivation of citizens on behalf of the aesthetics of modernity made "Indonesian" ICDPs distinct from the transnational regulative discourse on the need for integrating development with conservation. The progressive temporality of the developmental state structured Indonesians' conservation biology in the 1990s at least as much as the natural temporality of biological evolution.

In May 1997 I experienced these particularities firsthand in the Togean Islands of Sulawesi, the location of a new national marine park. There, several Indonesian conservation biologists, interested in preserving species diversity in the new park, were holding an ecotourism practicum. The biologists had invited people from five Togean village communities to attend the meeting. They had asked two state representatives, the regent and the regional director of tourism, to speak. I arrived at the meeting in time for the opening ceremony, which began with a prayer and a speech by the regent. Then Daud (a pseudonym), the biologist who was running the meeting, introduced the purpose of the practicum. "This work is for the development of all of us and for our nation," he explained. We would learn about tourism, conservation, and how to employ conservation as a form of economic development and self-improvement.

First to speak was Pak Pujo (a pseudonym), the director of tourism. He began by describing the moral and technical rationales of tourism at the basis of ecotourism. "There are still some people who are not responsible [*tidak bertanggung jawab*] and who destroy the environment," he said. Tourism, he suggested, can provide a solution to this problem. We might be confused or have an "unclear understanding" about what tourism actually means, however. "For this reason, the government has created Law 9 of 1990 Concerning Tourism." From Law 9, we should be able to understand that tourism is connected with governance and therefore is the responsibility of the state. "We live in a rule-of-law state [*negara hukum*], and therefore we should follow its laws. In the law, you will find everything ordered there," he explained. He told us that in Indonesia, law begins with the president; then it descends to the ministers; next it goes to the national level, then the region, and finally the local level of government, which includes his office, the Office of Tourism, Level Two.

Along with tourism's positive influences are the negative ones. Tourism, we learned, presents many dangers. It can have "cultural side effects" and therefore requires particular attitudes and proper conduct. Tourism can "ruin the social contract," Pujo warned, and we must be vigilant. "Togean people practice and follow Islam, and Islam is a religion that instructs us in our daily lives." The people must follow the Quran, which means that they should not harm nature. But, more importantly, it means that Togean people should not follow culture brought in from outside. He invoked the nation-ideal: "We have our own culture. Indonesian culture. Pancasila culture. We have to be careful. If we see something wrong, don't follow that just to get closer to our guests. We have to remember that they are from the West and we follow Eastern culture. For example, they wear those 'mini' clothes." He drew his hands across his thighs as though he were delineating a bathing suit. Again he invoked the name of God, this time in the name of nature conservation: "God does not grant us permission to harm the earth. The earth is not a gift of our ancestors; they are only letting us borrow it."

The way to have successful tourism, Pujo concluded, would be to follow the seven important principles: (1) safety (*aman*); (2) order (*tertib*); (3) cleanliness (*bersih*); (4) freshness (*kesejukan*); (5) beauty (*keindahan*); (6)

friendliness (*rama-tama*); and (7) remembrance (*kenangan*). And then he gave us advice for the upcoming national elections:

> At our election [*pesta demokrasi*], it should be remembered that our development is the result of the New Order. It is the result of Golkar [Sekretariat Bersama Golongan Karya, the regime party]. When I was on the boat coming here, I heard the ship's bell, which reminded me of our upcoming elections: one ring meant stop, and three rings meant go backward [references to the two other legal political parties]. But two meant forward [*maju*]! Of course, it is your choice what party you choose.

What struck me most about Pak Pujo's speech on ecotourism was that it had very little to do with either tourism or ecology. Rather, it was a package of officially sanctioned messages on the direction of national development. Daud explained to me how Pak Pujo's presentation fit into his plans for biodiversity conservation, however. In the past, the government and NGOs were "allergic" to each other, he said. But now they try to work together, and the NGOs have to make concessions to the government position. They could try to influence the government just a little bit by introducing the idea that conservation is important, however. For example, Daud had given Pak Pujo the idea of a guide association and promised to help with planning the content of the program. Daud explained to me that the instructions from the central Jakarta offices were "70 percent Pancasila and only 30 percent tourism." "You can't eliminate the Pancasila content altogether," he explained to me, "or else the local officials will just throw your work into the trash. But maybe you can shift the balance, sixty–forty, and throw in something about conservation."

This example of Indonesian biodiversity conservation in practice illustrates how conservation could never be guided solely by the scientific temporality of biological evolution. The state's culture of progressive development was an irrefutable part of the pragmatics of conservation biology in Indonesia. In moving from the state's Pancasila principles to conservation principles, Daud was able to shift the balance in the direction of conservation science but was unable to turn the tables on the national temporality of the "engine of progress."

Moreover, Daud himself, as an Indonesian citizen as well as a natural scientist, possessed a subjectivity formed in dialogue with Indonesian developmental nationalism. We can see this attitude in Daud's own efforts on day two of the seminar, when he presented his ideas for integrating conservation and development in a presentation titled "Developing the

Capacity of the People." Daud began with two questions: "What does it mean to build our capacity?" and "Why do the people have to be strengthened?" The audience was slow to respond to his questions. One participant said, "We are fishing for the right answers first, for the answer that you want from us." Another person called out, "The people need to be strengthened because they are weak."

"Good," Daud encouraged. "And what are the people's weaknesses?" He turned to the blackboard and wrote down the responses as people called them out to him:

- Weak in education

- Weak in economy

- Weak with laziness

- Weak in communication media

Daud himself added to the list without noting it on the board: "Weak in our ability to overcome outsiders who are reef bombers and cyanide fishers."

"Why are we weak?" Daud asked then, and something unexpected happened. A young man stood up and asserted, "We have a problem with government. If our government was just, we would be given access to school without school fees. Many people here are smart enough to go to school, to college even."

Nervous laughter filled the room. Daud underlined *education* several times with his marking pen. "We need more education," Daud replied. Then he moved to the next item on the list: "What about economy?" The same participant spoke up again: "If the government organized more work opportunities and organized our education, there would be more work, and we would be able to do it."

Daud intervened on the side of the state: "But we aren't like a developed country [*negara maju*]. The government can't give us everything. We must learn to help ourselves."

Daud then asked, "What about laziness? Why are we lazy?" Again, the outspoken young man raised his voice: "Try building a junior high and high school here. If we are sent to town far away, that only adds to the costs that our parents can't afford. We lose the chance, so we become lazy."

By this time, the mood had become uncomfortable. Another participant jumped in: "Make the people more hardworking. If we are more hardworking, we won't be lazy." "Good!" Daud answered. He looked around the room to see whether everyone agreed. Heads nodded in agreement.

Daud next asked us to define the word *nature* (*alam*). People called out the elements of nature: "Forests!" "The sea!" "Stars!" "The moon!" Daud expanded on these suggestions: Nature is composed of "ecosystems" (*ekosistem*), and an ecosystem is a group of "biotic communities" (*komunitas biotik*). Indonesia has forty-seven types of ecosystems, he told us, including the sea, beaches, mangroves, and mountains.

Then he asked, "Why should we protect the animals and their habitats?" People remained silent. "Because of the food chain," Daud answered. "The plants are eaten by the herbivores [*herbivore*], and the herbivores are eaten by the carnivores [*karnivora*]. If the chain is broken, all will be broken."

He asked us to think of the trees. What will happen if we cut down trees? He was especially concerned about the forest on the island of Malenge because it is home to the Togean macaque, an unusual primate. But Daud oriented his response toward some of the participants' concerns: there will be erosion, floods, and the wells on the island will dry up. "The trees are an easy example," he told us, "but the sea is a much harder one. The sea is more difficult to understand because the system begins with plankton [*plangton*], which are tiny, and you can't see them."

Daud was asking us to use the environment without ruining it, for example, by not using bombs and poisons. "If we use a bomb or cyanide for fishing, we are quickly full one time, but later there will be nothing—there is only a momentary enjoyment. You are happy once, but the coral is broken and ruined," he argued. He turned to a participant, Pak Ahmad, and asked, "Isn't this true?" Ahmad agreed. "So do we need to bomb or not?" Daud asked us rhetorically. "Noooo," we answered.

It is impossible to understand evolutionary science in Indonesia without understanding the state's effect on scientists; in Daud's practicum, the science of biodiversity conservation was inseparable from official or bureaucratic nationalism. Daud's English-based scientific lexicon—*herbivora, plangton, ekosistem*—which Togean people were unfamiliar with, was a language that shamed people into silence and at least superficial compliance with scientific and state order. His mention of "laziness" had the same effect. The purposive forward motion of the ICDP fit with the state's desire to facilitate the flow of conservation and tourism capital. The practicum "socialized" state-approved meanings of law, economy, and morals; at the same time, the conservation message was shaped to fit desires for economic investment. As those who must be developed, Togean people represented for Daud the inadequate "human resources" (*sumber daya manusia*) of the developmental state. Daud's evolutionary biology is inseparable from the social engineering that characterized the ICDP. Daud's own interpellation into Indonesian state developmental time was compulsory, and he partially recognized it as such.

EXHIBITING THE NATION

> To Pramoedya, locked on Buru, the Indonesian revolution of 1945 is the
> absolute. It is, indeed, what may be beyond all the constructs of history. It may
> be the "flying to the unknown." It may be the moment when time stops.
>
> —*Rudolph Mrazek*, Engineers of Happyland

The popular nation has been theorized as an affective framework that
provides an alternative to the progressivist state. During the Indonesian
Revolution, a sense of the nation as protector and representative of "a people" and the transformation of the colonial administrative unit "Dutch East
Indies" into the independent nation of "Indonesia" depended upon con-
vincing Indonesia's diverse peoples to see themselves as one. Rudolph
Mrazek (2002) describes the Indonesian Revolution as the archetypal
moment for this nation-ideal. The revolution is the moment when time
stopped, "beyond all constructs of history," when the populist standard of
the nation was fixed through struggle against foreign hegemony. The poetics of popular nationalism should be seen as an antidote to official nationalism, which, especially during the Suharto period, tended to exclude
many of Indonesia's citizens and appropriate difference as an ideological
"resource" for state *techne*. "Nation" and "state" have always existed in tension in Indonesia. However, the revolutionary ideals of the nation were
reinvigorated during the last decade of the Suharto era, when Indonesians
began to rethink the nation-state. We cannot understand Indonesians' science without understanding their conversations on difference inspired by
the form of the popular nation.

In November 1993, LIPI sponsored a scientific conference in which
nationalist ideals of inclusion provided a counterpoint to state norms of
progress. The topic of the conference was Bajau people,[4] an ethnic group
living in the coastal regions of eastern Indonesia (including Togean Island
National Park) and known stereotypically for sea cucumber collecting and
for living aboard small boats. Bajau people were at the center of debates
over Indonesian biodiversity conservation and whether people who live
near the species scientists want to conserve would become conservation
partners or opponents of biodiversity conservation. For this reason, representations of Bajau and other rural Indonesian people were integral to the
practice of evolutionary science in Indonesia.

The scientists who attended the three-day conference were scholars of
Bajau people's "ecological adaptation, nautical skills, resource management,

maritime wisdom, and particular sea lore" (Sejati Foundation 1994:34). The LIPI event described its purpose as "the re-introduction of Indonesia's cultural and ecological diversity as national assets" (1994:34). Many of the scholars were interested in social evolution, some were knowledgeable about biological evolution, and others were cultural anthropologists with expertise in Indonesian cultural diversity, history, and politics. Another group came from activist NGOs working to preserve Indonesia's environments and defend politically marginal peoples.

One aspect of the conference was a museum exhibition also titled "Bajau." The exhibition was constructed around a replica of a Bajau village set in a water reservoir filled with floating canoes brought from Sulawesi. Displays explaining the distribution of Bajau communities around Southeast Asia, Bajau origin stories, Bajau terminologies and lexicons, the Bajau environment, Bajau sea cucumber collecting, and medical practices and beliefs all surrounded the central "Bajau village." Museum archaeologists, ostensibly in charge of Indonesian prehistory, oversaw the exhibition's installation, and "ecological adaptation" was the scientific framework used to describe Bajau lifestyles. The catalog text read, "Today, the seafaring culture of the Bajau remains an example of these early maritime communities. Indeed, their present-day practices are direct links to Indonesia's maritime past" (Sejati Foundation 1994:3).

Many aspects of the exhibition presented Bajau people within a social evolutionary narrative of the nation. In representing Bajau people anachronistically as a remnant of Indonesia's prehistory, the exhibit was a spectacle of elite Indonesian progress and superiority reminiscent of universal expositions and world's fairs. The "native village" display, like that in the Bajau exhibition, is a conventional trope of ethnic exhibitions dating from the nineteenth century. In "native villages" presenting "native peoples" in *tableaux vivants*, spectacles of non-Western societies attempted to educate Euro-Americans in racial and cultural superiority (Barkan and Bush 1995:25). They did this through a social evolutionary model proposed as both the deep past of Europe and the living present of the world's non-European peoples. In the Indonesian exhibition, Bajau people were likewise made to represent Indonesian prehistory rather than the contemporary nation.

Shelly Errington has observed that although the idea of progress has come under suspicion in the global North, the idea of cultural evolution has had a new life breathed into it across the global South:

> Governments of third-world (or "developing") countries have
> tended to embrace the idea of progress with enthusiasm.

Originally called "modernization," more recently "development," the idea of ceaseless forward economic and technological movement has been given new life by an alliance composed of authoritarian third-world regimes, transnational corporations, international monetary and development agencies, and consultants from the industrialized state economies. Like early discourses of progress, these late-twentieth-century avatars invent objects that appropriate and refer to the primitive and the past, although these are more likely to take the form of glorification of national heritage rather than primitive art...or cultural theme parks celebrating ethnicity or national history, or decorated and themed airports and hotels. (Errington 1998:5–6)

The mode of representation in the Bajau exhibit replicates familiar social evolutionary hierarchies, but the exhibit also accomplishes something different that is more particular to contemporary Indonesian nationalism. The exhibition not only raises the question of the place of ethnic diversity in Indonesia's past but also asks about the role diversity will play within Indonesian national futures. For example, in a section of the exhibition titled "Issues Affecting the Bajau Today," Bajau people are presented as modern researchers and experts who participate in national economic advancement. "In collaboration with local Bajau researchers, LIPI and Sejati research presents the ecological and social-cultural issues affecting the Bajau today," the curators wrote. The contemporary environmental problems that Bajau people face in concert with other Indonesian citizens are also represented. In one part of the exhibition, for example,

> the visitor can learn about how changes in marine ecology influence the whole of Bajau society. The visitor could study how marine (traditional) resource management would be applied to wider development projects. Equally, the collected research would show the commercial potential of marine resources, and this includes marine tourism, for Indonesia's national development. Most importantly, the main hosts of the exhibition, two Bajau representatives from North Sulawesi, would always be present to answer questions from the public and to recount their immediate experience. (Sejati Foundation 1994:38)

Public programming for the exhibit included a discussion with Abdurrachman Wahid—leader of the Muslim organization Nahdlatul Ulama, who would later become Indonesia's fourth president—on the importance of cultural diversity in Indonesia; a visit by fishermen from Jakarta Bay to discuss issues in common with Bajau representatives from Sulawesi; and special events for business leaders and schoolchildren.

Despite its anachronistic native village display and its language of ecological adaptation, the Bajau exhibit contains a mode of representation that challenges elite Indonesians to rethink Bajau people's place within the story of the nation, "creating something new within the most traditional political forms" (Rose 1999:280). In conversation with Abdurrachman Wahid or in discussing environmental problems, Bajau people, too, become inheritors of the Indonesian Revolution and participants in creating new Indonesian futures. Although the exhibit fit well into a social evolutionary framework, its authors were attempting to solve problems other than those addressed by turn-of-the-twentieth-century Europeans in their native village displays. Barkan and Bush, who explore primitivism as a particular form of modernism, claim: "As primitivism reappeared in text after text, each new ideological mix proved unpredictable" (Barkan and Bush 1995:)

The ideological and idiomatic form of the Bajau exhibit included an egalitarian and populist spirit of a nationalist awakening that challenged Suharto-era tropes of the primitive as an obstacle to national progress. It held up the ideal of Indonesian pluralism for urban visitors to explore and evaluate. Bajau people, with their "marine nomadic" lifestyle, come to represent not only the ancient archipelagic roots from which the nation grew, the antique proto-Indonesia known by the name Nusantara, the nation's "subjective antiquity in the eyes of nationalists" (Anderson 1983:5), but also the nation's hopes for the future. Rather than an abstract field for the evolution of species, the maritime worlds Bajau people inhabit became part of the representation of "Indonesia" in a determinable form, constituting for nationalists a grounds for the nation's genesis and replication. In the Bajau exhibit, we witness the utopian temporality of the national public sphere emerging from within a conventional exhibitionary form and in opposition to the developmental temporality of the state.

CONCLUSION

Foreign scientists in Indonesia, like those searching for Flores Man, for the most part seem unaware of the role their own social investments, including Euro-American nationalisms, play in their own scientific practice. It has been the work of science and technology studies to point out such social investments. My project here takes those investments for granted and has been interested instead in the role of the postcolonial nation-state in Indonesians' evolutionary science. This should not make Indonesian scientists seem somehow strange or unusual; they are no different from Euro-American scientists in this regard. Rather, learning of these investments allows us to understand how the nation-state and its temporalities create for Indonesian scientists more than the simple nationalistic "bias" that foreign scientists regularly accuse them of having. Although Euro-American scientists are uncomfortable with what they often view as nationalistic animosity, what I have shown in this chapter is that both nation and state are responsible for an intricate and contested shaping of the social field of evolutionary science in Indonesia.

In the exhibitions around the theme of Bajau or in the figure of Daud as development worker, we are able to see what Pheng Cheah calls the mutual haunting of state and nation. "Even as the postcolonial nation haunts the state in its promise of reincarnation, it is also shadowed by the state," he writes (Cheah 2003:382). For Cheah, the popular nation, that utopian ideal of inclusion, is "haunted by figures of finitude that are the very opposite of freedom: death, specters and ghosts, lifeless machines, and other forms of nonspiritual *techne* or nonrecursive prostheses" (2003:382). In other words, the popular nation is haunted by the bureaucratic state; even when Indonesian scientists aim to be inclusive, we can see state forms of bureaucratic domination incorporated into their efforts. Likewise, Anderson's "popular nation" is subverted by "official nationalism," only every now and then reemerging as a utopian nationalist dream. Nationalism, in Indonesian paleontology or conservation biology, is not a distortion of scientific practice. It is a condition of possibility for Indonesian science; it can also become a figure of exclusion.

The pretense that the Hobbit or the coelacanth can be understood in abstract evolutionary time and space, disconnected from their sites of discovery in Indonesia or without recognition of the involvement of the Indonesian people and their national histories, represents the inability of the popular nation to protect its people from foreign trespass. Yet paradoxically, the state can also be a figure of death for the ideal nation. The oppression of people living in the Togean park in Pak Pujo's "seven important principles" and Daud's "four weaknesses" ("nonspiritual *techne*") is an example of how the state can limit the nation-ideal and the lifeworlds of scientists. Even though the workshop was designed to include Togean people in the "national" park, it ended up excluding their "universal free selves." Where the bureaucratic state extends itself into the practices of saving biodiversity, the conservation of species is not successful because it does not include "the people" in the project of conservation in a life-affirming way.

To use Mrazek's words, "The numbers, the maps, and all the other gadgets of the watching technology were applied so that the matter *is not touched*" (2002; emphasis added).

For both Mrazek and Cheah, each working through the writings of nationalist author Pramoedya Ananta Toer, national liberation inherently involves a freedom from the alienation brought about by the state's role as prosthesis of transnational capital. The four "weaknesses" of Togean people are an example of such alienation. The idea of ecotourism, with its expatriated profits and shift in use-values from Togean people to Euro-American tourists, is another. The opportunity for the Togean environment to be conserved for popular well-being is lost through Daud's own imbrication in a state project of control by means of a transnationally recognizable "economic development."

In the introduction to this volume, Ferry and Limbert employ the OED's second definition of the word *resource* to describe material used for the defense of a national collectivity, for the "support of a country." I would argue that within the project to conserve biodiversity, the state represents not only transnational capital but also, importantly, national capital. During the Suharto era in Indonesia, it became more beneficial for the state to claim resources in the name of elite Indonesian capital than to share them for the benefit of the nation and its people. The state's interest was in progressive, developmental time (*pembangunan*), in other words, rather than in the romantic flowering (*perkembangan*) of its national ideals.

Despite the seeming difference between the temporality of evolutionary time (absolute and beyond human history) and Indonesian history (either developmental or utopian), one can draw parallels between them. Anderson writes, "Our own conception of simultaneity has been a long time in the making, and its emergence is certainly connected, in ways that have yet to be well studied, with the development of the secular sciences" (1983:24). Both biological evolution and nationalist awakening share a logic in which "being is transformed into becoming, essence into existence, and the past and the present are rendered provisional in light of the force of the future" (Grosz 2004:7). The Indonesian nation that flowers through popular nationalism into an enduring but fragile Indonesian identity, or the essence of the insular maritime past that becomes the existence of the national archipelagic concept Nusantara, is similar to the provisional and emergent nature of forms of life through biological evolution. Like all new forms of life, what the nation will become is never entirely certain—it is set in constant motion, always in a process of possibility and becoming, always vulnerable to extinction by the state or instrumental reason. This idea is very different from a claim that societies "evolve" to fulfill a teleological destiny as represented by modernism or economic and social development.

If national being is like the being of species, then the inverse is also the case. If, as Anderson claims, the nation is "a secular transformation of fatality into continuity, contingency into meaning" (Anderson 1983:11), we might also understand evolution and the origin of species this way. Not only are biological species arrestable as an empirical thing in scientific or homogeneous empty time (where "man makes the species"), but they also gather social meaning through their relationship to time. The "tree of life" gives present meaning to a series of contingent and chance events within evolutionary time. Prior evolutionary events are irrecoverable once a species has gone extinct. Future speciation demands preservation of maximal species diversity—we have the requirement not only to discover and identify new species but also to *conserve* them, transforming fatality into continuity, meaninglessness into value.

Grosz describes the temporality of Darwinian evolution as relations of simultaneity and succession. She writes, "Time inhabits all living beings, is an internal, indeed constitutive, feature of life itself, yet it is also what places living beings in relations of simultaneity and succession with each other insofar as they are all participants in a single temporality" (Grosz 2004:5). Biological evolution is not the fulfillment of a messianic plan. Rather, although it is possible to speculate on the past, the future of speciation is open and contingent. Speciation is best not carried forth as a rationally planned force. The radical contingency and unpredictable vitality of life are what must be saved. Here lies another analogy between evolutionary process and the nation.

The evolutionary sciences in Indonesia enter the sphere of vital politics closely associated with the nation-state. Because species and specimens are found within the confines of nations by scientists with national identities, it is meaningless to attempt to understand the temporality of biological evolution separately from the temporalities of human history, even when human histories appear much more fleeting in duration. Valuing human and evolutionary temporalities together, along with the work of Indonesian scientists as Indonesian subjects, opens up possibilities for richer understandings of heterogeneity and difference. Knowing of the political and cultural processes that give life value and valuing life as the "mobilization of maximal difference" are each crucial for transcending finitude. If we fail, extinction is forever.

Acknowledgments

Many thanks are due to Elizabeth Ferry and Mandana Limbert for their expert and collegial guidance on the project "Natural Resources and Their Temporalities." I would also like to thank Kiko Benitez for his helpful reorientations around the idea of the nation. The School for Advanced Research provided an invaluable institutional setting in which to produce this volume.

Notes

1. Anderson's book *Imagined Communities* is readily identifiable as the work of an Indonesia scholar. My intention is to apply his rubrics of popular and official nationalism to the Indonesian context only. Popular nationalism is not always a progressive force, as the cases of Nazi Germany and contemporary US nationalism clearly demonstrate. I agree with the argument of Pheng Cheah (2003) that progressive possibilities for the nation exist in postcolonial Southeast Asia.

2. President Suharto came to power in Indonesia in 1966 through a coup that was blamed on the communists but that many believe was of his own making. He was known as a brutal dictator, responsible for the deaths of almost a million Indonesians. He was also known as the "father of development" and instituted a pro-Western economic regime. The Suharto era came to an end when he stepped down in 1998 after massive popular protests and cries for reformation. By this point, the level of corruption in Indonesia had become too great for foreign economic investment in the country. His fall from power was precipitated by the Southeast Asian financial crisis of 1997.

3. Much has been written on acceptable forms of national ethnic difference in Indonesia. The state has supported the existence of differences it has viewed as "aesthetic" and "cultural" while repressing expressions of political difference based on ethnicity. See especially Pemberton 2004 and Volkman 1990.

4. The name *Bajau* is an exonym; the people themselves use the name *Sama*. I have chosen to use *Bajau* here to avoid confusion, because it is the name of the museum exhibition. In much of my other work, I use the endonym *Sama*.

6

George Forrest's Rhododendron Paradise

Erik Mueggler

I will begin with two images of suspension. The first (figure 6.1a) is a photograph of a rope of twisted bamboo spanning a gorge. A human figure, difficult to discern, dangles from the rope's center in what seems a terrifying position. Consul G. Litton described this bridge in a secret report to the British Foreign Office, adopting the tone of a hard-bitten sojourner for the empire: "These single rope bridges of the upper Salwen are far more difficult to cross than the double ropes of the Mekong. After being trussed by cords on a bamboo half-cylinder or runner fitted over the 'bridge' it is necessary to haul oneself hand over hand; as one is tied with face to the sky and back to the 'bridge' this is a difficult operation" (Foreign Office 1906).[1]

The original print is in the archives of the Royal Geographic Society, filed with many other photographs of suspension bridges—of twisted liana cane, of ropes and planks, of timbers and iron chains—over the three great rivers that run in parallel gorges north to south through northwestern Yunnan. The reverse is stamped with the photographer's name, George Forrest, and the date, 1905. At that time, in the confident opinion of the Royal Geographic Society president, the Salween remained the last great riverine puzzle on earth, its northern reaches yet unexplored by any European (Forrest 1908:265).[2]

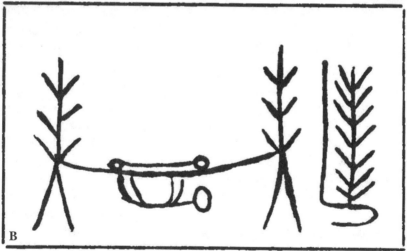

FIGURE 6.1

A: *Bamboo rope spanning a gorge (courtesy Royal Geographic Society)*. B: *Line drawing from a handwritten manuscript used in a Naxi funeral ritual (Janert 1965:238)*.

Ever since Britain annexed Upper Burma in 1886, British cartographers and diplomats had been working to survey and negotiate the borders of this new addition to the empire. This was a military and ethnographic project as much as a cartographic one. Between the Irrawaddy basin and Yunnan were interposed a large number of small, semi-independent states, many prosperous and well organized. Some had confederated to oppose the chaotic last kingdom of Burma, and these confederations resisted British domination (Thant 2001; Woodman 1962). The subjugation of the Shan and Wa states brought the great cartographic undertaking of the India Survey into contact with the ongoing project of the Qing Empire to map its own dominion. In 1897, under considerable pressure from the British, the Qing court approved a comprehensive treaty granting the British a treaty port in the border town of Tengyue and agreeing to jointly survey a precise boundary in the future. Over the next few years, map after map was produced. In the south, in the Wa states, five different boundaries were proposed; in the north, near the upper Salween, another "five colored map" was created, with a line of a different hue for each proposed boundary (Hong 1997; Xie 2000).

As acting British consul in Tengyue, G. Litton represented the British in a joint boundary commission in 1904. His Chinese counterpart was Shi Hongshao, trade commissioner (*daotai*) for western Yunnan. Litton believed that the gigantic, unsurveyed mountain range between the Salween and Nmai, an eastern branch of the Irrawaddy, was a natural and proper boundary (Foreign Office 1905). Shi maintained that this range, the Gaoligong, and regions to the west of it were under the jurisdiction of native hereditary officials (*tusi*) of the Nu, Qiu, and Lisu peoples, whose ancestors had been granted titles by the Ming and Qing courts. It was to challenge this assertion and to establish that the range was the "natural and ethnological divide" between the two empires that in October 1905, Litton, accompanied by two Lisu Indian army regulars and tens of Lisu porters, each carrying sixty to seventy pounds of rice, walked up the gorge of the Salween (Foreign Office 1905, 1906) (figure 6.2).[3]

Litton's other companion was George Forrest, a Scott employed by the British seed firm Bees Ltd. to scour Yunnan for hardy alpine flowers (figure 6.3). He had been in Yunnan for just over a year—a decidedly mixed experience. Two months previously, the Foreign Office had informed his mother and his fiancée of his death. He had been visiting a small French Catholic mission on the upper Mekong when an army of Tibetans attacked. Two French priests were killed, and Forrest barely escaped, hiding by day and traveling at night. Three weeks later, he showed up starved, wounded, and clothed in rags near the town of Yezhi on the Mekong. He had lost all his possessions, including a large collection of botanical specimens and seeds. Although still weak from this experience, he was happy to accompany

FIGURE 6.2

Consul G. Litton and Indian army regulars, 1905 (courtesy Royal Botanic Garden, Edinburgh).

Litton as his naturalist and photographer. "Surely I shall secure something new on such a long stretch of untouched ground," he wrote on October 10, 1905, to his scientific mentor at the Royal Botanic Garden, Edinburgh (Royal Botanic Garden).

Forrest and Litton investigated the gorge's geography, its climate and zoology, the ethnology of its inhabitants ("Wild Lisoos with poisoned arrows"), and their political affiliations ("no sort of government or control

FIGURE 6.3

George Forrest, 1905 (courtesy Royal Botanic Garden, Edinburgh).

of any sort or kind") (Forrest 1908:244, 256). At the bamboo-rope bridge, where villagers were feuding over control of the bridge, they discharged their firearms, subduing all into "awestruck silence." They then climbed the east bank of the river to the summit of the Mekong–Salween divide, where they accomplished the main objective of their journey:

> Here a surprise awaited us, for the view to the west was perfectly clear, and the whole of the great Salwin–Irawadi divide was spread out before us. From a little below the pass this range could be followed to the north as far as the eye could reach, until at a distance of about 100 miles from where we stood, and in approximate lat. 28 30' N., it was merged into a huge range of dazzling snow peaks, trending westwards. (Foreign Office 1906)

"Not the least doubt remained in my mind that this was the true frontier between India and China," Litton continued. He did not live to argue the case further (expiring in his sedan chair shortly after this journey), but his description of this "vast wall" gradually became sedimented into the landscape. It was repeatedly quoted in insistent British proposals, vigorously opposed by Qing negotiators, that the Salween–Nmai watershed should become the border. Until 1910 the British treated the divide as a provisional border. That year, the British occupied the village of Pianma, west of the divide, and declared the range the de facto border, arousing popular nationalist outrage throughout China. The border was not finally established until 1960, long after Burmese independence.[4]

The second image (seefigure 6.1b) looks like a cartoon-strip version of the first (see figure 6.1a). It is a line drawing of a rope stretched between two trees. An inverted human figure dangles from the rope and the "bamboo half-cylinder" that Litton described. To the right is some kind of tree. A square frame bounds the drawing. The image is from the title page of a handwritten manuscript used in a funeral ritual called, in the Naxi language, *lònv*. The figure within the frame is this word, written in what has become known as the *dongba* script, a writing system used by Naxi ritualists, or dongba. The left side is the word *lò*, meaning "to cross or pass over," the first syllable of the word *lòk'ö*, "to cross a rope bridge." The right side is the word *nv*, the term for the effigy of a deceased person (Rock 1955:4; 1963:237, 351).

Naxi performed lònv for dead children. In a family courtyard, a ritualist read the manuscript with this title, describing the soul of the child—unable to eat, unable to see or hear, unable to use hands or feet to put on clothes. The soul was escorted across a rope bridge that spanned a river separating the world of the living from the world of the dead. Then the rope was cut with a knife, severing the link between worlds and preventing the mourners from following. All of this was performed both in words and gesture. The lònv manuscript specified the things to be used in the rite: a strip of black hempen cloth as the rope bridge, a fir tree to which the rope was tied, and so forth (Rock 1965:238–239). This rite was performed in conjunction with a common and widespread ritual of mourning called *zhimá*, in which ritualists escorted a dead soul across the landscape of Yunnan, through known and unknown places, north toward the lands whence the ancestors had come, and eventually to Ngyùná Shílo Ngyu, the vast mountain of Shílo, the place where the world of men met the world of gods.

This manuscript was written or (more probably) copied in the nineteenth century in the Lijiang Valley, near the great bend of the upper Yangtze (or Jinsha) River. In the early twentieth century, the upper Salween was about two months' travel from the Lijiang Valley, farther than it was from Rangoon. Of course, there were rope bridges much closer to Lijiang, along the Mekong and Yalong rivers. Still, the upper Salween and its rope bridges were embedded in the ritual imagination of Naxi farmers. In particular, a small ritual to bring rain seems to have been performed frequently near Lijiang in the early twentieth century. In this ceremony, held by a spring, a ritualist chanted to the spirits who brought rain, inviting them to descend from all the great rivers and lakes in all four directions. In the west, these spirits were asked to descend from villages in the lands of the upper Salween down to towns along the Mekong, around the mountainous lands to the north and east, and down across the Yangtze to the Lijiang plain. The source of this journey, its highest point, was the great snow mountain Nundù Gkyinvlv, the crown of the Salween–Irrawaddy divide, the center of the "huge range of dazzling snow peaks" that Forrest and Litton spotted at the apex of their journey, shining from a hundred miles farther to the north (Rock 1952:607, 613).

RE-SOURCES

These two images might be said to belong to two archival regimes. In each, a mountain of inscriptions was interleaved with the earth in particular ways. And the mode of that interleaving was structured by particular technologies of perception. The modes of perception that engaged Forrest and Litton were archival modes: cartography, ethnology, botanical exploration. One might think of the images, texts, and specimens this journey produced as diagrams of these modes of perception. British rule in India depended upon the production, on an unprecedented scale, of such diagrams—in maps, surveys, systems of classification. At the same time, every encounter with the earth has the potential to nurture modes of being not circumscribed by extant power-laden diagrams. Litton and Forrest's glimpse of that great snowy range of peaks beyond the Salween was negotiated in uneven diplomatic arguments, contested in several armed battles, and eventually cemented into the earth as immutable fact. But it had another life as well. Over the next three decades, that glimpse would keep returning to Forrest, shepherded back to him by unstable encounters with the archival regime of Naxi ritual practice. And these encounters eventually made possible a mode of relation with the earth quite different from what Bernard Cohen (1996) called the "survey mode" of creating knowledge for the empire.

The manuscript from which the drawing comes was part of a regime that dominated religious practice in the region within the great loop of the Yangtze River, the center of what is now called the Naxi ethnicity. The texts collected and copied by Naxi dongba formed a rich repository of knowledge about the landscape of northwestern Yunnan. This regime did not produce and organize knowledge for the purposes of rule (although it once may have). It mobilized this knowledge to manipulate relationships between human and nonhuman entities in order to regulate the social well-being of people and communities. It did not survey the surface of the earth; it palpated its depths, communicated with hidden presences, and divined traces of a past that had vanished from the surface. In all these ways, it diagramed modes of perception that were so far from those to which George Forrest devoted his energies as to be incomprehensible to him. Nevertheless, there were points of contact and friction, at which one of these regimes deformed the other, creating new and compelling possibilities for it.

Some science studies scholars argue that we must begin to think of relationships between humans and nonhumans in new ways. Bruno Latour has made this point at great length. Latour argues that we can no longer afford the "modernist settlement" that gave us a strict division between the social and the natural, human subjects and nonhuman objects. Instead, we need to develop new methods to understand ways in which human and nonhuman beings have always coexisted socially. One such method might be to examine the routes and networks of relationships that bind them, even in contexts that might appear to be structured by strict subject–object distinctions. A rich example is Latour's (1999) attempt to trace the chains of reference that lead from the soils and plants of soil science to its scientific facts. As we work along these complex routes linking the social and the natural, gigantic, monolithic Nature dissolves into natures, many participants in a collective.

Anthropology is given a didactic role in this argument. Latour is concerned with "the West": anthropology offers us the perspectives of "non-Western cultures," for which nature has never been an issue and which "have preserved the conceptual institutions, the reflexes and routines that we Westerners need in order to rid ourselves of the intoxicating idea of nature" (Latour 2004:43). But of course "the West" is also an imposed settlement. The work of collecting—of fashioning a collective world of humans and nonhumans—might also be, at the same time, the labor of tracing networks of historical relationships that have always spanned the supposed divide between the West and its others. Along many of these routes, divides between social and natural, or subject and object, that seem to define modernity were also deformed or transmogrified.

In the introduction, Ferry and Limbert explain that this volume is about resources and time. They relate the word *resource*, through its etymology, to the French word *source*, referring to the place on the earth's surface where a flow of water originates. The concept of resource, they state, "suggests both the continuous generation of something from an originary point, as water emerges from a spring, and the potential for creating something else, as water nourishes growing plants." This chapter taps into this part of the conceptual terrain explored in this volume. It is about two intertwined searches for a source—two intersecting ways in which a portion of the earth's surface was organized around a point of origin in space and time. What interests me about this story is the evidence it presents of an ambiguous intertwining of two apparently incompatible regimes of knowledge. This intertwining was not made possible by conceptual parallels in notions of origin, source, or resource. It was made possible by intersecting practices—of walking, collecting, writing, and reading—all grounded in the earth's material form. A dramatic form: four great rivers emerging from some of the earth's highest mountains, flowing closely parallel, separated by enormous ridges, running down a terrain that gradually and consistently sloped from north to south. It was a form that seemed to give the earth agency, making it a forceful player in the history of the human societies of this region. I think of telling this story as a way of raising questions about the agency of nonhuman actors in social relations and, for the purposes of this volume, particularly actors that have been drawn into social relations as sources or resources.

In telling this story, I have several questions in mind. In what ways might a more nuanced view of such historical relationships of encounter deepen our understanding of the social lives of nonhuman beings, in particular the social life of the earth? In what ways has the earth, as a social being, served as a source or resource for experiences that circumvent established ways of thinking and living a divide between the social and the natural?

REGIMES

During his first, eventful expedition to Yunnan, George Forrest shipped about fifty-five hundred specimens of plants and seeds home to Edinburgh. His employer, Bees Ltd., raised plants from his seeds and began to advertise some of the most spectacular for sale as "novelties." At the Royal Botanic Garden in Edinburgh, Regius Keeper Isaac Bailey Balfour and his staff devoted much of their time to naming and describing new species from the duplicate specimens Forrest sent to the garden. Before his expedition, Forrest had affianced a young worker in the garden's herbarium, Clementina Trail. Shortly after his return to Edinburgh in 1907, they married. In January 1910 he began another expedition, again for Bees Ltd. He planned to spend three years in Yunnan. But because of financial disagreements with Arthur Bulley, the founder and owner of Bees Ltd., he spent only a year. For most of this time, he camped near a village named Nvlvk'o, at the foot of the great Yulong range of Lijiang.

ERIK MUEGGLER

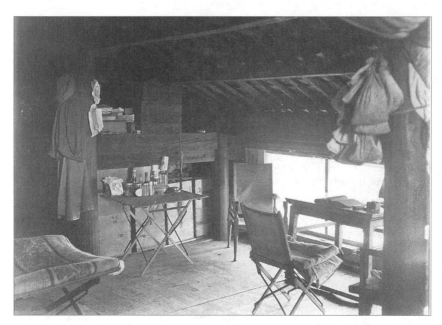

FIGURE 6.4
Forrest's "garret" in Nvlvk'o (courtesy Royal Botanic Garden, Edinburgh).

Forrest wrote home almost daily, always as though he were alone. Indeed, he was lonely, wishing himself at home with Clem and their infant son. But he was never alone. Tracing his steps on each toilsome search or climb were three or four unnamed men from Nvlvk'o carrying his camera, tripod, rifle, and baskets of plant specimens. More Nvlvk'o men joined him in camp, where he showed them how to arrange, press, and dry specimens. He laid the most desirable of these aside, and in the autumn he brought them out, one by one, to discuss their characteristics and locations with the men. Then the Nvlvk'o men walked the range again, in parties of four or five, gathering seed and bearing it in baskets back to camp. There, they placed the seed in paper packets, which they numbered, labeled, and packed into crates for shipping. They shipped two thousand plant specimens and seeds of many hundred species. The Nvlvk'o men also collected bats, birds, frogs, leeches, about two thousand species of insects, and eighteen snakes, bottled in spirits (Maclean 2004).

In May 1912, Forrest returned to Nvlvk'o on an expedition funded by J. C. Williams, a wealthy gardening enthusiast with an estate in Cornwall. He rented a house in the village. He lived on the second floor, in one long room that he called his garret (figure 6.4). For Forrest, this room had the advantages of a wooden floor, in contrast to the mud floor below; windows overlooking the courtyard; and a degree of privacy. But for the men who worked in the courtyard on the collections of specimens and seed, it must have seemed a strange choice. Most homes in Nvlvk'o had only one story, with roof beams directly above the main floor. In those few with two, the second story was used to store grain and meat and sometimes to stash an extra unmarried son or two. A household head would never have chosen to sleep in this storage space.

Houses centered on a raised hearth on the ground floor. Sleeping and sitting areas occupied three sides of the hearth, where a family ate and entertained. A male household head slept on the innermost side, away from the door, usually along the south wall. If he was married, his wife slept to his right, along the east wall. Between them was a small shrine. This arrangement indexed the central division in Naxi kinship, between patrilateral "bone" relations and matrilateral "flesh" relations. Male visitors in the household head's patrilineage—his "bone"—were expected to sit along his side of the hearth; men and women from his wife's patrilineage—his "flesh"—sat on his wife's side; non-kin guests sat opposite the "flesh" side. On formal occasions, people sat according to their seniority in their agnatic groups, the most senior closest to the shrine. The open side of the hearth, closest to the door, was where the work of cooking and serving food took place. Most of this work was performed by women, typically by unmarried daughters, who had an ambiguous status, full members of neither the bone they were to leave nor the one they were to join (Mckhann 1992:254–255).

In Forrest's house, his cook and servants occupied the hearth, climbing the ladder to his garret to bring him food and tea; his collectors filled the rooms and courtyard with their activities of drying seeds and pressing specimens. He had neither bone nor flesh relations, and his place in the garret offered no opportunities to create fictive or ad hoc substitutes. The work of producing and ordering social relations went on below, outside his awareness. Most important, his place in the garret offered his companions no comprehensible perspective on his relations with them: it gave them no opportunities to see themselves from his place. Perhaps he sensed and cultivated this. He arranged the garret to suit himself: a table before the open window for reading and writing, his camp bed with its head to the opposite wall, another table laden with bottles of liquor and medicine against the side wall, bags of seeds suspended from the beams, a line for hanging photographic negatives. This was a space for nurturing social relations of another order—with the family, patrons, and sponsors who received his letters and photographs.

FIGURE 6.5

Forrest's camp on the Yulong range, circa 1906 (courtesy Royal Botanic Garden, Edinburgh).

With this house as his base, Forrest conducted two explorations: an intensive search of the Yulong and Cangshan mountain ranges and an extensive search of territories to the north. As he had the previous expedition, he walked the Yulong range himself, concentrating on primulas (figure 6.5). The Nvlvk'o men explored the Cangshan range, to the south, near Dali, and mounted extensive explorations to the northeast and northwest. Parties of two or three collectors, one mule, and one muleteer made expeditions of about three weeks each. As many as three parties were out at one time. On returning home, the men would linger for a few days to review the collections and begin the work of drying and labeling (figure 6.6). They would then head out again, often extending the search farther from Nvlvk'o and often looking for specific species that Forrest instructed them to gather. In September and October, the last parties of the season gathered the seeds of plants located on previous searches.

Forrest participated in none of these expeditions. He seemed not to know or care how the men slept and ate. He provided no tents or bedding;

FIGURE 6.6

Collectors from Nvlvk'o, after a journey, with specimens (courtesy Royal Botanic Garden, Edinburgh).

the mule bore presses and specimens; the men carried little on their backs. Sometimes they slept in the open on their goatskin capes, wrapped in felt blankets. Most often, however, they were almost certainly guests in the houses of local people. When those houses were Naxi, they entered spaces familiar to them, where relations among household members were laid out around the hearth and where their own status, as they sat opposite the flesh side of the hearth, representatives of the bones of potential marriage partners, was also clear. Things were more difficult and ambiguous in the houses of Han, Tibetans, and other Tibeto-Burman peoples of the region. Naxi distinguished themselves from their neighbors by preferring or prescribing patrilateral cross-cousin marriage—anathema to these other peoples (Mckhann 1992). Consequently, household space, always at play in kinship practices, may have been difficult to comprehend and negotiate in the houses of non-Naxi hosts. With these hosts, the men from Nvlvk'o spoke the lingua franca, Yunnan Chinese, which many people in the region spoke imperfectly or not at all. In areas occupied mainly by Han, asking for hospitality may have been difficult and embarrassing: many Han looked upon all Tibeto-Burman peoples as inferior and uncivilized.

The linguistic and ethnic landscape of northwestern Yunnan had been shaped in the fifteenth and sixteenth centuries by the conquests of the Mu kings. The Mu were a lineage of local chiefs, based in Lijiang and named first by the Yuan and later by the Ming and Qing as native hereditary officials (*tusi*). During the Ming, the Mu carried out an aggressive and extended military expansion into territories occupied by "Xibo" (Tibetans) and "Yifan" (other Tibeto-Burman peoples). Officially, they were suppressing "brigands and nomads." In each important place they conquered, the Mu garrisoned soldiers from the Lijiang area and created official posts for members of their own lineage group. These garrisons grew into small Naxi settlements, scattered over much of the vast, mountainous northwestern portion of Yunnan. Despite waves of immigration into the area in the eighteenth and nineteenth centuries, people in most of these settlements continued to speak the dialect of the Naxi language spoken in the Lijiang Valley and to follow kinship arrangements and religious practices similar to those of Naxi in Lijiang. In the former territories of the Mu kings, the only dense concentration of people who shared language and kinship with the Nvlvk'o men was within the great loop of the Yangtze. But throughout those territories, the men from Nvlvk'o could find scattered hamlets of people who spoke their own language, held similar assumptions about kinship, sent their dead over the same mountain routes, and shared names for each feature of the landscape.

Forrest believed himself to be undertaking a systematic search of the province, concentrating on areas richest in species and gradually developing a comprehensive phyto-geographical archive of the region. But scattered evidence in his letters and field notes gives a different picture. He made several plans to expand his operations to the east and northeast, beyond the ancient routes of conquest of the Mu kings. All failed. In some cases, his men returned from brief forays into the country beyond to report it dry and unproductive. In others, they simply explored places other than those Forrest asked them to—places within the former territories of the Mu kings. The only exceptions to this pattern were on the main route from Burma—the hinterlands of Tengyue and Dali—with which Forrest had familiarized himself before he employed any men from Nvlvk'o.

Two regimes of social relationship, among humans and between humans and the earth, then, were anchored in that house in Nvlvk'o. From the garret, a new geography of Yunnan was being added to the imperial archive, with the mass shipment of seeds, specimens, notes, and descriptions to Edinburgh. From the courtyard, ancient connections between Lijiang and its former hinterland were being renewed as the Nvlvk'o men fanned out through the region, walking old routes of conquest, building relations of friendship and possibly kinship with the descendants of ancient garrisons, working through Naxi-language lists of names for routes, villages, streams, and mountains. On the ladder between flowed a stream of specimens and gestures, a trickle of verbal description and instruction, a steady current of cash. Compared with the rich activity of social relation within each regime, this flow was severely restricted. As a result, the participants in each regime had no more than a dim awareness of the details of the other. Thin as they were, however, these streams of words, flowers, and coins energized each regime, setting it in motion. Over the next few years, still in mutual ignorance, these regimes began to assert force on each other. Mapped onto the landscape—as was inevitable—these forces began to pull more and more strongly north.

RITUALS

At home, people in Nvlvk'o had a rich ritual life, centering on written texts. Naxi-language writing took two forms. The most common and widespread is often described as pictographic, although it combines iconic and symbolic elements. It is now known as dongba, the Chinese transliteration of *dtomba*, the Naxi name for the ritualists who wrote and read it. In form, dongba books were modeled on Tibetan books, with elongated pages bound between covers, stitched on the left side. In most, each page was ruled lengthwise into three rows; each row was divided into rectangular panels. Within each panel were figures of gods, demons, humans, animals, heads, hands, limbs, insects, plants, mountains, tools, weapons, foods, ritual objects. The panels and the signs within them were read left to right. The other script, far less common, was *geba* (*ggobaw* in Naxi). It too was written on pages ruled into rows and panels, but it was purely phonetic. Syllables were represented by conventional graphs with no iconic qualities.[5]

In many ways, dongba textual practice was an archival practice. Dongba were incredibly productive of writing. Some twenty-seven thousand manuscripts still exist, a fraction of those extant before the Cultural Revolution, when tens of thousands were burned.[6] Most books were written to be read aloud at rituals intended to maximize the fertility of villages and households, escort the dead to the lands of the ancestors, exorcise ghosts and demons, or accompany marriages. Some were for divination. Most rituals required several books, some thirty or forty. According to contemporary observers, dongba ritual was in decline in the Lijiang basin in the early twentieth century, although nearly every village still contained at least one ritualist. One rough estimate is that dongba comprised some 8 percent of the Naxi population (He and Guo 1985:39). Many dongba had libraries of hundreds, even thousands, of books. In the area around Nvlvk'o, every lineage group required specialists to read texts during three important ritual forms: ordinary funerals, funerals for love suicides, and yearly "sacrifices to heaven." Yet scores of ceremonies were no longer performed. Some dongba took every opportunity to sell off excess texts, but many continued to cultivate their libraries, reading and copying manuscripts no longer in use. Some could read and perform ceremonies that had not been enacted for generations.

In the early twentieth century, the most important contexts for reciting texts were rituals of mourning. The funerals of bone or flesh kin were among the most important occasions in anyone's life, occasions for a tectonic shift in the world of social relationships. These shifts required work: the affective labor of learning to live in a world suddenly bereft of foundational elements, the social labor of reordering relationships along new axes. Although Forrest's collaborators spent years away from home, they participated in many such rituals. At the death of a father or brother, when the rite could not proceed without them, messengers were sometimes sent out to find them and bring them home.

The most common ritual of mourning was called *zhimá*, or "teaching the road." It was performed for anyone who died a "normal death"—not by violence or suicide. On an astrologically propitious day shortly after the death, kin, neighbors, and friends, often numbering in the hundreds, gathered in the courtyard of the deceased, bringing gifts ranging from a small bag of grain to a sheep or horse, depending on their relationship with the dead. For two or three days and nights, they drank, danced, sang, wept, ate, and offered sacrifices before bringing the coffin from the house and burying it. "Teaching the road" used words and gestures to guide the deceased soul through the geo-cosmological landscape archived in dongba textual practice. The soul was released from the purgatorial realm in which it had fallen at death and moved through this landscape to the lands of the ancestors and gods. To this end, most significant acts in the rite took the form of speaking to the dead. Close kin lamented with verses that recounted their warm memories of the deceased. Friends and neighbors sang songs describing the life and death of the deceased, the gathering of mourners, and the road to the world of the ancestors (Mckhann 1992:272). And dongba recited texts.

In the zhimá of the early twentieth century, dongba recited approximately forty texts (Rock 1955:xv). Other participants overheard these recitations with varying degrees of comprehension. There were many other foci of attention: the dance, the lamenting mourners, the work of butchering, cooking, and distributing sacrificial meat, one's own cup of alcohol. Some mourners listened intently; others heard the verses go by with half an ear; many heard little or nothing. But ordinary mourners did recite some texts themselves. Central among these were songs for the deceased that recounted the origins of the heavens and earth, of winged, hoofed, and clawed beasts, of winged demons, and of death itself. For senior men, a category to which, as persons of leading economic and social status, Forrest's collectors were very likely to belong, these songs were central to the experience of the ritual.

In the 1930s, the botanist and ethnographer Joseph Rock, living in Nvlvk'o village, took unusually careful notes on the performance of one such song. It began the night before the coffin was to be buried, in the central room of the house, where the coffin lay, head to the door and feet to the wall. A dongba sat at the coffin's head, on its left side; next to him sat men representing the friends and neighbors of the deceased; on the coffin's right side sat senior men of the deceased's bone and flesh kin. Before them were long tables laden with food and wine. The dongba read the funeral song; the men repeated each verse, through twelve pages of the manuscript. All then filed outside to join the hundreds of mourners assembled in the courtyard around a big log fire. They made an open circle, joined hands by interlacing fingers, and danced around the fire at the pace of a slow walk. The dongba led them through the remaining five pages of the text, which they sang while dancing. For the rest of the night, they repeated the song as they danced around the fire, taking turns to rest.

On this occasion, the song was "Song for the Dead, the Origin of Sorrow" (*Mun ndzer á' lá' dzhu*) (figure 6.7). It told the story of Ssussa of Ssùlò, who, panning for gold in the river, saw his reflection in the river and understood that he was old. He was a rich man; he had chests of grain, trunks of silver and gold. But he had no years. So he set off for the south to buy years:

from the Ssùlò River's head	*ssu gyì gkv nnu' dtù*
to the Ssùlò River's tail	*ssu gyì man la' t'u*
from the Ssùlò River's tail	*ssu gyì man nnu' dtù*
to the fields of Bberdder	*bber dder llu' la t'u*
from the fields of Bberdder	*bber dder llu' nnu' dtù*
to the river's winter ford	*ts'u gu k'u la' t'u*
from the river's winter ford	*ts'u gu k'u nnu' dtù*

to the river's summer ford	*zhù gu k'u la' t'u*
from the river's summer ford	*zhù gu k'u nnu' dtù*
to Ndawgv village	*ndaw gv dù' la' t'u*
from Ndawgv village	*ndaw gv dù' nnu' dtù*
to Gvssugkò meadow	*gv ssu gkò dù' la' t'u* [7]

And so on, in alternating, repetitive cadence, the verses reeling off in linked pairs, imitating the walking cadence of the dance. Ssussa's route south was given in sixteen place-names. He walked from the source of the Ssùlò (Wuliang in Chinese) River, in Muli County, Sichuan, to where it empties into the Yangtze at the northern apex of its second great bend. Then he continued south to Bberdder (Baidi in Chinese), crossed the Yangtze at the Naxi village of Ndawgv, climbed through a string of meadows and passes that lead over the Yulong range, descended to the market village of Baisha, near Nvlvko, continued on to Lijiang town, and then, in a single leap, arrived in Kunming, the provincial capital. At Baisha, he circled the market three times, finding wood, grass, wine, and food, but no years. In Kunming, the biggest market in the world of ordinary experience, he found fine satins and brocades, but no years. Then he turned and found that the market had dispersed, the great Dianchi Lake had dried up, the black rocks had split, the green bamboo had yellowed. This was the origin of sorrow: the realization that, riches or no, death will come and sorrow will follow. This was a journey in the realm of ordinary experience: it took the listener down rivers, along paths, and over passes that he or she may well have already walked.

This much the mourners sang, in its first iteration, inside the house around the coffin. Dancing in the courtyard, they sang the second part of the song, about the dance:

in sorrow we guide the dead	*dzhu la' zhì bpú bbue*
dancing we tread on demons…	*ts'o la' ts'ù szèr bbue…*
this crowd of sons of sorrow	*dzhu zo ch'i ddù' hóa*
slim-waisted they sway	*t'ú' ts'ù t'u' nyu nyu*
by custom they sway and dance	*nyú la' ddu' ts'o ndu*
we guide the crane to the clouds	*gko bpú gkyì gkyi bbue*
guide the tiger to the mountain peaks	*la bpú sso gkyi bbue*
guide this ancestor up above	*yù' bpú ggò gkyi bbue*

FIGURE 6.7

Pages from the "Origin of Sorrow" text (Jantert 1965:364).

to the dazzling white cloud gate	*gkyì k'u p'èr lv la*
flying, the crane will return	*gko ndzì la' bbue ma'*
all the winged creatures	*ndu mun ndu ch'i dzù*
guide the crane back to the clouds	*gko bpú gkyì gkyi ssà'*
but his power must not pass…	*non ò khu' muan chèr…*
to the glittering golden mountain gate	*sso k'u shì ghú'gh ghu'gh*
dancing, the tiger will return	*la ts'o la' bbue ma'*
all the clawed creatures	*dshì mun ch'i dzù la*
guide the tiger back to the mountain	*bpú sso la' gkyi*
but his power must not pass	*non ò khu' muan chèr*
we guide the ancestor to the gods' land	*yù' bpú hà' dù' t'u*
he must cross nine ridges	*ssu bbu ngv mbù ló*
but his power must not cross	*non ò mbù ló k'u muan chèr*
he must ford seven rivers	*p'à' gyì sher hò nder*
but his power must not ford them	*non ò gyì nder khu' muan*

To dance was to winnow the dead soul, separating it from its "power" (*nonò*), these skills and capacities the deceased displayed in life. The song gave examples: the ability to sing and follow along when others are singing, to count and record numbers, to sing wedding songs, to sing while walking in the mountains. These powers were to remain with the soul's sons and daughters. They were to the soul as the clouds are to the sky, the grass to the land, gold to the Yangtze, snow to fir branches, dew to bamboo leaves, a saddle to a horse, a yoke to an ox. They were a load to be borne; freed of them, the soul could travel faster (Rock 1955:98, rubric 3).

"Song for the Dead, the Origin of Sorrow" is a clear example of the close relationship among walking, voicing, and mourning at the heart of Naxi rituals of grief. The singing or chanting voice was invested with the power to move entities through the archived landscape. This movement was the focal aim of the rite, toward which its immense repertoire of words, acts, and artifacts was bent. All the possibilities for reconfiguring affect that mourning contains were to be found in this movement over the known and experienced landscape through imagined cosmological realms, to the soul's final destination.

The ritual as a whole effected a similar movement. Dongba taught that the ancestors of Lijiang Naxi had migrated from homes far to the north, somewhere in the grasslands of eastern Tibet. The rite of "teaching the road" sent the soul back to this ancestral homeland. Its texts recounted the life of the deceased, from boyhood to death; prepared the soul to undertake the journey; and guided it along the road. They emphasized the power of the voice in compelling the soul to move: "Use your fingers to clean your ears of wax; strike them with your white palms to clear out the rest. Your ears are now clear; you can hear my good voice" (Rock 1955:109).[8] They gave long lists of place-names, guiding the soul back along the routes the ancestors had taken in their migrations south. Such a path might begin in the Lijiang Valley with a detailed and comprehensible roster of place-names, cross the Yulong Mountains, ford the Yangtze River, and proceed north up the Zhongdian Plateau. The texts grew less comprehensible as they proceeded farther north, naming villages that had long since vanished. The final clusters of names were clearly mythological as the path took to the sky on the golden bridges and silver chains along which the first ancestors had descended from heaven.

In these texts, the structure of writing imitated that of walking. Each place-name occupied a panel, followed by a name on the next panel. When the names were repeated, as in the "Origin of Sorrow" song, the repetition occurred within the frame of a single panel. This footstep-like pattern was emphasized in performance. Voiced at a rapid clip, each verse went by at about the same pace as a footstep in a deliberate walk, and the simple syntactical and semantic parallelism of the verses tended to line them up in alternating pairs, like walking feet. The written text turned a list of place-names into a visual map depicting the stages of the journey in successive panels.

A text-like map supplemented these map-like texts. Dongba inherited or copied *hà'zhip'ì* (gods' roads), elaborately painted strips of hempen cloth, thirty to forty feet long and about a foot wide.[9] In the morning, after a night or two of dancing, singing, and chanting, a dongba unrolled a gods' road, one end at the coffin's head, the other extending to the north or northeast. Like dongba texts, the gods' road was divided into panels. Within each panel was a painting of a place through which the dead soul would pass. At the coffin's head, the scroll began with the realm of demons: the nine black spurs of hell, the tree of spines on which dead souls were impaled, and the many tortures to which demons subjected them. Souls were boiled in oil and stabbed with swords, their heads pierced with spikes, their tongues pulled out with pincers and plowed with oxen. After the realm of demons came that of humans: thirty-three cities and villages through which the soul had to pass. One panel mapped out the four directions and five elements of this realm; others showed temples, gatherings of dancing dongba, and Dibba Shîlo, founder of the dongba cult, riding triumphantly on his white steed. After the realm of humans was the realm of mountains and forests: seven golden mountains guarded by tigers and eagles. The final section showed the thirty-three realms of the gods.

The dongba presiding at the "teaching the road" ritual made dough figurines of demons and gods and placed them on the panels that corresponded to them. Standing before the coffin, they chanted eight texts that corresponded to the gods' road, moving a miniature effigy of the dead soul along the road and overturning the figurines of demons as it passed. Sometimes dongba supplemented the gods' road with models of the geo-cosmological realms, made of papier-mâché, earth, and wood. In all these representations of the road—texts, maps, and models—the threshold between the worlds of mountains and rivers and the world of the gods was Ngyùná Shîlo Ngyu, the "vast mountain of Shîlo," at which Dibba Shîlo had descended to earth leading 360 disciples and yaks loaded with books.

It was as though a text, although very like a map of a journey, was not like enough. For this final enactment of the dead soul's journey, the text had to be stretched out in a line, a road in miniature with miniature beings moving along it. It was not quite writing, for it could not be read directly. But it was not quite a road either. It was something in between—a mediator for these parallel acts: eyes and mouth moving along a written page, feet moving along an actual road.

The landscape archived in dongba texts was central to Naxi rituals of mourning. Participants in rituals plunged into this archive to manage grief and to reconstitute the social world damaged by it. They moved it with eyes, voices, ears, and dancing feet, taking on its hundreds of names, overcoming the difficulties and obstacles attached to each. These rituals of mourning must have given the landscape a distinctly archival dimension for the men from Nvlvko as they followed the routes of the Mu armies northward, gathering flowers for Forrest. The archive lent the mountains and rivers a powerful orientation: it inclined them northward and upward (a single word, ggò, expresses both in dongba texts). These journeys may have offered opportunities to bring archive and experience together again—opportunities to rediscover old place-names in conversation with Naxi residents along these routes; opportunities to imagine treading paths parents and grandparents may have trod as they worked up through the earth archive on their way to the lands of the ancestors; opportunities to push up the incline in the direction that all these texts, songs, and dances pushed, toward the sources of the rivers, the highest mountain meadows, that "glittering golden mountain gate."

SEARCHES

In July 1917 Forrest and a team of Nvlvk'o men settled for the season in a small village in the far northwestern corner of Yunnan, on the west bank of the Mekong. It was Forrest's fourth expedition and the beginning of his second decade of collaboration with the Nvlvk'o men. The village—a few houses, a Buddhist shrine on a promontory, and a small French Catholic mission—was called Tsiriting.[10] Small parties of men ranged up and down the Mekong–Salween divide. They found rhododendrons everywhere, many new. There were so many species and varieties that distinctions seemed to melt away. In October, Forrest wrote in a letter to the *Gardeners' Chronicle*, "The wealth of Rhododendrons is almost incredible and the number of new species and forms more than confusing. I have really given up attempting to define the limits of species; each individual seems to have a form, or an affinity, on every range and divide differing essentially from the type." Each plant seemed to be not a token of a type but a point in a continuum. Species and varieties became, in strict terms, indescribable: "There is scarcely any ligneous vegetation but Rhododen-dron, the flowering season a riot of colour, gorgeous beyond any description; mountain sides splashed with colour like a giant palette" (Forrest 1917).

Slipping through continua rather than arranging itself into taxonomies as usual, Forrest's language pushed him toward intense feeling, which seemed to him to exceed anything language could express. Four years earlier, the primulas of the Yulong range had given him a similar experience. On July 17, 1913, he had written to Williams, "It is not that I am unobservant, or that I do not appreciate the beauties of nature, quite the reverse. I think most often I feel too intensely for words, on such occasions words fail me, they seem bald and unsatisfactory" (Royal Botanic Garden 1913).

Now, on the upper Mekong, he began to dream of a place where the entire, tangled puzzle of *Rhododendron* would naturally unravel—the place where the genus had originated and from whence it had diffused into its numberless variety. "What I have seen," he wrote to a scientific mentor at Edinburgh in July 1917, "points to the fact that we are approaching very close to the optimum of the genus, which I reckon is not very far from here, probably some short distance n[orth] and w[est] of the mountains of Sarong [Tsharong, now Dzayül County, TAR]" (Royal Botanic Garden 1917a).

The preceding year, at Edinburgh, he had been introduced to the "age-and-area" hypothesis of the American ecologist J. C. Willis. Willis proposed that in a region with no well-marked barriers to diffusion, the area occupied by a given species would depend on its age: the older the species, the wider its range (Willis 1915, 1916a, 1916b). Forrest interpreted this to mean that the more species of a genus in an area, the closer that area to a point where all the species of that genus would originally have evolved. It was a strange idea—it would have appeared strange even to Willis and his followers. It assumed the existence of an infinitely generative point where species were continually coming into existence. In the past, Forrest had searched for sites where particular species congregated most densely, assuming these to be the "centers of origin" of those species. Now, after exposure to Willis, he assumed that all or most species of a genus would have originated in a single small area, where the genus itself had evolved from an ancestral form. His mentors at Edinburgh, always mindful of his fragile ego, gently encouraged him in these ideas.

By the end of the season, Forrest had added two thousand new species and varieties to his collection and located the generative center of *Rhododendron* more precisely. He could find it on the map—or, rather, just off the edge of the map, in territory the India Survey had not yet fully filled in. On November 1, 1917, writing from Tsiriting, he asked the Edinburgh scientists to trace with him a route through the map, toward this place:

> If you are interested in my plans, procure sheet no 91 of India and Adjacent Countries, which gives the Tarong [Tsharong] Yunnan frontier. Follow this, the Mekong Salwin divide, from Tzekou [Cigu], which you will find almost on lat 28º N. long 98º 50' E., to a point at 30º N. lat 97º 40' E. long, where it breaks more northwards, forming the eastern confines of a basin in the shape of an irregular elongated ellipse extending over almost 2 degrees of latitude from 29º to 30º N. (Royal Botanic Garden 1917b)

He could not stop thinking of the "revelation" he would experience were he to journey a hundred miles farther north. He wrote to Balfour on November 1, 1917, "I have dreams of mountain ranges clothed in Rhododendrons and naught else, and though it may seem absurd, in parts even here it amounts to that. I have the feeling that, if I get further north next season, I shall double my catch" (Royal Botanic Garden 1917b). On March 26, 1918, he wrote to Balfour, "This is the spot I have been trying to tap for many years. If I or my men do not reach it I shall not die happy!" (Royal Botanic Garden 1917b). He began to think of this place as a key that would make legible the entire, difficult, disarticulated geography of the region. He wrote to Balfour on July 7, 1918:

The whole lesson of my nine years of exploration of this region is told in a very few words, when speaking of that genus. Travel northwestwards and the species are ever on the increase; break eastwards or south and there is a marked decrease in numbers immediately! From some point northwest of Tsarong, the genus spreads out in a fan-shaped drift southeast, gradually thinning off in numbers as the lowlands or plains are reached! (Royal Botanic Garden 1918a)

The next season, despite a serious battle between Chinese and Tibetan forces in Tsharong, three men from Nvlvk'o and one Tibetan collector from Tsiriting made two journeys up the Mekong–Salween divide into southern Tsharong. "I wish I could be with them," Forrest wrote in the spring of 1918. "Tsarong is closed to Chinese and Europeans alike," he explained to his syndicate. "However, my men carry their passports on their faces, all of them being Mossoo [Naxi] or Tibetan" (Royal Botanic Garden 1918b, 1918c, 1918e). The party crated eighty to ninety species of *Rhododendron* and hundreds of species of other genera to send to Forrest at Tengyue. In the summer of 1919, another party, of three Tibetan collectors from Tsiriting, walked into central Tsharong. Residents received them hospitably, despite the recent fighting. But no precipitation had fallen on the mountains for more than seven months; the ground was dry, the flowers few, the alpine meadows burned up. The men moved southwest, to the range that divided the Salween from the Qiu (now Dulong), a northern tributary of the Nmai. When hearing from a missionary of the men's move, Forrest immediately shifted his hopes for the center of origin of *Rhododendron* to this range. "Strange how they should decide to prospect there," he wrote in the summer of 1919, "for that is the country I should try to reach could I get north from here…! As viewed on the map it looks very hopeful, far enough north and such an extensive system of huge ranges, that there must be much that is new to us in it" (Royal Botanic Gardens 1919a, 1919b).

In dongba texts, rhododendrons gave off the scent of primordial battle.[11] They took form in a cloud of smoke emerging from the burned corpse of a vanquished enemy during a war at the time of the earth's creation. Along with birch for arrows, spruce for spears, and mulberry for bows, they were among a few plants fashioned into weapons in the battles fought during the formation of the cosmos. Armor and shields were woven of their strong, sinuous branches, and sword sheathes carved from their black limbs.

These battles were concerned with a primordial division of the cosmos. This was not a division between social and natural, human and nonhuman, or domestic and wild. It was a complex negotiation of overlapping claims of rule or ownership asserted by many different alliances of beings over many others. Dongba texts described hundreds of wars and battles over such claims, to which there was never permanent settlement, only perpetual contestation. Frequently, lines were drawn between the warring parties, often between black and white: black regions were claimed by evil beings (ghosts, demons, humans), white regions by good (gods, ancestors, priests). Lines of garrisons and forts were built between white and black regions, reminiscent of the lines of towers that once divided the realm of the Mu kings from those of their enemies to the north and west. As soon as any such line was described, however, it was breeched by one force or another; a claim of redress was made, and a battle was joined.

Rites of healing continued these ancient battles. Texts described how armies of gods, ancestors, priests, demons, and ghosts marshaled the inanimate material of the world to their causes by assembling it into beings or part beings with limited capacities. And they showed ritualists how to imitate those acts in their own battles. To collect plants and assemble them into ritually powerful beings was to gather and focus the ambiguous nonhuman forces inhabiting the landscape, making possible exchange and negotiation between them and humans. This exchange made use of a ritual language of plants, a language that articulated affect and bodily sensation with the properties of plants. Rhododendrons were prominent in these rituals. An example is the rite of Dtona, intended to drive away demons of slander afflicting a person or a household. Among the instruments assembled for this rite were beings called Ngawbpa. These were torches assembled from twigs of several trees, of which the black rhododendron (*mùnnà* in Naxi) was the most important. Dongba texts contained graphs for at least twenty varieties of Ngawbpa: headless beings with twigs for torsos and powerful running legs and feet. Some had horns of yak, cattle, or goats sprouting from their twig bodies; others, beaks and talons of chickens or fangs of dogs. Some could see and call; others could laugh or spit at demons. One text described them as "fast as the clouds and winds, swift as the fish in water, ferocious as a tiger, able to devour an ox in the forest...the trees of the enemies are smashed; the gates to their cliff-dwellings are destroyed, their animals killed; their houses are burned" (Janert 1984, vol. 7, pt. 2:282). Ngawbpa were both substitutes for slanderous enemies and allies against the demons of slander. As enemies, they were burned and beheaded, their twig bodies set alight before being chopped to bits while dongba recited texts about burning and beheading slanderous neighbors. As allies, they were called upon to drive the demons of slander back into enemy lands.

Like all ritual instruments, Ngawbpa had a geneaology and a place of origin. Their father was a black rhododendron sprouting from the mountain of Shílo; their mother, a thin-leaved willow at the mountain's foot.

Nvlvk'o villagers must have found Forrest's preoccupation with plant specimens strange. As they learned to tag the specimens with numbers corresponding to his notes and to give their own notes on the locations and situations of the plants, they also learned how specimens were inserted into chains of reference connecting them on the one end to specific locations of the earth and at the other end to a mysterious but enormously authoritative abstraction: scientific botanical taxonomy. Their participation in Dongba ritual practice may have provided a model for making sense of this. There, too, individual plant specimens, gathered from the mountain, were inserted into chains of reference. They were made tokens of species types, linked to specific passages of text, given points of origin on the earth's surface. And all of this was undergirded by the enormous authority of Dongba textual practice, with its complex taxonomies of gods, species, stories, and techniques.

It should hardly seem surprising if these men found the clues to what Forrest so avidly sought in this other authority, if they mapped his obsessions onto this other cartography. And in this other cartography, rhododendrons always pointed back along the road north to the threshold between worlds, the great mountain of Shílo.

Back in Edinburgh in early 1920, Forrest dazzled the Rhododendron Society with black-and-white lantern slides of his latest expedition. He spoke of the "nucleous and radiating point" of the *Rhododendron* genus. As one travels north toward Tsharong on the Mekong–Salween divide, he said, the mountains rise higher and higher,

> the sacred mountains of the Doker-la [Dokar La] and Ka-gwr-pu [Khawakarpo] surpassing even the Lichiang range in altitude and rugged grandeur, and…there is scarcely any ligneous vegetation but Rhododendron, the flowering season a riot of colour, gorgeous beyond any description; mountain sides splashed with colour like a giant palette. (Forrest 1920:23)

Yet all of this "is but a tithe of what is to come, not only of Rhododendrons, but of many other genera—Primula, Gentiana, etc." (Forrest 1920:17). He had heard from Baptist missionaries who had traveled north

FIGURE 6.8

Chao, Forrest's head collector from Nvlvk'o (courtesy Royal Botanic Garden, Edinburgh).

of Tsharong in Kham of "an undulating plateau of vast extent and high altitude, enclosed by higher ranges, everywhere clothed in Rhododendrons, great and small, to the exclusion of almost all else" (Forrest 1920:20).

By July 1921 he was back in Yunnan's far northwest, in a village of scattered Lisu and Tibetan dwellings, about four miles south of Tsiriting. The

Nvlvk'o collectors worked up and down the Mekong Valley, south to Yezhi and north to the Dokar La, Khawakarpo, and beyond. But continued clashes between Chinese and Tibetan forces made central Tsharong too dangerous. Again, Forrest shifted his aspirations to the divide between the Qiu and Salween. Of this area, he had told the Rhododendron Society, "I do not consider it rash to say that when [it] is explored it may prove as prodigal in its flora as Tsarong" (Royal Botanic Garden 1921a).He arranged for Chao (figure 6.8), his head collector from Nvlvk'o, who had worked with him since at least 1912, to lead "his particular gang" of eight or nine Nvlvk'o men to this range. The party climbed the great, glaciated Qiu–Salween divide to a pass around sixteen thousand feet. Beyond, to the north, they glimpsed a mightier range yet. It was, Forrest believed, the same range he and Litton had seen during their exploration of the upper Salween in 1904 (Royal Botanic Garden 1921a).

They returned to Forrest's base on the Mekong for a few days and set off again, this time with tens of Tibetan porters carrying food. Nearly everywhere else, the Nvlvk'o collectors had relied on locals for food. But they had discovered that food was very scarce in the upper Salween and Qiu valleys. The peoples living there, whom the Chinese called Nu (or Lu) and Qiu after the river valleys they inhabited, grew only maize and only enough for four to five months of the year, subsisting for the rest of the year by hunting and gathering (Royal Botanic Garden 1921a, 1921b).

The Nvlvk'o men worked their way up and over the Qiu–Salween divide and down to the timberline. Chao wanted to descend to the bed of the Qiu, but Forrest, fearing fever, had forbidden it. Again, they caught sight of the great range beyond. Forrest wrote in September 1921:

> [They] speak of having seen, during a clear blink of the mists which enfold these altitudes...a huge snow-capped range inclined transversely to that on which they stood and lying several days journey to the northwest. Consul Litton and I on our journey up the Salwin in the autumn of 1905 at the furthest point north attained a glimpse of the same range, and a most awe-inspiring sight it was, though distant fully 100 miles to us. (Royal Botanic Garden 1921c, 1921d)

It was a wishful confusion. Litton had insisted that the mighty range he and Forrest had seen was an extension of the Salween–Nmai divide—the "vast wall" that would be a natural barrier between the British Empire and its Far Eastern neighbor. But that single glimpse had haunted Forrest for nearly two decades, and he began to associate it with his own promised land—now the northern extension of the Salween–Qiu divide, considerably to the northwest of Litton's "vast wall." On these two journeys, Chao's "particular gang" gathered forty-five species of *Rhododendron* and about one hundred of other genera. "Not bad for what is, so far, merely scratching a new area!" Forrest exulted (Royal Botanic Garden 1921c, 1921d).

The taxonomists at Edinburgh examined the collections of this season and wrote Forrest in Nvlvk'o that they contained several new species of *Rhododendron*. It did not take more than this news to set him off on the topic of his particular Eden. By now he had settled firmly on a strategy for moving the precise location of that Eden from Tsharong to the Salween–Qiu divide—now farther north than his men had yet penetrated, among the great peaks they had glimpsed through the mists. He wrote to Balfour on March 23, 1922:

> That fact is further evidence of the opinion I have so often expressed…that the nucleus of the genus—its radiating point—lies somewhere in Central or Northeast Tsarong…. Though looked at and measured by the eye on the existent maps that seems but a comparatively short distance from where we terminated our last season's exploration, yet it is an immensity judged by the plant life of the region. I can never hope to get there, I think. However, I may safely make an addition to my prophesy of past years that the northern spurs and peaks of the Kiu chiang [Qiu River]–Salween divide, where it breaks up and loses itself in the higher Zayul and other cross ranges of Southwest Central Tsarong, is going to prove the richest ground of all. How much I now regret the lack of knowledge which confined me to Central and West Yunnan in the early years of my work! (Royal Botanic Garden 1922a).

Chao's party had made the long journey back to Nvlvk'o late in the winter. In early March, they set off again for the Salween–Qiu divide (figure 6.9). Forrest promised them a bonus of one Mexican silver dollar for every new species of *Rhododendron* gathered in flower and a half dollar for every *Primula*. For two months, they worked the great mountains between the Qiu and Salween. In late July, they met Forrest in Tengyue with some two hundred species of *Rhododendron*, nearly all in flower. But Forrest had no way of telling how many were new. With so many species flowing in over the previous few years, the Edinburgh staff had fallen far behind, and the genus was a tangle. Forrest guessed that Chao's new collection held twenty

FIGURE 6.9
Party of collectors from Nvlvk'o on the road (courtesy Royal Botanic Garden, Edinburgh).

to forty new species. Presumably, although he mentioned it nowhere, he paid Chao and his men a bonus of at least twenty Mexican dollars (Royal Botanic Garden 1922a, 1922b).

Forrest and his collaborators had brought a region into being—or rather, a stratum of a region, in the form of a systematic archive of assemblages of words and things. Between Forrest's first expedition, from 1904 to 1907, and his third, from 1912 to 1915, this region-making project became increasingly ambitious. By 1913 Forrest was making plans to deploy teams from Nvlvk'o strategically throughout the region to "sweep North-west Yunnan clear" of all the species in which his sponsors might take interest. The archive in Edinburgh would be a full record of the region, with a type specimen of each species indexed to its area of distribution. By 1917 this idea had begun to take on a focus and an orientation. That most charismatic of genera, *Rhododendron*, appeared to show a pattern of diffusion from the far northwest, where numbers of species were most concentrated, toward the southeast, where they became progressively less concentrated. Given contemporary scientific knowledge about the processes of differentiation and dispersion, this need not have implied that the genus was focused on one identifiable location, but Forrest took exactly this to

FIGURE 6.10

Dongba pictographs. Left to right: *Nundu, the upper Salween (the three-leaved plant is the symbol for Rhododendron, here used phonetically); Nunkhi, the Nu people of the upper Salween; and Nundu Gyinvlv, the great snow mountain of Nundu (Forrest's rhododendron paradise) (Rock 1963:564).*

be the case. After 1917 he became obsessed with finding this "promised land" and experiencing the "revelation" he felt it would offer. In 1923 Isaac Bailey Balfour, Forrest's mentor and surrogate father, died while working out a thorough revision of Rhododendron. He was the only person on earth who knew the genus well enough to verify Forrest's claims about it. Forrest made three more expeditions to Yunnan, the last ending with his death in 1932. But he gave up the idea of ever again penetrating as far north as his paradise of rhododendrons.

SOURCES

As Chao and his party worked their way north up the Mekong from the Tibetan village of Tsiriting, they found villages of Naxi scattered along the way. The most northerly lay some five days from Tsiriting in the valley of a stream that joined the Mekong at an important group of salt wells called Yanjing (Tshakhalo in Tibetan). When, instead of walking north, they passed over the Dokar La into the Salween River valley and then over the range beyond into the Qiu River valley, they found no Naxi settlements. Nevertheless, these mountains and rivers had once been conquered by the Mu kings. As a result, they were embedded in the archival regime cultivated by Naxi ritualists. In dongba texts (figure 6.10), the people of the Salween were called Nunkhi and represented by the symbols for a yellow pea (*nun*) and a man (*khi*). Their land was Nundù, land of the Nun. The highest mountain on the Salween–Qiu divide was the Nundù Gyuinvlv (Kenichempo in Tibetan), the great snow mountain of the Nun. Beyond this mountain, in the Qiu River valley, lived the T'khyukhi, represented by a drawing of a sword boring a hole (*t'kyù*, "to bore") and a man (*khi*). Their land was the T'khyudù, land of the T'khyu (Rock 1963:564).

This far-flung geography had been made present to the Nvlvk'o men even at home, and even in the trivial circumstances of daily life. Just below Nvlvk'o was a meadow with a spring. If the rainy season had not begun by June, villagers would sponsor a small ritual there called *khu'ma*, "desiring rain." Most people from Nvlvk'o had probably seen this rite performed several times. At the spring, dongba recited fourteen texts calling upon the original dwellers of the land, *ssu* and *llu*, to arise from rivers, lakes, and streams throughout the former Mu realms and to sweep across the land toward the Lijiang Valley. Only one of these texts was specific to the khu'ma rite. It was clearly written to be performed in Nvlvk'o and nearby villages, because it named the springs and cliffs of the Yulong range in the immediate vicinity of the village as "our own mountain and valley spirits" (Janert 1984, vol. 4:1504; Rock 1947:611).

The text described the effects of drought: "When waters of silver and gold dry up, the heart of a skilled man aches; when waters of turquoise and cornelian dry up, the liver of a wise woman aches."[12] It called upon the ssu kings and chiefs: Màmí Bpalò, who holds an eagle; Bpawua Ts'òbpò', who leads a red tiger on an iron chain; Làbbu T'ogkó, who holds a golden mirror; and dozens more. It implored them to call up the ssu of mountains and valleys, of springs and villages, of the wastelands, of the clouds and peaks—armies of ssu soldiers, twenty-five thousand strong. It asked the ssu of the ponds and streams of the Yulong range for cloudbursts—thirty-four place-names in the immediate vicinity of Nvlvk'o. It called on the ssu of the regions to the northeast, describing a circular path from the mountains around the beautiful Lugu Lake of Yongning into the Lijiang Valley and toward Nvlvk'o. To the southeast and southwest, it traced two more winding paths, taking in mountains and villages along the southern borders of the former Mu realms and tending in toward the Lijiang Valley and Nvlvk'o—another thirty-four place-names.

When these lists of places swept around to the northwest, they were flung much farther, west to Weixi (Nyinà in Naxi), then far up into the lands of the upper Salween (Nun in Naxi) and Qiu (T'khyu in Naxi) and the great mountain range Gyinvlv between:[13]

alpine meadow spirits of Nyinà	*Nyi nà ghugh szi gkò*
alpine meadow spirits of Dze nà à ho	*Dze nà à ho ghugh szi gkò*
spirits of meadows with bubbling springs	*Ts'u ts'u gkò*[14]

mountains of Lazhermberlèr	*La zher mber lèr ngyù*
mountains of Gkawgkàwssma	*Gkaw gkàw ss ma ngyùsnow*
mountain of the Nun lands	*Nun dù Gkyi nv lv*
great snow mountain of the T'khyù lands	*T'kyhu dù Zher nv lv*[15]

After winding through several villages with Naxi names, the route ascended to Odso Lvmanà, literally, "the place of the black and white rocks in Tibet." Odso Lvmanà was at the foot of Ngyuna Shílo Ngyu, the "vast mountain of Shílo"; it was the first place the founder of the dongba cult, Dibba Shílo, had come when he entered the world of men.[16] The trail then wound down into Weixi and toward Lijiang—seventeen more place-names. Finally, the text called on the ssu of the north, along the Wuliang River in the Muli district, wandering through Bberdder (Baidi in Chinese), across the Yangze River and the Yulong mountain range, and into the Nvlvk'o area again—another sixty-two names (Rock 1952:607–619).[17]

Naxi ritual practice gained its effective force by bringing the great geo-cosmological archive of dongba textual practice into the intimate realm of daily life. In rites like khu'ma, every act of recitation was a movement through this archive, drawing its listeners along long, looping, rhythmic paths of place-names. These paths connected daily domestic life with the nonhuman substrate of life, which could not be experienced bodily, only through speaking or reading. In this archive, the lands of the Nun and T'khyu were at the outer limit of the human, associated with the wildest of things: bear and boar, tiger and leopard, crane and eagle, spruce and rhododendron. These lands were mentioned only in texts that appealed to the original nonhuman inhabitants of the land, the ssu and llu, who commanded the forces of nonhuman life.

Chao and his men clearly had the sense that they were trespassing beyond the outer limits of the human as they crossed the great ranges into those river valleys for the first time in 1921. Echoes of their voices reverberate in Forrest's recitation of their report to him of their journey. In a letter to Balfour of September 3, 1921, his prose shifts into a style far more vivid and compressed than his usual efforts:

> I can believe every word did they paint it even more luridly. Roads of no kind, deep jungle-choked and panther-haunted gorges separated by razor-backed spurs and bounded by breakneck precipices and dense forests at the lower altitudes; cane brakes and boulder-strewn marshy moorlands with snow drifts

and eternal mists at the higher, and above all, a chaos of screes, ragged peaks, and glaciers! (Royal Botanic Garden 1921c)

In Naxi rituals of grief, places like this divided the living earth from what lay beyond—the "glittering golden mountain gate" through which the tiger passed in the song of the origin of sorrow, the "nine ridges" and "seven rivers" the deceased ancestors crossed. These were the places where mourners faced the lands of the gods, then voluntarily turned their faces away, letting their grief carry them only this far toward the ineffable. In principle, each such journey ascended to Ngyuna Shílo Ngyu, the "vast mountain of Shílo," the final threshold of the human world. As the men from Nvlvk'o made forays into the mountains around the upper Salween and Qiu river valleys in search of the center of *Rhododendron*, they came as close as they ever would to Odso Lvmanà, where Shílo, the founder of the dongba cult, descended to earth, and the great mountain, origin of worlds, that towered above it.

CONCLUSIONS

To the end, Forrest believed himself to be involved in a straightforward mission to apply the taxonomical language of botanical science to this empty portion of the globe. All his letters, field notes, and journal articles give the impression that this was an uncomplicated extension of a carto-graphic and taxonomical regime in place since the eighteenth century. Now and then, moved by the incapacity of language to express his feelings about this landscape, he allowed these taxonomies to slip and blur. But he never allowed his relationships with his collectors to move toward any kind of hybridity: he remained resolutely ignorant of their prior knowledge of plants; he took no interest in their ideas about the geographical form of the region; and he viewed the rituals that brought these forms of knowl-edge together as a meaningless and irritating waste of time.

Nevertheless, the points at which desire and longing began to shape his scientific practice were also, it seems, openings to the knowledge of his collaborators. These were points at which the great archive of geo-cosmological knowledge that shaped their ideas about this landscape began also to change his, opening them up to new possibilities. As the men from Nvlvk'o made ever more northerly journeys over many years, they were forging connections with the geography embedded in their ritual life. They were walking back along the routes of their ancestors, back toward their own center of origin. Often, these were routes they had already taken, through that dense interleaving of text, voice, and motion that formed their rites of mourning. The great mountain of Shílo was the orienting edge of this geography. It was off beyond the geographical archive of ritual practice, somewhere past the Nun and T'khyu river valleys, the point from which ancestors had come into this world and toward which the dead returned. In particular, it was an orienting point for their affective lives because they were bound up in this geography—the point at which, in the work of mourning, they had to turn back were they not to follow the dead. For Forrest, the source of *Rhododendron*, somewhere beyond the upper Salween and Qiu, was also the orienting point of his sense of the region's geography. He needed this center to make sense of the genus *Rhododendron*—and indeed to make sense of his decades of exploration. In particular, it was an orienting point for his affective life because it was bound up in this geography, his longing for an aesthetic paradise, his life goal.

It should not be surprising that this convergence was laden so heavily with affect. Many historians of colonial science have noted that intimate relations among humans were threatening to that enterprise, particularly to the authority of European scientists. Controlling the intimate and affective aspects of their relationships with their indigenous collaborators was extraordinarily important to colonial field scientists. Yet relations among humans and between humans and nonhumans are always embodied relations and, as Hugh Raffles (2002:326) notes, always mediated by affect, as well as by power and discourse. Lonely George Forrest was always careful to maintain the exclusionary relationships with his collectors that he believed science demanded of him. Yet he eventually found ways to create meaningful affective relationships—of longing, of desire, and of ecstatic involvement—with the ultimate nonhuman object of his science—the earth. I have argued that this particular relationship could not have come about without the guidance of his collectors. Despite himself, Forrest learned from them how to create a social relationship with the earth.

Collectively, the chapters in this book are meant to move us toward new ways of understanding resources. Colonial science and ethnography were instrumental in producing for us that strict division between the social and the natural that seems to shape most discussions of "natural resources." Yet it is possible that intimate histories of colonial science might show scientists to have been involved in a rich variety of social relations with the nonhuman participants in their science. One route toward such intimate histories might be a closer examination of the networks of relationship that formed between scientists and their indigenous collaborators, many of whom had long-established social relations with the nonhuman beings that were being transformed into the natural objects of science.

Acknowledgments

I am most grateful to Jane Hutcheon, Leonie Paterson, and Graham Hardy, all librarians at the Royal Botanic Garden, for their frequent, cheerful assistance with the research for the project of which this chapter forms a part. I carried out this research with the help of a British Academy Fellowship, under the generous sponsorship of Roy Ellen. The MacArthur Foundation also provided funding. The chapter was written during a fellowship at the Center for Advanced Studies in Behavioral Sciences. I thank the participants in the SAR advanced seminar for their wise advice.

Notes

1. In 1908 George Forrest presented an edited version of Litton's report, accompanied by Forrest's photographs, to the Royal Geographic Society (Forrest 1908).

2. The great scientific traveler Xu Xiake solved this puzzle for Chinese geographers in the seventeenth century. On Xu Xiake's exploration of the Nujiang, see Xu Xiake's diaries (Xu 1999) and Joseph Needham (1959:524–525).

3. Note on orthography: Place-names in northwestern Yunnan are often in many languages. In this chapter, for the sake of readability, I most often use standard Chinese place-names, in the Hanyu Pinyin orthography. Where appropriate, I supplement these with Tibetan or Naxi names. For Tibetan place-names, I use the simplified system of phonological transcription introduced by Tournadre and Dorje (2003:475–480). For Naxi names and terms, I have used a simplified form of Joseph Rock's system of transcription, given in Rock 1963:xxxi–xxxvii.

4. In northwestern Yunnan, the final border followed the Gaoligong ridge, which divided the Salween and Irrawaddy watersheds except in two locations: Pianma, which China successfully retrieved from Burma, and, in the far northwest, the Dulong (formerly Qiu, known to the British as the Tarong and to Tibetans as the Drong), a tributary of the Irrawaddy, divided from the Salween by the highest point of the Gaoligong range (Foreign Office 1906).

5. The most comprehensive printed edition of dongba texts is a one-hundred-volume interlinear translation made in more than two decades of work by the Lijiang Dongba Culture Research Institute (He and He 1999). Joseph Francis Rock also produced many interlinear translations, some of which I refer to here.

6. Some seven thousand of these are in Western libraries; twenty thousand or so are in libraries in Lijiang, Beijing, Nanjing, and Kunming.

7. This and the next passage from "Song for the Dead, the Origin of Sorrow" are from Rock 1955. Rock's translations of dongba texts vary enormously in quality. Or, to be more precise, aspects of them vary; his full English renditions are reliably horrible. In his translation of this text, Rock took unusual care to have the entire

pictographic text copied, give the full vocal transcription of the entire text, and give a full explanation of every single pictograph. This has allowed me to provide an English translation that I think better reflects the original.

8. I have taken some liberties with Rock's translation, aided by his detailed footnotes, which include many of the pictographs for this text.

9. Several "gods' road" scrolls have been preserved and published. The Lijiang Naxi Culture Research Institute published a fine example as color photographs in Li 2001. Rock gave one to the Library of Congress, which has published it on the Internet as photographs (http://hdl.loc.gov/loc.asian/asnaxi.nza079). Rock published two scrolls as photographs (Janert 1984, vol. 7, pt. 2:plates 1–31; Rock 1937).

10. Forrest romanized this name to Tsedjrong.

11. The texts mention three types of *Rhododendron*: *mùn* or *mùnnà*, *shwua*, and, less frequently, *mùnlua*. Joseph Rock identified *mùnnà* as *R. decorum*: small, with rough black bark, glabrous leaves, and fragrant white flowers, growing abundantly on the Yulong Mountain at around nine thousand to ten thousand feet. *Shwua* was both *R. rubiginosum* and *R. heliolepis*, larger and more tree-like, with narrow leaves, glabrous on top and scaly on the bottom, and with pink, red, crimson, or lavender flowers. *Mùnlua*, again according to Rock, was "any of the large Rhododendrons growing at 14,000 feet elevation in western Yunnan, alpine regions, flowers pink, leaves with brown tomentum beneath, like *R. adenogynum*" (1963:292).

12. Rock and his collaborator, the dongba He Huating, created a transliteration and partial translation of khu'ma in *The Na-khi Naga Cult and Related Ceremonies* (1952:607–619), using a manuscript in He Huating's library that he refused to part with, Rock's number 1,782. This manuscript is reproduced as a hand copy in Janert 1984, vol. 4:1501–1506, drawn by a dongba with whom Rock worked after He Huating's death. It is incomplete. Janert 1984:1507–1516 also includes an untranslated hand copy of manuscript 8,586, more complete than 1,782. I have consulted both manuscript reproductions, in addition to Rock's translation, for my own translation.

13. For this passage, I follow Rock's transcription (1952:613). Rock's translation of this passage is only partial, so I also refer to the manuscript copy in Janert 1984, vol. 4:1516, which, however, does not correspond exactly to Rock's transcription.

14. My translation of this line is uncertain because Rock's transliteration (1952:613) does not match the manuscript in Janert 1984, vol. 4:1516.

15. Here, the manuscript contains an additional phrase, which does not appear in Rock's translation.

16. This place, also called Berder Odso, was mentioned in many other dongba texts. For instance, every dongba kept a book called *Gkó'ó* (*Throwing Out the Grain*), used at nearly every ceremony to which gods or spirits were invited, including the

muanbpo, or "sacrifice to heaven" ceremony, in which every nearly man in Nvlvk'o participated every year. It described the roads along which ancestors had scattered grain for the gods. The ancestors scattered grain down the mountain of Shílo and then into Berder Odso before descending into places close to the Lijiang Valley. Dongba identified Shílo as Tönba Shenrap Miwo (ston-pa gshen-rab mi-bo), the mythical founder of the Tibetan Bön religion. Berder Odso was the Tibetan Barlha'ösä (bar-lha-hod-gsal), through which Tönba Shenrap Miwo had passed on his way to the world of men.

17. Here I have also followed the numerous notes from other parts of Rock 1952 indexed to these pages.

7

The Temporal and Spatial Politics of Student "Diversity" at an American University

Courtney Childs, Huong Nguyen,

and Richard Handler

Universities are cultural resources. Their mission is to transmit cultural resources to students and, through them, to the wider societies in which they are located. Thus the students themselves can be conceived of as cultural resources, or perhaps as resources to be cultured over time. This process of cultural transmission is conceptualized in terms of the standard Western temporal scheme of progressive motion from "the past" through "the present" into "the future." As storied president of the University of California Clark Kerr once wrote, "the ends" of the university are "the preservation of the eternal truths, the creation of new knowledge, [and] the improvement of service wherever truth and knowledge of high order may serve the needs of [humanity]" (Kerr 1963:38). Kerr thought that such a mission always verged on contradiction, as universities struggle to reconcile "the tug of the anchor to the past with the pull of the Holy Grail of the future" (1963:38). But on the whole, he thought that the university, and especially the American university, did a masterful job of changing itself quickly "while pretending that nothing has happened at all" (1963:45).

Kerr's rhetoric suggests the socio-evolutionary narrative that structures, even overwhelms, university mission statements. Like the nation-state and other powerful institutions in modern societies, the university can be given a distinguished, albeit hazy, "Western" pedigree: the Greeks, of course, the medieval Christian Church, the city-states of the Italian Renaissance, Paris, Oxbridge, the German Enlightenment. And like individual nation-states (Handler 1988:40–43), individual universities have specific pedigrees that usually include a dated birth or founding, a cohort of "founders" or ancestors, and a subsequent history that may include ups and downs but, in general, traces an upward trajectory of "growth" and "development." Also like nation-states, universities do not like to envision their own demises; rather, they rarely imagine anything other than a future of ever-greater accomplishment.

The cultural resources that universities transmit to their students are deemed to have both absolute value and utilitarian value. That is, the knowledge created and conserved in the university is at once its own reward and of service to society. The tension between "absolute" and "utilitarian" evaluations of knowledge is an enduring one in modern culture, yet for generations, academicians have worried about the "corruption" of the university by the utilitarian concerns of students, parents, donors, politicians, and, impersonally encompassing all of these, "the market."

At the turn of the twenty-first century, the struggle between "business" and "culture" in the university is often experienced (and bemoaned) by academicians as "the corporatization of the university." By this is meant the increasing pressures that professors and administrators believe they face both to tailor their "product"—education—to the needs of the market and to organize themselves institutionally in ways that emulate or demonstrate "sound business practices." Their ostensibly compliant response to corporatization stems from their belief that marketplace rationality is necessary for institutional health (for example, Zemsky, Wegner, and Massy 2005) and sometimes also from the knowledge that their donors and sponsors will require at least the appearance of such rationality.

As anthropologist Bonnie Urciuoli has shown (1999, 2003, 2005a, 2005b), one of the primary results of corporatization in the university is the creation of a rhetoric of "skills" that is used to market and justify the liberal arts to the wider society. The knowledge conserved and created in the university may be good in and of itself, but it is undoubtedly good for workplace success. In the new global economy (as the clichés have it), employers need workers who have been trained not with yesterday's knowledge but with skills that will allow them to adapt endlessly to new technologies, flexible production practices, and shifting market niches. Those skills are for the most part traditional ones: the ability to think critically, to speak and write clearly, and to solve problems. There are also human relations or managerial skills: the ability to get along well with others, to work as a "team," and to be a "leader" in a "diverse," "multicultural" world. It is with the last of these issues, "diversity" construed as a cultural and educational resource, that the present chapter is concerned.

Our primary ethnographic information comes from field research conducted informally and formally during the 2003–2004 and 2004–2005 academic years at the University of Virginia (UVA) by Courtney Childs and Huong Nguyen, both of whom were acting simultaneously as "native" students and as anthropologists. Childs had worked with Sustained Dialogue, a student organization whose mission is to serve "as a catalyst for bringing together different types of people and opening lines of communication between racial groups" (Sustained Dialogue 2007). Sustained Dialogue has been highly acclaimed by the university administration, but Childs quickly became disenchanted by the ease with which participants blamed UVA's racial tensions on "self-segregation." She resolved, therefore, to study ethnographically students' notions of self-segregation (Childs 2005:2–4). Nguyen served as president of the Asian Student Union (ASU) during 2003–2004. The exhaustion and frustration generated by a year of work in that capacity led her to undertake anthropological research on minority student leadership in her fourth year. Handler supervised both student anthropologists' research and theses, and all three conferred together during the two years of activism and research.[1]

We begin by reviewing the "time-saturated" rhetoric that characterizes most of the university's public relations literature. Next we focus on the university's public discourse of diversity, noting how that topic is assimilated into the standard temporal narrative of progress. We then turn to the ethnographic heart of the matter, using the research of Nguyen and Childs to examine some of the ways in which "minority" and "mainstream" undergraduates conceptualize diversity and racial tension in relation to space and time.

THE RHETORIC OF DIVERSITY AT MR. JEFFERSON'S UNIVERSITY

The university's founder, Thomas Jefferson, is a unique piece of cultural property. Given his historical importance in the United States, his devotion to the ideals of the European Enlightenment and thus to the culture of the modern university (in Kerr's sense), and his participation in the American slaveholding system, he is a challengingly polysemous institutional symbol and totemic ancestor. In many rather charming ways, he is routinely invoked in the daily life of the university; its natives seem at once at ease with his name and ever-so-slightly self-conscious about their name-dropping practices (Nguyen 2005:43–44).

Many public relations and planning documents emanating from the university's central administration begin with a reference to Mr. Jefferson, just as many ceremonial events conclude with a toast to him. The preferred rhetoric is time saturated. Mr. Jefferson is at once the university's "anchor to the past" and the inspiration for its progressive vision. We (faculty and students in the present) are his "heirs." The university is constantly in motion, ceaselessly striving to improve and develop, although in most cases, spatial terms—verbs of activity and motion—refer metaphorically to nonspatial projects (the improvement of the curriculum or the accomplishment of research). Even when progress, expansion, and renovation refer to buildings—that is, to literal places and spaces—there is always a metaphorical overflow, an implication that those places and spaces will be important because they will house cultural work that is ultimately not spatial. University buildings thus are cultural resources. But more importantly, they are sites in which to produce more cultural resources.

In the university's planning for its future and in its current assessment of its overall progress, diversity is a prized resource, but one that needs to be developed. Progress on this front, however, seems elusive. There is no doubt that the student body has been significantly "diversified," starting with the admission of African American students in the 1960s and women in 1970. Currently, women compose 55 percent of the student body; Asian and Asian-Pacific Americans, 11 percent; African Americans, 9 percent; and Hispanic/Latino students, 3 percent. Like other elite research universities, UVA works hard to recruit minority faculty and administrators, with some success but far less than the institution would like. The curriculum has changed and continues to change in those areas of scholarship influenced by cultural studies, social history, gender studies, and critical race theory. And the organizational structure of the university continues to sprout new units functionally designed to enhance diversity.

But the elusiveness of progress in this area is represented, to diversity's well-wishers, with depressing frequency by ongoing "incidents." When Childs and Nguyen were students (2001–2005), the most prominent of such incidents were a fraternity Halloween party to which two members came in blackface, dressed as the tennis players Venus and Serena Williams; "the Daisy Lundy incident," in which a black candidate for the presidency of Student Council was physically attacked, with the perpetrator yelling, "No one wants a nigger to be president"; and the vandalizing of a black student's car, with a racial epithet written on the window (for an overview, see M. Turner 2005). For whatever reasons, many more racial incidents were not deemed important enough to attain the status of the named, dated, and publicly recorded incidents just listed. There is also a kind of oppositional discourse that doubts the truth of the reports of such incidents.

The blackface and Daisy Lundy incidents were among the most public of the catalysts that prompted UVA president John Casteen to appoint a Commission on Diversity and Equity in the spring of 2003. Its work was reported in the 2003–2004 *President's Report.* Enunciating major planning goals, the report moves easily from its discussion of Mr. Jefferson and "the useful sciences" to the topic of diversity. The commission, we are told, has formulated a plan to create "a safe and nurturing atmosphere for all students, staff, and faculty, regardless of race, ethnicity, gender, or sexual orientation." The plan "has challenged us to adopt diversity as a way of life in the same way we embrace honor. Our response to acts of intolerance must be as strong as our response to acts of lying, cheating, and stealing." As we will discuss below, "honor" refers to UVA's student-run Honor Committee, an institutional site of racial struggle. That honor can be paired, ahistorically and apolitically, with tolerance in this document suggests the many ways in which diversity can be sanitized for selected audiences (University of Virginia 2003–2004).

Urciuoli has argued that a sanitized version of diversity has displaced older, historically situated meanings of the term in recently corporatized higher-education rhetoric. She notes that in the rhetoric of multicultural student organizations (those that address the needs of minority students), the word "*diversity*...retains some sense of race-like historical specificity" (2005b:164); that is, minority students and their organizations understand diversity in terms of group identities and the historical struggles associated with people marked by those identities. Urciuoli contrasts this connotation of the term to that prevalent in corporate rhetoric, in which diversity refers to individuals abstracted from such histories. In this perspective, every individual has "core traits" (such as age, ethnicity, and gender) and "secondary traits" (such as education, military experience, and first language) that distinguish him or her as a unique person (165). Individuals bring such traits into the workplace as "assets" that can be used to accomplish corporate tasks. Combined into "teams" and directed by "leaders," diverse workers pool their individual assets, which become, in this perspective, resources for corporate success. Thus "dry-cleaned of residue from history, structural inequality, and discrimination" (165), all individuals are equally diverse, and the corporate pursuit of a diverse workforce is little more than an instrumental routine for recruiting qualified employees. At Hamilton College in New York, the site of Urciuoli's research, the historical and political sensibility of the multicultural organizations has no counterpart in the rhetoric of the fraternities and sororities, which describe their missions as isomorphic with that of the college as a whole, concentrating on "the development of skills in leadership, scholarship, friendship, and community service" (167).

Urciuoli further argues that diversity has been assimilated into a discourse about skills that liberal arts institutions use to assert the value of education to the wider society and especially to corporate employers. The increasing salience of college rankings (such as those of *U.S. News and World Report*) puts diversity, understood in terms of individual assets, at a premium in the world of higher-education administrators, especially admissions officers. Although there are several ways institutions can "move up in the rankings," the one of importance here is the recruitment of "better" students. The rankings claim to be able to assess, numerically, the student population. Diversity is one of several desired and countable attributes for a student body (others are test scores, high school class ranks, grades, and so forth); more diversity thus means a higher ranking. Urciuoli connects diversity to skills because both are among the scalable qualities that a school claims for itself and can claim of its students:

> For itself, the school claims...*excellence, distinction, rigor, diversity, leadership.* Qualities located in students include (1) desirable practices that the school promises to inculcate in students such as *skills, effective communication, critical thinking;* (2) desirable qualities that the school...promises to further develop in students such as *leadership, citizenship, responsibility;* (3) desirable qualities that the school seeks as fixed properties of students, specifically *diversity* and *multiculturalism.* (Urciuoli 2003:390–391)

Such claims both respond to the ranking system and create more data to be "assessed." Whether this system affects the liberal arts curriculum (after all, most professors would agree that their courses foster "critical thinking") is an open question; but, as noted, the effect on diversity policies is to push the emphasis from questions of historical struggle and social justice to issues of numbers and "human resources."

Minority students not only increase a school's diversity index but they also serve as a resource for other students. The public relations images disseminated by institutions of higher education feature people of color more prominently than many campus residents would find them in daily life. This exaggerated image of diversity stems partly from the social ideology of the universities, but it also speaks to their desire to attract "better" students, to improve their rankings. The premise here is that better institutions have a "more diverse" student body and that mainstream or upper-middle-class white students (those with high test scores and the family wealth to afford an expensive education) will be disproportionately attracted to institutions with high rankings (Urciuoli 1999, 2003:386). Moreover, minority students are thought to contribute to the education of the other students by bringing into the community "diverse perspectives"—about which the less culturally exotic mainstream students can learn, such knowledge then becoming an asset in the corporate job market. In these ways, then, minority students come to be conceptualized as resources for the entire educational community.

ENTERING A WORLD OF DIVERSITY

Nguyen and Childs noted, in their experience as prospective college students and then as college students and researchers, that diversity is marketed differently to mainstream and minority students. For prospective students who are white, diversity is touted as a resource that will make their education more "well-rounded." Prospective students who are not white, however, do not have the same luxury of choosing, or forgoing, an education that is well-rounded in this sense. They *are*, after all, the human resource that will diversify the institution they attend. As such, they look for signs that institutions are "welcoming." In short, white students receive (and look for) the diversity pitch; nonwhite students elicit (and look for) the "tolerance" pitch.

As matriculating students make the transition from high school to the University of Virginia, one of the most important "choices" they are asked to make concerns housing. Although they do not fully understand it, they are about to enter an institution of segregated spaces. There are two groups of dormitories for first-year students: the "Old Dorms" of McCormick Road and the "New Dorms" of Alderman Road. It is an open secret that those dorms have "racial reputations," as columnist Patrick Harvey wrote in the *Cavalier Daily*, a student newspaper. Using 2002 statistics, Harvey reported that the population of New Dorms was 30 percent minority, whereas only 12 percent of the students in Old Dorms were minorities. The dorms, Harvey concluded, are a "self-segregating mess" (*Cavalier Daily*, September 29, 2003). Childs (2005:13–15) found in her interviewing that incoming white students see Old Dorms as welcoming, traditional, Jeffersonian, and "more social" than New Dorms; they see New Dorms residents as "less involved" (in student activities) than Old Dorms residents. Incoming nonwhite students, on the other hand, see Old Dorms as white, traditional, conservative, and even racist. They find New Dorms to be more racially diverse and hence more welcoming. Reflecting on his first-year experience, another student researcher, Alberto Gullaba, describes New Dorms as a "multicultural haven" and Old Dorms as its "white mainstream counter-part." Gullaba (2004:26) found it disconcerting that wealthy white students, uniformed in collared shirts and khaki pants, clustered in the Old Dorms.

The students who first experience these racialized spatial distinctions in the dorms soon learn that white and nonwhite persons are segregated in many domains of student life at the university. Although more than half of undergraduate students seek private housing after their first year, the 40 percent who stay in university housing tend to choose particular dorms based on their racial and ethnic identities (Gullaba 2004:49–60). But the decisive institution for reproducing spatial segregation is the "Greek system" of national fraternities and sororities. As Gullaba notes in his poignant memoir of the racial dynamics of his student experience, the initial racial division of Old Dorms–New Dorms is reinforced in the second semester during rush, when students seek entrance to fraternities and sororities. Gullaba, a Filipino American, describes the New Dorms residence staff's work to promote multiculturalism becoming ineffectual in the face of rush, as his white acquaintances disappeared, "off to a world on the opposite end of Central Grounds, a place far more stimulating than the multiculturalism of New Dorms" (Gullaba 2004:35). The standard conversational icebreaker of his first semester—"Where are you from?"—was replaced by "Where [which fraternity or sorority] do you want to pledge [join]?" And Gullaba describes himself wondering, "What happened to all of my white friends? Where did they go?" (35–36).

Only 30 percent of UVA undergraduates join Greek organizations, but the system is hegemonic nonetheless: like the Old Dorms–New Dorms distinction, the Greek–non-Greek distinction maps racially segregated populations. Not all non-Greeks are nonwhite, but most Greeks are white, and Greek culture is understood by most students to be "traditional," as that word is understood at Mr. Jefferson's university. (There are nonwhite Greek organizations too, and they play an increasingly prominent role in Greek life [see Kelman 2006], but the distinction between the "traditional" and the "multicultural" Greeks is sharp, reinforced by the fact that only the traditional organizations have houses.) Rugby Road, the site of the traditional fraternity houses (large, appropriately decaying, brick buildings), is considered Greek (and white) space by the students; indeed, nonwhite students speak routinely of their discomfort in traversing that space.

Additionally, Greek students participate heavily in the most traditional, most powerful, and most well-financed of the student organizations: the honor system, Student Council, and the judiciary system. Thus their control of racialized space extends in crucial ways into the metaphorical space of the university's organizational chart.

MULTICULTURAL STUDENT ORGANIZATIONS IN SPACE AND IN STRUGGLE

Administratively, diversity in student life is sited in the Office of the Vice President and Chief Student Affairs Officer. The office has six departments, only one of which—the Office of African-American Affairs—is explicitly marked in racial terms. Four others—those devoted to "residence life," "student health," "career services," and the university radio station—are functionally specific. The sixth department, the Office of the Dean of Students (ODOS), is the most functionally diffuse, with overall responsibility for the nonacademic aspects of student life. ODOS is composed of five units, four of which are functionally specific, devoted to "alcohol and substance education," "fraternity and sorority life," the student center (Newcomb Hall), and orientation programs for new students. The fifth ODOS unit is devoted to "student life" in general. It is within this unit that "programs" for minority students other than African Americans—Asian and Asian-Pacific American, Hispanic/Latino, and "LGBT" (lesbian, gay, bisexual, and transgender) students—are sited. From the perspective of many minority students, then, the markedness they experience is reflected in and reinforced by the university organizational structure, in which, among the boxes within boxes, there are a handful of lower-level, lightly staffed units dedicated to their needs. (However, many mainstream students criticize the university's support for such units, which they feel contribute to "self-segregation.")

Beyond the university bureaucracy, are dozens of racially or multiculturally marked student organizations, including at least thirty-five Asian and Asian American groups. Student organizations and clubs (whether or not racially marked) serve a bewildering variety of purposes or "missions," from the purely social or recreational to the cultural, political, and religious. In Nguyen's own experience and in her interviews with Asian American students (2005:19–24), she found that like most students, Asian American students sample a range of organizations during their first year (often becoming "too involved" and "overextended" in the process). Like the process of pledging a fraternity or sorority and the curricular process of sampling courses and then choosing a major, the choice of a student's extracurricular activities is understood as a key moment in an educational career that leads to fully individuated adulthood. Sampling organizations allows students to discover and refine their personal and social interests, in the American tradition of the "voluntary association" of like-minded individuals acting in concert, as social critics since Tocqueville have discussed at length.

Choice in these matters, however, is overdetermined (as social scientists never tire of pointing out). It is no surprise that racially marked students choose racially marked organizations (or that white students enjoy the luxury of choosing fraternities, sororities, and organizations that are racially unmarked). As one of Nguyen's informants put it, "I tried things with no racial connotations, and it didn't work because it made me so uncomfortable.... Every time I sat in Honor [Honor Committee] meetings, I felt like an outsider in the group.... My opinion is that organizations that don't cater to racial groups are pretty much white" (Nguyen 2005:20). Other interviewees told Nguyen that minority students who enter mainstream organizations are frequently relegated to the minority or diversity subsection and are discouraged from pursuing higher (unmarked) leadership positions. They claimed that a kind of covert racism pervaded the atmosphere of such clubs; an African American interviewee told Childs that UVA "traditionalism" unites "Honor, Student Council, and Old Dorms," all of which work together to exclude minority students (Childs 2005:21).

Minority students, then, frequently end up in minority student organizations, where they find a space they consider "comfortable" (Nguyen 2005:21). Racially marked or minority organizations are in some ways like the unmarked organizations for mainstream students, and in some respects they are different (as the linguistic concept of markedness implies). As Urciuoli notes (2005b:164), organizations for marked students have a political and cultural mission that unmarked organizations do not have. Nguyen found in her work that Asian American groups were concerned with three functions or missions: fellowship (to provide the interpersonal "support" that minority students may need in a potentially hostile environment), cultural and educational "outreach" (the classic situation in which the stigmatized must present themselves to the "normals" in ways that ensure the latter's comfort [Goffman 1963]), and political action, especially within the university. For their part, unmarked organizations also promote fellowship, and they too have political and cultural goals. But they are not charged with "normalizing" their members by publicly staging cultural diversity, and their political action ostensibly represents, or speaks to, the entire community on behalf of the entire community.

Racially marked student organizations are organized like their un-marked counterparts. Despite the special needs and problems they address, they afford the same kind of opportunities for self-development (and similar items to be listed on curriculum vitae) as those afforded to members by unmarked groups. Like mainstream students, minority students expect to develop themselves and their "leadership" and "communications" skills through their extracurricular activities. Both mainstream and minority students think of leadership in terms of organizing activities and solving problems. The clubs themselves exist (in the native viewpoint) to fulfill a mission, solve a problem, make a contribution, and generally improve the university. In a fundamental way, then, leadership, "problem solving," and good works are underpinned by the socio-evolutionary narrative discussed above: the mission, broadly construed, of student organizations is to achieve progress, whether in student life, university governance, or the wider society.

It is well known that many Asian American students do not arrive on university campuses thinking of themselves as Asian Americans (Espiritu 1992; for Hispanic/Latino students, see Urciuoli 1999:293–294). Rather, their identities are more locally or nationally specific ("Filipino"; "Pakistani from Toronto"). Nguyen found in her research that some Asian American student leaders got involved in organizations such as the ASU in response to their experiences of racial discrimination at UVA but that their understanding of antiracist activism stemmed from prior experiences in their home communities. In other words, these students understood their own activism as part of an ongoing historical struggle; the context and the labels at the university were new, but the underlying issues were familiar ones.

These minority student leaders nonetheless find themselves participating in the corporate rhetoric of "leadership" and "communications" that has permeated student organizations and university administration generally. Nguyen describes her own experience in the following terms:

> I...ran for the position of ASU president because I believed that I could do a better job than the two presidents before me. There were so many problems, I remember thinking, but if there have been so many ideas for change, how come UVA remained so problematic?...The answer...I decided, was apathy. If the other ASU presidents had only done their jobs in addressing it...if they had actually gotten everyone to understand the problems, then everyone would have come together, and then we really could have gone far. Where they failed, I resolved, I was going to succeed. (Nguyen 2005:22)

To understand the frame of mind represented here, we need to open a parenthesis on the topic of corporate models of communications and leadership. According to Urciuoli, in the discourse of American management and administration, "*communication* means information transmission in organizational interactions that promote the best interests of the company or of those running it" (2005b:161). As Handler and Gable (1997: 150–153) learned in their study of the organizational hierarchy at the Colonial Williamsburg Foundation, there is an assumption among corporate officers and managers that conflict is a function not of competing interests but of poor communications. Problems such as labor unrest or disputes between managers and staff are *not* the product of unavoidable clashes between people whose class-based interests are contradictory; indeed, in American culture it is thought that there are no such contradictory interests separating social classes. Rather than class conflict, administrators look for "win–win" solutions—responses that ostensibly give all people what they need but that, as Urciuoli suggests, are formulated to harmonize with managerial definitions of collective well-being. (The irony is that in corporate and now university discourses, this ideologically loaded use of the term *communication* coexists with the rhetoric of critical thinking and clear writing [communication] as neutral "skills" that colleges teach and that employers want. As Urciuoli acerbically remarks, in the corporate world, "actual critical and precise thinking and writing can get people fired pretty damn fast" [2003:407].)

The term *leadership* is similar. The term is drawn from the rhetoric of industrial relations and social engineering to indicate "a person who uses a skill set to bring about results" and especially a person who knows how to organize and motivate other people to achieve common (read "corporate") goals (Urciuoli 2005b:164). From the perspective of the traditional liberal arts, with their emphasis on the critical analysis of values, what is striking about the rhetoric of leadership is the paucity of discussion about values—that is, the notion that leadership is a good, a valued skill in and of itself, regardless of the ends to which the skill is put. From the liberal arts perspective, then, faculty members and even administrators are bemused and sometimes shocked by the alacrity with which inexperienced young students put themselves forward to be leaders, with no self-consciousness at all of their lack of wisdom to function as leaders in the chosen domain.

One might suspect that adolescents playing at adult leadership roles would not be able to accomplish significant results, but UVA celebrates its emphasis on student leadership. Melding with the rhetoric of Jeffersonian democracy, the administrative discourse on leadership emphasizes that the university allows its students an unusual degree of self-governance and leadership opportunities compared with peer institutions. As one dean told Nguyen, what "makes UVA different" is the high degree of "trust" administrators place in students: as "students learn how to make good decisions, how to motivate others to work toward a common goal, and how to manage a budget," they acquire "skills" that will put them "head and shoulders above students from other institutions" as they compete for entrance into the workforce (Nguyen 2005:36–38).

Administrators' trust in students reaches its apotheosis in the student-run Honor Committee, the most controversial of all the components of student self-government and the one in which many, if not most, faculty have the least confidence. To give the bare details of a complex situation, "honor offenses" by students at UVA ("cheating" on academic work and also "lying" and "stealing") are investigated and judged solely by other students. Conviction at an honor trial means automatic dismissal from the university. This "single sanction" does not appeal to many faculty, who believe that complex classroom and life situations require a range of responses. Moreover, the Honor Committee is renowned for bungling its procedures (as one would expect in a system run by inexperienced amateurs). Finally, the Honor Committee functions in a racially charged atmosphere, in which "spotlighting" students of color often leads to a higher frequency of charges against them than against mainstream students. In such a situation, the fact that few students realize, and no one discusses, the nineteenth-century origins of the Honor Committee in the slave South's notions of honor and racial purity is a piece of historical amnesia that is nothing short of astounding (see Ayers 1984:9–33 for an overview of Southern honor). For all these reasons, then, many professors boycott the system and deal with classroom cheating in their own ways. Indeed, the system is almost dysfunctional, although the university continues to celebrate it as a central example of its Jeffersonian culture and student self-governance.

The disconnect between the on-the-ground dysfunctionality of the Honor Committee and the public celebration of its functionality brings us to the central difference in the experience of student leaders of racially marked organizations in comparison with leaders of unmarked organizations. As Nguyen found, both in her own experience and in her interviews with other Asian American student leaders, a year of hard work as a leader resulted not in a sense of accomplishment but in "exhaustion, disillusion, disempowerment, and discontent" (2005:30). The apathy and ignorance about matters of racial justice that Nguyen and other leaders sought to address seemed to them to be impervious to their best efforts to bring about change through education. Because minority organization programs are marked as being of and for minority students, they almost never reach the wider audience that, the leaders feel, needs to be educated. Thus one Asian American student leader described his work as "Sisyphean" and not very successful: "We student leaders have made only the slightest dent in the problem" (Nguyen 2005:32–33).

Additionally, part of the minority student leaders' dilemma stemmed from their mediating position between mainstream university culture (especially the culture of leadership) and the minority groups they represented. As ASU president, Nguyen found it tiring to be "constantly called upon by various [mainstream]...clubs and offices to sit in on their innumerable diversity planning efforts....My opinion, it seemed, was enough to stand for...[that of] all the undergraduate Asian-American students" (Nguyen 2005:29). But most demanding of all was the effort required to maintain a publicly positive attitude, not only toward the university community at large but also toward younger Asian American students to be recruited for diversity work and organizations. Nguyen reflected, "When... asked about what it is like to attend the University...as a public figure I was conditioned to say that it is a lot of fun. When *really* asked what it is like... however, I would eventually disclose that it is somewhat like running head-first into a brick wall" (2005:28). Nguyen and her colleagues, we might say, ran headfirst into history, an open-ended history in the making, not the history of the socio-evolutionary narrative. In their "diversity-related programs," they found, happy endings were not guaranteed. Progress was not inevitable. The "incidents" continued to occur.

RACE AS PSYCHOLOGICAL SPACE: THE COMFORT ZONE

If the minority student leaders whom Nguyen studied are torn between competing historical narratives—one about inevitable progress, the other about contingent struggle—the mainstream students of Childs' research seem mostly to want to avoid the history of racism altogether. Their easy recourse to "self-segregation" as an explanation for the university's racial "problems" depicts racial tension as a spatial, not a temporal (historical) phenomenon. Moreover, the notion of self-segregation psychologizes the problem, making it a function of students' attitudes and choices. These ideas are condensed in the "key symbol" (Ortner 1973) that Childs found at the center of her interviewing: the metaphor of the "comfort zone."

To understand the spatialization of race at the university, we must first recall that in American culture, race is thought to be visible. Laypeople, as well as social and natural scientists, assume that race manifests itself in phenotypic features (primarily skin color) that cannot *but* be visible. Race may or may not be a social construct in this perspective, but its visibility is a natural fact. People cannot help noticing race, so the fact that some societies use skin color to create social categories is not surprising. Such a belief ignores the extensive anthropological evidence concerning societies in which skin color is *not* used as a basis of social categorization. It also ignores the fact that visual cues are themselves culturally created and learned (see Segal 1991); one is not born knowing how to move or decorate one's body in the style of a particular group, nor is one born knowing how to recognize such cues in others, or even knowing that skin color itself should be taken as a sign of "race." Finally, it ignores the fact that in the United States, the race of the unmarked group is often *not* visible, at least to those in the group. Most white Americans, for example, do not think of racial segregation when they see crowds of white people. In sum, in American culture, race is thought to be visible, which means, as we shall show, that Americans easily imagine it as a natural phenomenon, deployed timelessly (unchanging) in space. But they find it difficult to imagine race emergent in time—that is, as the ongoing production of a contingent social history.

When Childs interviewed students about their notions of self-segregation, she found that students responded by describing their experiences of *seeing* it. Moreover, they saw it sited in specific places, the most notable of which is widely known at the university as the Black Bus Stop (BBS). One student told Childs, "When I think of self-segregation, I have a very visual picture in my mind with the Black Bus Stop" (Childs 2005:29). Geographically, this bus stop occupies a position of interchange between several areas of "grounds" (the campus, in university lingo) that are heavily used by students. On weekdays, on the hour (when students are hurrying from one class to another), the BBS is something of a bottleneck, with crowds of students packed together waiting for the next bus. It is not clear to us that black students frequent the BBS in numbers greater than would be statistically representative; it is clear, however, that their presence there is noticeable to white students, who are made uncomfortable by it, as they repeatedly told Childs.

In her interviews, Childs found that such discomfort led to awkward discussions of "guilt" and "racism." The interviewees expressed embarrassment as they described the "loudness" and "attitude" of the black students at the BBS. "I feel like I'm being stereotypical, but it's true," one student said. She went on to describe her own feelings of "exclusion," "intimidation," and "anxiety" at the BBS because she worried about what the black students there might be "thinking about [her]." "I don't want them to look down upon me, or think that I'm a bad person." Another student told Childs, "Maybe I'm just carrying the guilt of...white people everywhere, [but] sometimes I wanna...scream, 'I like you, I'm not a racist!'" (Childs 2005:30).

The anxiety these students expressed is underpinned by an ambiguity concerning the social causes of their anxiety. On the one hand, white students experience guilt at their own discomfort—a guilt they link to a racism they wish to disavow. As several students told Childs, they preferred to think of themselves as "colorblind" and wished that they lived in a world in which everyone was. In this frame of mind, they blame all students equally for UVA's racial tensions. All students, white and minority, they claim, unnecessarily make use of racial categories instead of realizing, as one interviewee put it, that "when it comes down to it, people are just people." On the other hand, the very notion of a black bus stop suggests that many students believe they can "see" self-segregation and that black students, not white students, are the ones who practice it and thus cause the university's racial problems. This kind of blame-the-victim argument is common among white students, who chide not only minority students for choices that harm the community (as we will discuss in a moment) but also the university for supporting minority programs.

Many minority students buy into this model as well. A black student interviewed by Childs understood that white social spaces and events were not marked as racially segregated: "If you look at Old Dorms Quad, you can see hundreds of white folk laid out in the sun....*I* don't have any issues with it....Just lie out in the sun, it's your area, that's where you socialize. And that's fine, that's the White Tanning Spot, whatever." This student also explained ways in which black students feel excluded from mainstream spaces and activities, much like the experiences Nguyen's informants described regarding their participation in organizations such as the Honor Committee. Given such experiences, it made sense to Childs's informant that black students had carved out some "black-friendly" social spaces for themselves. But in reasoning thus, he seemed to accept the BBS as a statistical and social reality that had been created by the active choices of black students: "Instead of lying on the Lawn [the most central and sacred part of Mr. Jefferson's 'grounds'], black people decide to sit at the bus stop.... But because we decide to put a name on [our social space] and put *black* in the name, it becomes an issue" (Childs 2005:33–34).

Although many of Childs's interviewees spoke about self-segregation as a black–white issue, some talked about Asian American (and more rarely, "international" and Hispanic) students as an intermediate category. Here "model minority" thinking came into play. White students told Childs that they were less "uncomfortable" around Asian American students, who were, in their opinion, "less vocal" and more "integrated into white society" than African Americans. Childs's informants were well aware of the presence of Asian American student organizations at UVA; indeed, they tended to judge their Asian American peers in terms of "different levels of Asianness," as one put it, with those students who are "more Asian" being considered more likely to participate in Asian American groups and activities. Typically, informants realized, on the one hand, that minority students might need a "support group" in the unfamiliar environment of the university. On the other hand, they thought that clustering together in racially marked groups discouraged the "reaching out" that is necessary for UVA to ease its racial tensions (Childs 2005:34–35). In sum, from the mainstream perspective, the ideally diverse student is a person of color who is not a "clumper" (a term we heard admissions officers use) but who "builds bridges" to other groups.

The foundational site of personal composure and racial unity is what students call the comfort zone. It is from a student's comfort zone that he or she can reach out and build bridges. In the native understanding, students can choose to do this, although there is much equivocation about whether the choices are conscious or unconscious. Clumpers—minority students who choose to participate in minority student groups—can always be accused by mainstream students of self-segregation, and self-segregation in turn can be blamed as the root cause of UVA's racial tensions. When minority student organizations display safe cultural differences to edify the larger community (as in culture festivals), they are building bridges. When they take political action, they are stirring up dangerous racial trouble.[2]

Student discussions of the comfort zone start from the presumption that each individual is a naturally bounded unit. Indeed, the comfort zone is, in the first place, the person, the "I" within a body. Each individual is imagined to be "inside" his or her comfort zone, and it is believed that it requires "effort" to "step out" of that "box." The comfort zone is, in the second place, a social space occupied by like individuals, with likeness in this case imagined in racial and cultural terms. As one student told Childs, people should be "comfortable in your own kind....It's a comfort zone and a natural gravitation." She continued, "It's natural for people to just shift into groups" (Childs 2005:36). This idea is nothing other than the hegemonic model of the nation or race as a collection of naturally similar individuals (Handler 1988). Beneath that model lie two unexamined (and we would argue, erroneous) assumptions: that social life depends upon similarity, not difference, and that the similarities that bind people into groups are natural, biological, or inner, essential, and unchanging—that is, not the contingent product of history.

Although students say that they can choose to step outside their comfort zones, they acknowledge that it is difficult. Both mainstream and minority students accuse each other of being afraid to venture beyond the comfort zones provided by their own "kind." They also admit their fears in this matter, as well as what they have to gain by overcoming them. As one of Childs's interviewees, a white student, put it, by "not stepping out," students lose an opportunity for "life experience" that can teach them about others. But minority students and their organizations are more visible, or marked, than white students in this regard. It is all too easy for whites to see minorities as "self-segregators" and to claim that they are "putting themselves in such a diminished part of the world," as one administrator told Childs. It's "no wonder," he continued, "that the black students [are] feeling uncomfortable."

The metaphor of the comfort zone psychologizes and naturalizes racial tension. Rarely do students connect "discomfort" to institutional racism or historical struggle. Indeed, they often translate the recurring racist incidents of university life into "excuses" that minorities can use to reinforce their psychological barriers. In this mainstream perspective, such incidents are "not the norm"; they are "isolated." But minority students "exploit" them by placing "too much emphasis" on them. It is not the incidents, then, but the exploitation of them that causes people to "start drawing lines." One of Childs's interviewees, a white man, went so far as to say that he felt victimized by the Daisy Lundy incident because in its wake, white males "get looked at differently." In his view, this was just another facet of self-segregation—"a strain on race relations" that "doesn't help foster people wanting to get together and integrate more" (Childs 2005:47–48).

As we noted at the outset, the student organization that has garnered the most praise for its work encouraging harmonious race relations is Sustained Dialogue (SD), the local offshoot of the International Institute for Sustained Dialogue, headquartered in Washington, DC. SD promotes ongoing small-group discussions among students to confront "racism, self-segregation, ignorance, [and] racial tension." The very fact that SD uses the word *racism* on the opening page of its website distinguishes it from most student groups. But the fact that it pairs racism with self-segregation suggests that the psychological model we have outlined will dictate the terms of political discussion—as Childs found to be the case in her two-year experience with the group. Thus, although the site discusses social problems, it focuses on individual choices and "human relationships" as the solution to those problems: "Participants must be willing to expose themselves to criticism and share their beliefs in full honesty, and most of all, they must be willing to change, for no one who enters the process emerges the same person" (Sustained Dialogue 2007). Indeed, Priya Parker, a cofounder of the group at UVA, has explicitly argued that the kinds of institutional changes that minority student groups recommend in response to racial incidents "miss the point." According to Parker, "these responses aim at addressing institutional and representational issues, and ignore the more obvious issue of student racial climate, the actual *attitudes*, perceptions and patterns of behavior between racial groups" (Parker 2004:93; compare Childs 2005:50–54).

In its belief that individuals who "open themselves up" to criticism and share information about inner "attitudes" are the key to solving the problem of racism, SD reproduces the ideology of the comfort zone. Not only does this ideology psychologize and spatialize race relations, but also, in it, space itself is less social than psychological. The work that SD aims to accomplish seems to result from the simple act of opening mental doors. There is little discussion of the political content of people's attitudes or of the potential for struggle between people holding ultimately incommensurable points of view. Indeed, when Childs trained to be a group facilitator, she was cautioned against becoming "too theoretical" (read "political") and told instead to focus on "personal experiences" (Childs 2005:51). Stepping outside the comfort zone seems to require no more than bringing mental rooms ("imaginary space," as Whorf [1956:150] described the Western conception of the mind) into proximity, opening their doors and, from the security of one's inner comfort zone, peering into the room of your neighbor. One student "testimonial," posted on the SD website, states: "We all go to school seeking new experiences and people, but often don't like to step outside our comfort zones. Sustained Dialogue…through simple communication, creates great friendships. Cultures, religions, and entire lives are shared merely through human interaction."

In the atemporal, spatial-psychological ideology that structures the mainstream discussion of diversity as a resource at UVA, there is no place for the idea that racial struggle *is* a form of communication, an ongoing argument about the allocation of resources and rewards in our society. Indeed, the very idea that a community such as the university can include people who are irreconcilably different—not racially or biologically but socially and politically—is beyond the pale of the nationalist imaginary that defines what a community should be. When community is defined in nationalist terms, as people who are more similar than different, the kinds of marked cultural and racial diversities we have been discussing cause acute anxiety, unless they can be imagined as safe educational resources to be used for the greater (read "mainstream") good. The spatial-psychological ideology of diversity and the nationalist ideology of community dovetail with the corporate ideology of communications, as the work of SD suggests: the answers to social problems are not struggle and institutional change but "clear communications," which magically will make all our troubles disappear—irrespective of the content of what is communicated.

HOW TO TALK ABOUT RESOURCES IN TIME

When diversity is conceptualized as a resource, it is easy for Americans to talk about how to develop, manage, or improve it. Such talk in turn fits into the socio-evolutionary model of a unidirectional, universal history (away from the primitive past and toward ever-greater progress) that has dominated the teaching of history in the United States since the turn of the twentieth century (Segal 2000). The socio-evolutionary narrative of human history attaches itself easily (in the modern, secular imagination) to the evolutionary narrative of natural history. Our prehuman ancestors evolved to the moment when they became fully human, with a set of mental traits and social behaviors that mark us to this day. Then these newly hatched humans muddled around for millennia in "prehistory" before the genius of Greek–Western rationality launched us on our current, irreversible trajectory. This grand temporal scheme unites the socio-evolutionary narrative of progress toward greater diversity with the atemporal spatial-psychological model that many mainstream students use to understand racial tensions: those tensions are not a function of a social history but of the natural human inclination ("hardwired" at some moment in the deep evolutionary past) to "gravitate" toward one's "own kind." "Clear communications" can overcome that inclination, not so much by grappling with difficult differences and competing interests but by proving to us that, as members of one community, we are really all the same!

Given that universities constitute one of the few domains in contemporary society where alternative models of history are discussed, it is striking to see how easily official institutional discourses content themselves with socio-evolutionary celebrations. Perhaps this situation is not surprising, because these official presentations are aimed at a public that must be constantly cajoled into supporting, politically and financially, the institution. At best, administrators can mention UVA's "Southern" history of slavery, Jim Crow, and segregation. For example, the president's Commission on Diversity and Equity (discussed briefly above) took one sentence to recognize that past: "The University of Virginia, founded in an era of slavery, and built with the labor of enslaved people, finally began to accept African-Americans in tiny numbers in the 1960s" (University of Virginia 2004). But, true to the genre of socio-evolutionary history, that past has already been superseded by the progress represented by those first African American students, whose acceptance would seem to erase the fact that earlier generations of African Americans were included ("accepted") as laborers. Mentioning the evils of the past does not lead to a discussion of the persistence of that past and its relationship to present-day problems. Rather, briefly mentioning past evils in a list that includes progressive steps taken since their time reconfirms the inevitability of progress.

In Nguyen's work as a student leader, she noticed a similar deployment of the socio-evolutionary sensibility at the many administrative meetings she attended following the occurrence of "incidents." Administrators described such incidents as disheartening events, but there was never any discussion of their structural inevitability—that is, no discussion of the ways in which the unresolved inequities of the past continue to structure the events of the present. Indeed, this sort of historical amnesia marks the commission's internally contradictory statement about the acceptance of African Americans in the 1960s, which at once mentions and renders invisible the slaves of earlier times. As Nguyen, following Cheng (2001), has pointed out, the mainstream institution has always depended upon a minority presence (minority resources, we might say), whether as slave labor or as embodied diversity (Nguyen 2005:43–51), both to build the place and to bear witness to its tolerance and humanity.

Notes

1. Of the thirteen thousand undergraduates at UVA, about ten thousand are enrolled in the College of Arts and Sciences. The remaining undergraduates are distributed across the engineering, nursing, commerce, and architecture schools. Most of the students Childs and Nguyen studied and interviewed were in the College of Arts and Sciences, although the student organizations they analyzed included students from all the undergraduate schools.

By state law, two-thirds of the undergraduate population must be Virginia residents. Including students in graduate and professional schools, the total enrollment at UVA is about twenty thousand.

2. Here we follow Urciuoli's earlier work on "racialization" and "ethnicization." Urciuoli points out that every acceptable ethnic group in the modern United States (such as Italian Americans and Irish Americans) was at one time considered to be a race. Assimilation into the middle-class mainstream requires people to present only those cultural differences that are "safe" and "clean," such as ethnic food and cultural festivals. Difference that threatens the political-economic status quo (such as Spanish-language ballots) is considered "dangerous" and "dirty," a function of "race," not "culture" or "ethnicity" (Urciuoli 1996:15–40).

8

The Claims of El Pueblo

Possessions, Politics, and Histories

Paul K. Eiss

There was once a peaceful Mayan people who lived at the foot of a stone temple, offering incense to the gods to the music of priestly chanting. One day, on the coast nearby, strange beings arrived, mounted on ferocious beasts. They imprisoned the leaders of the little pueblo and subjected them to horrible tortures, searing their feet with hot coals. The Spanish ordered their Mayan translators to ask the leaders of *el pueblo*, "Do you know where we can find gold?" But the Mayan translators, betraying their overlords, simply told the prisoners in Maya, "Nuc ma ti' [Tell them no]." As the interrogation and torments intensified, the valiant leaders continued to respond "Ma! [No!]," until death took them. Their valor was widely recounted in the pueblo for ages to come. Inhabitants honored the men who had demonstrated "the greatness of el pueblo's spirit," by telling and retelling their story. "U NUC MA! [Their answer was no!]," they would recall, eventually adopting those words as the name of their pueblo.

We might read this story about the origins of the name of the Yucatecan town of Hunucmá as an example of what Fogelson has called epitomizing events—that is, "narratives that condense, encapsulate, and dramatize longer-term historical processes" (Fogelson 1989:143). At the same time, it is important to recognize the limited constituency of this tale of Hunucmá's origins, unlike the events and "nonevents" Fogelson discusses. The story of

"Nuc ma ti'" may have had some currency among town residents one-half century ago or more, and it was recorded in written form in a small collection of poetry published in 1983. But in contemporary Hunucmá, it seems to be known by only a handful of residents.[1]

My purpose, however, is not to demonstrate the significance of this story for contemporary populations but rather to consider what a reading of it might suggest about the workings and construction of "el pueblo" as a collective entity, as well as the place of resources and of history in that construction. This question is a complex one in Latin American and other Spanish-speaking contexts, in which the term *pueblo* not only signifies a political abstraction, "the people," but also is commonly used to refer to small population sites (typically, rural villages), as well as communities (whether inhabiting such population sites or wider collectivities). In similar terms, among anthropologists, historians, and political theorists, studies of el pueblo have tended to diverge into studies of (1) place (this village or town and its immediate surroundings); (2) community (whether local or broader); or (3) political abstraction ("the people").[2]

Each of these takes on el pueblo tends to translate the term into distinct terminologies and domains of interpretation. Some of those who privilege the first meaning, for instance, might assimilate the term to the study of local patterns, places, landscapes, histories, and practices of settlement or habitation. For those exploring its second connotation, el pueblo figures as a kind of communal organization and collective identity. Thus, for some, el pueblo is emblematic of a "folk," "peasant," or "local" consciousness that emerges organically from a state of isolation or of being "small scale" (what Robert Redfield [1941] modeled in his work and what Benedict Anderson (1983) refers to as "face-to-face" communities). Others, following Eric Wolf (1955), would explore the concept in terms of the articulation of local institutions with wider political and economic structures and relations of exploitation. For those who explore el pueblo in its third and seemingly most abstract sense, as "the people," the term refers to popular political identity and agency, in relationship with or opposition to socially or politically dominant groups or the state. Invocations of el pueblo in broad terms—*el pueblo mexicano, el pueblo trabajador,* or *el pueblo maya*—thus are taken as expressions of "nation," "class," or "ethnicity," voiced either as a means of distinguishing "insiders" from those of other nations, classes, or ethnicities or as a means of distinguishing such groupings in civil society from an opposing political entity—that is, "state" or "government."[3]

Despite the differences among these analyses of el pueblo—as place, community, or political abstraction—they share a fundamental limitation.

All begin by observing one of the ways in which el pueblo emerges as a claim over a domain—over a place, over a population, over political legitimacy or voice—and then proceed to identify that claim with the "meaning" of el pueblo. But instances of, and references to, el pueblo do not all fit easily into one or another of these rubrics. Consider a few examples. A man from the small town of Tetiz hacks away at underbrush, preparing to plant maize in what he has identified as "lands of *el pueblo.*" A cleric declares a revolution against Spanish rule and issues a proclamation of independence decrying the "enslavement of *el pueblo*" and calling for its liberation. Thousands of people walk in a religious procession under a hot sun, following a religious icon of the Virgin of Tetiz, whom they often call the Virgin of El Pueblo. A female strike supporter stones a police officer in the town of Hunucmá, shouting triumphantly, "You see? *El pueblo* has balls!" Indigenous Maya speakers arm themselves and seize San Cristóbal, the capital of the state of Chiapas, shouting the Zapatista rallying cry: "¡El pueblo! ¡Unido! ¡Jamás será vencido! [The people, united, will never be defeated]" A man carefully collects donations for a religious confraternity, explaining his elaborate precautions: "Well, you see, this is money of *el pueblo.*" A group of men from Hunucmá charge onto a plantation at dusk, torching fields and shooting overseers, and later describe the action as one aimed at the "liberation of *el pueblo.*" A man leads a populist campaign for the presidency, calling it a struggle against the "exploiters of *el pueblo.*" A year later, as president, he faces street demonstrations organized by his wealthy adversaries, with marchers chanting "¡El pueblo! ¡Unido!..."

Despite the differences among all these instances of el pueblo and the domains in which they emerge (material, symbolic, political, religious), a few features seem common to them. First, el pueblo is more than *either* place *or* people *or* political abstraction. In some instances, el pueblo may lodge neatly into one such domain or another, but in other cases, el pueblo may articulate or transcend them. In the story of "Nuc ma ti'," for instance, to read el pueblo as referring to *either* people *or* place *or* politics simply would not make sense. To understand this tale and perhaps to explore the meaning of el pueblo more generally, we must begin by rejecting such schematic distinctions.

Second, el pueblo figures in the "Nuc ma ti'" story, and in many or most of its appearances as listed above, as something that belongs and that has belongings (resources, among other things)—something that possesses and is possessed. The problem of understanding el pueblo thus is not one of cataloging the many meanings of *el pueblo* and the contexts in which the term is used. Nor is it one of identifying the resources with respect to which el pueblo is defined or even of exploring how certain classes of things come to be claimed as pueblo resources. Rather, it is that of understanding el pueblo in terms of possession—that is, both as a possessing subject, regardless of what is possessed, and as something that can *be* possessed.

To explore this topic in a comprehensive fashion would be to track the emergence and transformations of the concept of el pueblo across the Americas and beyond. Such a study clearly would be beyond the scope of this chapter. Instead, I offer a historical genealogy of the emergence and transformation of el pueblo in one region, a story that begins and ends with a name. I return to the "Nuc ma ti'" story to ask, How did the pueblo of Hunucmá come to possess, and how did el pueblo come to *be* possessed? What is the significance of its possession of a name—not just the name *Hunucmá* but the name *el pueblo*?

POSSESSIONS

El pueblo has many histories, and in Yucatán its deepest history is Mayan. Before the Spanish conquest, Yucatec Mayan society was organized into *cahs*, Mayan political and territorial entities that were dominated by lineage groups (*ch'ibals*), led by *batabs* (male chiefs). Lands were held under complex arrangements, both as collective and lineage possessions. The social geography of the cahs in western Yucatán, the region where Hunucmá is located, was fairly varied. Along the Gulf coastline were cahs active in fishing and salt production. The interior, marked by marshes and salt pools immediately inland from shore and by denser and drier forests farther inland, was populated by small cahs that produced maize and cotton for their own use and for trade (Bracamonte y Sosa 2003; Patch 1993; Restall 1997; Roys 1957).

As throughout the Americas, the Spanish conquest of Yucatán brought radical changes, some devastating. These ranged from warfare, forced resettlement, missionization, and tributary forms of exploitation, to the ravages of epidemic disease. In the Hunucmá region, disease practically annihilated coastal populations along major trading routes and, through Spanish practices of population resettlement, left the inland cahs as the region's principal population centers. Nonetheless, the cahs (*repúblicas indígenas* in Spanish parlance) remained the fundamental social, political, and territorial groupings, retaining access to most of the woodlands and other communal resources they had held before the Spanish conquest. Male members of the ch'ibals conserved their status as native elites, and the batabs continued to exercise power locally as long as they helped gather various kinds of tribute and helped enforce the Christianization and subjugation of Mayan populations. While Spanish clerics worked at eradicating practices that they considered to be idolatrous, native populations took the establishment of religious confraternities (*cofradías*), as an opportunity to further cement clan power and communal sovereignty, largely through feasting and other communal functions. Locally held icons of saints and the Virgin became highly valued cofradía and cah possessions, serving as foci of communal social organization, political power, and religious practice and sentiment (Farriss 1984; Restall 1997).

The cah was not simply a Mayan survival but rather became a colonial institution with a mediating role—one that "Mayanized" Spanish institutions while putting indigenous authorities and institutions to use in enforcing the terms of Spanish colonial rule (Farriss 1984). The cahs remained the primary institutions through which communal possession and political voice were exercised and through which local and lineage sovereignty over communal resources—woodland for subsistence agriculture or hunting, salt pools, wells, and the like—was preserved. But at the same time, they were the basis for political interactions with the corporatistic structures of the colonial state—mediating and moderating the terms of tribute extraction and other forms of colonial exploitation (Restall 1997).

The cah was thus an entity that articulated territory, community, religiosity, and the hierarchies and exercise of political power. Its ability to do so was largely dependent on Mayan archival and documentary practices. Mayan scribes produced the kinds of documents and records required by Spanish authorities while also guaranteeing communal claims to corporate status and land. One example of this situation is the genre of Maya-language cah documents and maps relating to the description and measurement of lands of the cah in territorial possession rituals. Another is what Restall (1997, 1998) has called "primordial titles" of cahs, which took the form of narratives that often incorporated territorial records within them. The narratives of such "titles" tended to focus not on the dislocations of the conquest or its aftermath but rather on the legitimacy of the cahs and their governing elites, stressing the continuity of their corporate claims to sovereignty and territorial integrity. Thus archives and documents, as well as the histories inscribed within them, effectively became communal resources—and among the most closely guarded at that.

From the late eighteenth century forward, however, the cahs were dismantled progressively, first in connection with late colonial administrative reorganization and reforms and more intensively following Mexican independence in 1821, through measures aimed at stimulating commerce through the privatization of communal lands. The last vestiges of the cahs were finally eliminated in Yucatán in 1868 (Bracamonte y Sosa 2003).[4] But even as the cahs lost juridical recognition as a basis for territorial or political sovereignty and even as *hacendados*, ranchers, and government officials worked at expropriating and privatizing communal lands, indigenous populations seized upon another collective entity through which to defend their possessions: *el común*. This Spanish term had a long prior existence, in Spain as in the Americas, as a fairly expansive way of referring to the totality of communal lands attached to rural populations, which could be claimed by populations not only on the basis of prior ownership but also on the basis of need (Vassberg 1984). At the same time, *común* referred to the communal entity in question—that is, as "commune." El común was not a corporate *ethnic* entity, like the cah, but rather a corporate *class* entity, one that grouped its members in terms of their relationship to land and labor, as well as place. Like the cah, it did not include wealthy Hispanic residents and landowners, but it did embrace both members of the indigenous republics and working commoners of mixed ethnic descent (mestizos and *pardos*) (AGEY-C 1815; AGEY-J 1856a, 1857; AGN-T 1815).

Notwithstanding such differences and the term's Spanish origins, el común was a concept that was exceedingly compatible with indigenous understandings of the cah. In fact, documents of the mid-nineteenth century suggest that Maya speakers often used *común* as a rough translation of *cah*, referring not only to common property but also to a form of corporate political organization and territorial possession, commensurate with those that had characterized the indigenous republics. Moreover, as with the cah, history continued to be central in the workings of the común; for working residents of the area, maps and historical documents of the cah remained critical communal resources for the defense of increasingly tenuous claims to both land and sovereignty in the name of the común.

So much for *cah* and *común*, but what about *pueblo*? To be sure, the term *pueblo* had entered into use in Spain by the twelfth century, when it was used to refer to agrarian settlements established in rural Castile at the initiative of local nobility (Velasco 1989). Such populations were equipped with common lands in their vicinity. In Yucatán as well, under colonial rule, in the course of their administrative duties, colonial officials applied the term *pueblo* to settlements under their jurisdiction. From the period of independence, however, *el pueblo* became charged with new meaning as the subject par excellence of anticolonial and liberation movements at the state and national levels (inspired in part by diverse revolutionary movements in the name of "the people" in the Americas and Europe). With the collapse of colonial rule, republican liberals and Creole nationalists called for uprisings against peninsular Spaniards in the name of el pueblo and, upon victory, assumed the positions and power the Spaniards vacated.

The rise of el pueblo as a collective political subject reshaped the terms of political collectivity in Yucatán, adding to its complex political lexicon. From around 1820 through the 1860s, historical documents from western Yucatán show its residents alternately making reference to *cah, común*, and *pueblo* according to their social and ethnic backgrounds and political motivations. Privileged Spanish speakers who resided in rural districts like Hunucmá took control over town councils in the name of el pueblo to capitalize on both the losses of Spanish officials and the declining power and authority of the cahs (Bracamonte y Sosa 2003; Güémez Pineda 1994; Rugeley 1996). The cah remained the primary point of reference for indigenous populations, although it lost its political effectiveness; el común was the way most indigenous and nonindigenous working commoners laid claim to communal land or communal autonomy, with varied success. Occasionally, however, el pueblo served as a point of reference for commoners as well, as they sought to use a liberal rhetoric of political rights to bolster their claims to the resources of cah or común.

By the latter decades of the nineteenth century, however, and especially from the 1870s forward, with the rise to the Mexican presidency of modernizing dictator Porfirio Díaz, el común, like the cah, succumbed to the unrelenting efforts of landowners, hacendados, and government officials at the state and federal levels to stimulate economic modernization through the expansion of commercial export agriculture. From the 1860s forward, this situation brought the expansion of henequen agriculture in response to rising international demand and prices for hard fibers and cordage. Fields of spiky henequen plants spread throughout northwestern Yucatán, on lands formerly held as communal woodlands, as elite families expanded their properties, secured capital from foreign lenders, converted cattle ranches and maize haciendas to henequen cultivation, and used their access to local government posts to facilitate the acquisition of land and labor (Joseph 1988; Wells 1985). By 1886 about 110 henequen haciendas had been established throughout the district of Hunucmá, making it one of the most important and productive regions in the henequen zone (*Razón del pueblo*, October 1886).

The concept of pueblo was transformed in tandem with these developments, as it became a preeminent framework of governance and an object of control and development in a period of authoritarian capitalist modernization. Henequen was commonly referred to as the principal form of "public wealth" in the region—that is, as a collective resource that generated public and private revenues that made possible the existence and progress of the *patria* as a body politic after decades of civil war and economic stagnation (Coronil 1997; Kantorowicz 1997[1957]). Rural gentry in Hunucmá, as in other rural districts of Yucatán, embraced a "patriotic" rhetoric that posed the regional and local commercial development of the pueblos and the construction of a Mexican patria at the national level as complementary endeavors. Landowners and hacendados used their control over town councils not only to foster their own enrichment but also to claim a highly visible role as political and cultural representatives of el pueblo, particularly during holidays, ceremonies, and public encounters with government officials. They presided over inaugurations of public works projects and schools in the pueblos, which were posed as effectively materially constructing el pueblo in the most grounded and abstract of senses. The inaugurations of such projects were timed to coincide with exuberant celebrations of national holidays. On the inauguration of a railroad line in 1883, for instance, one poet penned an ode to the transformation of Hunucmá into an "Eden"—that is, both a paradise and a place of beginnings. He declared that the rail would "bring glory to the country" and fortune to el pueblo, allowing "radiant Yucatán…to glimpse its future" (*Union yucateca*, April 4, 1883).

Thus landowners, merchants, and government officials defined cah and común not as they had been—through claims to collective possession of lands or other natural resources—but through the performance and possession of presumably distinctive, local *cultural* resources—that is, pueblo "traditions." Thus pueblo gentry organized lavish "traditional" fiestas on festive dates and during visits of government officials, with performances of regional traditions (notably, a folk dance called the *jarana*, in which daughters of local gentry were effectively placed on display as feminine signifiers of regional pride and pueblo authenticity). The inauguration of a marketplace in Hunucmá in 1884, for instance, was described in the press as a "fiesta of progress" in which "*el pueblo* succumbed to a joy as intense as it was legitimate." Yucatán's governor, accompanied by an entourage of genteel Mérida residents, attended the festivities, witnessing an exemplary demonstration of the civility and hospitality of the Hunucmeños, including dances in which "Hunucmá's beauties displayed their grace and beauty" (*Eco del comercio*, June 9, 1884; June 16, 1884; December 8, 1884). Such traditions were not invented de novo in this period but were reinvented (Hobsbawm and Ranger 1983) as "civilized" diversions central to both the legitimization of the local dominance of rural gentry and the redefinition of pueblo–state relations during the henequen boom. More than just a place, the pueblos became a staging area where modernity and tradition were collaboratively constructed and performed by state officials and local elites as they staked their claims to el pueblo.

Notwithstanding the rise to hegemony of hacendados and pueblo gentry, working residents of the Hunucmá region found their own ways of laying claim to el pueblo. Despite the privatization of many communal lands and other resources, such as salt pools and wells, some lands remained attached to the pueblos as a critical resource for subsistence agriculturalists (now as *ejidos*, a term restricted to lands within a legally prescribed one-league radius around each pueblo rather than the more expansive holdings of cah and común). Although many pueblo residents were reduced by circumstance to indebted servitude on the haciendas, through the late nineteenth and early twentieth centuries, subsistence agriculturalists, woodcutters, and hunters—both men and women—continued to travel great distances to the old forests, salt pools, and swamps of the común that lay beyond the reach of the haciendas. As penal files relating to disputes over contested land, forests, and salt pools suggest, indigenous populations and working-class mestizos referred to these resources, whether or not officially recognized, as *del pueblo* or *del común del pueblo*. Finally, even after indigenous cofradías had been stripped of their resources, pueblo confraternities (now called *gremios*) occupied the center of public and spiritual life for working populations, making religious icons and gremio funds resources whose possession defined el pueblo in ways that were not reducible to the versions put on display by local elites. Thus working populations in the region—most of them Maya speakers—came to use *cah* and *pueblo* interchangeably, in ways that differed from elite usages, to refer to forms of communal possession, both spiritual and material, that retained their importance even in a time of unbridled capitalist expansion.[5]

Communalist visions of el pueblo and of its possessions would find new life and political legitimacy following the fall of Porfirio Díaz and the social upheavals of the Mexican Revolution. Although communal land rights were formally restored in the 1917 Mexican constitution, only with the advent to power of President Lázaro Cárdenas in the late 1930s did wholesale and definitive agrarian reform take place in Yucatán (Fallaw 2001). With the creation of state-run henequen ejidos in the towns and pueblos of Yucatán, including the Hunucmá region, the collective ejido took on functions that might be likened to cah and común in earlier periods, serving as a corporatistic framework of communal possession through which sovereignty was exercised by indigenous working people in ways institutionally linked and subordinated to the state (see ASRA 1937). Yet the difference from earlier forms was just as remarkable, given the capitalistic relations of production that came to be entrenched in the ejidos, whose "patrimony" (Ferry 2005a) remained restricted to henequen fiber produced for export and sale in the international market.

Finally, even as it was materially reinvested as a material and political subject, el pueblo remained a subject of spiritual possession. In recent years, in the wake of agricultural crisis and the progressive abandonment of both henequen and subsistence agriculture by local populations (Baños Ramírez 1990, 1996; Villanueva Mukul 1990), the size and organization of communal religious organizations and cults of local saints have increased remarkably. The gremios continue to work through the collection and administration of monies of varied origin—from the clandestine poaching and sale of venison, from agricultural work, or, increasingly, from remittances sent to the gremios from migrant workers in the United States (Eiss 2002a). Principally through the annual fiesta, these communal monies, managed and sacralized in the gremios, continue to play an important role in defining the consciousness of el pueblo in terms of relations of material, spiritual, and cultural possession.

In light of the genealogies of cah, común, and el pueblo, we may read the story of "Nuc ma ti'" as a story about possession.[6] First, we may note the importance of physical features in the story—not just the geography of the coast but also the temples—as a way of evoking a presence and possession that antedate the Spanish conquest. Second, and perhaps more importantly, there is the gold itself—which serves both as a general signifier of possessions of material and spiritual value and perhaps as a reminder of the continued importance of communally possessed money in the making of el pueblo. At the same time, the story is remarkable for what it excludes or silences (Trouillot 1995). Thus the "Nuc ma ti'" story effaces the role of power, privilege, and exploitation in shaping claims over el pueblo and its possessions. It presents el pueblo as autochthonous rather than as an entity strongly influenced by "outsiders"—notably, the governments that alternately vested, disinvested, and reinvested cah, común, and pueblo as collective entities.

DISPOSSESSIONS

Yet this interpretation is limited. Gold, for instance, does not make its appearance in the story of Hunucmá's origins solely in terms of its value for the Mayan inhabitants of the region, but also in terms of its value for and potential seizure by the Spanish. If we were to read the story of "Nuc ma ti'" only as a story of possession, we would ignore experiences of communal *dis*possession—the loss of communal resources—that arguably give possession at least some part of its value in retrospect, whether at the moment of loss or in its wake. How is such loss recognized and culturally structured as an event, or potential event (see Limbert, chapter 2), of particular significance for el pueblo?

To address this question in the Hunucmá region is to return to the series of historic attacks on communal resources in the region, beginning with the late colonial disentailment of indigenous confraternities, the expropriation of cah treasuries, and the sale of many communal lands held by the cahs. In 1782 indigenous notables from Hunucmá complained to the king of Spain about the confiscation of the lands and cattle of religious confraternities, arguing that those sacred resources would be "wasted, without any benefit to the Virgin." Similarly, officials of another town in western Yucatán, also responding to the seizure of cofradía lands, warned the king of the "evils that will come in the future" if Spanish landowners and ranchers were to be allowed to seize "our lands and forests" (Bracamonte y Sosa 1994:171–174). A critical aspect of these processes of dispossession was the devaluation of history; the old documents and maps held by the cahs were increasingly disregarded by state officials. After cah officials of the pueblo of Kinchil sought to prevent a hacendado from seizing communal lands in 1818, for instance, state officials and courts ruled against them, dismissing and discarding the documents they had assembled, preserved, and marshaled in defense of cah lands as "a few confused maps made by Indians, or by inexperienced people" (AGN-T 1819). In the wake of privatization measures undertaken in the name of the new republic of Mexico a few years later, similar collective denunciations of material and spiritual dispossession were lodged in the name of cahs and their cofradías (Güémez Pineda 1994).

Precisely in this era of crisis, members of the cahs of the Hunucmá region seized upon el común as a way to reformulate communal sovereignty and defend communal resources from ranchers, hacendados, and government officials. Such strategies built upon old Spanish legal precedents, which defined común not only in terms of previous possession or ownership but also in terms of need. That is, at least in theory, both the historical fact of dispossession and the social fact of impoverishment resulting from such dispossession were valid criteria for claims of pueblo residents to land and other resources. Such precedents were put to use, however, in the particular context of independence-era Yucatán. Liberal Yucatecan Creoles, while avidly advocating for the privatization of communal lands, presented themselves as acting against the old regime on behalf of a long-oppressed, "enslaved," and dispossessed entity—el pueblo. Indigenous working populations, for their part, appropriated the liberal rhetoric on freedom and right but put it to a different use. In some cases, they equated the loss of lands of the común with the "enslavement" of el pueblo and their defense or recovery with the best means of realizing the right to "liberty" and self-sufficiency as "free" citizens of a new republic.

In this way, in Hunucmá as elsewhere, history remained important for claims over communal land, but with a difference. Now histories of the *dispossession* of resources, rather than solely their possession by the cah, became politically effective. The documents of the cahs remained critical for claims to común, but the framing narratives presented by cah officials and others in the name of el común, and sometimes el pueblo, were different. They came to emphasize poverty and the historic dispossession of common lands, both of which were legal criteria for rights to el común. Typically, such histories of possession and dispossession were framed temporally as a relationship between periods or conditions (whether past, present, or possible future) of slavery and liberty.[7]

Thus, when cah officials of Kinchil petitioned the government in defense of their común's lands in 1837, they based their plea not only on old cah documents but also on a statement regarding the size and poverty of the population and the history of recent land alienations in the area. They emphasized the danger to both común and pueblo as their ability to subsist was eroded progressively, adding a declaration that "the proposal of a few private landowners to buy or rent those lands is to kill, or at lease enslave *el pueblo*, making it the vassal of the buyer." This situation, they concluded, was "opposed to the liberty that the free and philanthropic Government that we enjoy offers, and to Kinchil's possession, since time immemorial, of its lands" (AGEY-PE-T 1837). "Liberation," it seems, had replaced lineage as the point of reference for legitimating both particular claims on resources and more general claims to political and social collectivity. Whereas the cah had been in a sense a colonial institution, integrated into the workings of Spanish mechanisms of domination and extraction, the común was oppositional—a hybrid of Spanish, indigenous, and liberal frameworks through which indigenous and working mestizo populations contested and threatened to arrest the dominant Creole vision of a polity built on agrarian commercial development and on the political exclusion and dispossession of both indigenous and nonindigenous working populations.

But by the 1850s, with the consolidation of the liberal state, claims to el común had become relatively inefficacious in legal terms, as demonstrated by repeated unsuccessful attempts by indigenous communalists to defend their control over woodlands in the area of Hunucmá (AGEY-J 1856a, 1857). In 1868 the cahs and their indigenous authorities were finally abolished by decree, leading on the one hand to the disappearance of the cah officials who had laid claim to the común so skillfully, and on the other to the practical exclusion of indigenous "citizens" from pueblo government and town councils, because all positions at the pueblo level were monopolized by Spanish-speaking, landowning gentry (AGEY-J 1853, 1856b, 1861). Sub-sequently, the expansion of henequen monoculture brought the rapid decline of independent subsistence agriculture and the intensification of indigenous indebted servitude (Wells 1985; Wells and Joseph 1996). Indeed, by the late nineteenth century, roughly 50 percent of the population of the Hunucmá district had become completely dispossessed of communal lands, residing on the haciendas as indebted servants on a permanent basis (Dirección General de Estadística 1901–1905).

As Hunucmá's gentry took effective possession of land and political power, working populations in the region faced a time of physical privation, violence, and exploitation—a history of dispossession. In this context, many working residents of the area abandoned their petitions to the government, instead mounting concerted campaigns of resistance. From the 1870s forward, insurgents struck at the people and properties that threatened to appropriate woodlands and other communal resources of the pueblos. They targeted the property and homes of landowners and knocked down stone walls that enclosed fields; they slashed henequen plants with machetes, torched hacienda buildings and houses in the pueblos, killed cattle owned by ranchers, and occasionally shot and killed prominent gentry. In several cases, pueblo residents attacked judges and state officials involved in the measurement and survey of lands. They even engaged in shootouts with federal troops, whom they fought with guerrilla tactics on a number of occasions from the 1870s through the late 1890s. Under interrogation, detainees sometimes described their actions as undertaken in defense of "lands of *el común*" or "lands of *el pueblo*" (AGEY-J 1889, 1891, 1892; *Razón del pueblo*, May 31, 1876; October 5, 1876; January 4, 1892; *Revista de Mérida*, May 3, 1892; May 17, 1892). Such usages suggest that in contrast to elite references to el pueblo, conceptions of el pueblo among working populations had become politicized and oppositional, anchored in possession but reshaped through the experience of historic dispossession, political alienation, and insurgency.

With the downfall of Porfirio Díaz and the onset of the Mexican Revolution in 1911, several reformist and revolutionary groups launched insurgencies aimed at political power in Mexico, inaugurating an era of partisan contention over the spoils of the regime's collapse (Wells and Joseph 1996). While a series of localized uprisings broke out throughout Yucatán, in the Hunucmá region, hundreds of men joined in a much more sustained, communalist insurgency, putting haciendas to the torch, bombing machinery, and ambushing hacienda administrators and soldiers. They targeted haciendas that had been established on lands of the old común more recently. In the few written messages they left behind and statements given under interrogation, they indicated that their actions were intended as part of a war against "slavery," aimed at "liberation." Their demands found echoes among elite and middle-class reformers, who embraced a rhetoric of martyrdom as they denounced the sufferings and dispossession of el pueblo and declared their own disposition to sacrifice themselves if necessary for the cause of el pueblo (T. Benjamin 2000). The victory of constitutionalist revolutionaries at the state and national level by 1914 brought radical reformists into power in Yucatán. They made explicit and constant references to el pueblo, both in denouncing its dispossession and degradation and in voicing demands for the restoration of communal lands and autonomy (Joseph 1988).

Through the ensuing period of postrevolutionary state formation, the rhetoric of dispossession returned from the margins, becoming a framework for recognition by and negotiation with the state. In that context, when revolutionary general Salvador Alvarado, who became Yucatán's governor in 1915, visited the town of Hunucmá, he was presented with a lengthy petition for the restoration of communal lands, written on ledger paper and signed by more than three hundred men of Hunucmá, many of them former insurgents (AGEY-PE-G 1915; *La Voz de la Revolución*, May 4, 1915). The petitioners made explicit reference to the possession of communal resources, evoking woodlands that they had held "centuries" before and from time immemorial, particularly areas of forest "known by the name of *El Común*." But dispossession was the dominant theme of the petition, one reiterated in references to the alienation of common lands in the recent and distant past, to the efforts of local landowners to "plant fear in the hearts" of those who dared enter the old woodlands, and to a resulting condition of "slavery" in which working pueblo residents found themselves "for centuries, in the hands of the powerful owner, who makes immense fortunes out of our sweat and badly paid labor." The petitioners demanded that the governor, and hence the state he represented, recognize them as speaking for el pueblo. Thus they called for the return of old common lands to "the benefit of *el pueblo*, allowing no one to claim them as property in order to conjure the evil that has caused so much harm to the property of *el pueblo*."

It is in light of this history of insurgency and the changing experience and rhetorics of dispossession in the Hunucmá region that we may reread the story of "Nuc ma ti'." Here, the significance of the gold in the narrative, or rather the loss of the gold, becomes evident. The same goes for the loss of lives as indigenous leaders become martyrs of el pueblo. Indeed, it is through the conquest itself and the retrospective retelling of its associated dispossessions that Hunucmá is named as el pueblo and enters into history, both as an object of dispossession and as a subject of martyrdom. Thus, even as the "Nuc ma ti'" story epitomizes the place of dispossession— the culturally, historically, and politically structured experience of loss—in the making of el pueblo, it anachronistically projects a modern consciousness of el pueblo and its dispossession, back to the moment of conquest. Hidden from view are the more recent losses of land and other communal resources that shaped the consolidation of el pueblo as a collective political subject.

REPOSSESSIONS

Once again, this reading captures only certain aspects of the "Nuc ma ti'" story. Relating a tale about the possession or loss of gold, or land, or life is not the aim of the tale. By the end, it becomes clear that the story is rather about how a place and a people came to have a name—Hunucmá— and with that name, a history. The telos of the story is *re*possession, and it is in the theme of repossession that we may find the most compelling narrative frame through which el pueblo, in Hunucmá and perhaps elsewhere, has been constructed and claimed as a contemporary social, political, spiritual, and historical subject. It is repossession, or its possibility, that lends a specific temporality to the political, material, cultural, and religious life of el pueblo, and it is in terms of repossession that explicit claims are sometimes made on and through history as el pueblo's most cherished resource (compare Childs, Nguyen, and Handler, chapter 7; Strassler, chapter 9).

There have been many kinds of "things," both material and immaterial, whose repossession has figured centrally in the shaping and reshaping of el pueblo as a political, social, and spiritual entity. Given the longevity of communalist struggles in the region of Hunucmá, land was historically one of the most important of those resources. The 1915 Hunucmá petition was effectively a demand for repossession, not only of communal lands but also of communal sovereignty and political recognition—desires flouted by landowners and government officials through resistance and inaction, respectively. With the advent of Lázaro Cárdenas to the Mexican presidency in the late 1930s, however, land reform again became a central concern of the government, and Yucatán emerged as one of the federal government's principal "laboratories" for large-scale collectivization of hacienda agriculture (Fallaw 2001; Joseph 1988). Under Cárdenas, repossession went from an insurgent demand to an official paradigm for the reorganization of society and state through the collectivization of henequen haciendas and the executive actions of "restitution" (*restitución*) or "donation" (*dotación*) of those lands to towns and pueblos throughout the henequen zone. Such actions were represented rhetorically (in speeches, land reform decrees, and so forth) as restoring possessions, long lost or stripped away, to dispossessed pueblos that now were to be transformed through their *repossession* as subaltern entities (ASRA 1937), whose endowment with resources came at the price of their tight subordination to agencies of state.

This arrangement would founder with the decline of the henequen industry and maize agriculture and the progressive dismantlement of the ejidos in the wake of neoliberal reforms enacted from the mid-1970s forward, most notably by Carlos Salinas in the late 1980s and early 1990s (Baños Ramírez 1996). As henequen and maize have declined, most residents of the region have abandoned the land in search of other sources of employment. From the 1970s forward, many found work at large-scale commercial chicken- and pig-raising farms that spread through the region. Others, more recently, have joined the ranks of transmigrants who journey far from their pueblos of origin to Los Angeles or Seattle in search of work. But in contemporary Hunucmá, the physical removal of residents from direct communal engagement with the land has not implied the decline of el pueblo. Rather, as the "Nuc ma ti'" story might suggest, the concept of el pueblo, once unmoored from the state-controlled collective ejidos and disarticulated from the land itself, has been opened to reappropriation and reinterpretation in a wide variety of contexts.

One of these contexts is that of labor, notably in the course of labor disputes with Avícolas Fernández, a Yucatecan poultry company. The company operated as many as fifty-seven farms, which by the 1980s were widely reputed to be characterized by intensely exploitative working conditions, including child labor, beatings, and the systematic and illegal repression of unionization drives. An initially successful attempt to form an independent union in 1990 triggered a violent response from company employees and strikebreakers, leading to a five-month-long violent conflict between workers, the company, and police and government officials centered in Tetiz

(Eiss 2003), a pueblo immediately adjacent to the town of Hunucmá. Strike organizers and pueblo residents represented that conflict not only as a union's struggle for recognition but also as a struggle of el pueblo for rights of which it had been dispossessed in becoming subjected to a new regime of "slavery" on the ranches. In one pamphlet, strikers declared their refusal to continue "bequeathing our misery [and] handing our children over to the voracity of the owner, so that he can continue appropriating everything that belongs to *el pueblo*." Increasingly, the strike came to be perceived as a movement for the liberation of el pueblo as a collective political subject. In one assembly, a sympathizer read a poem dedicated to "the heroic pueblo of Tetiz" as if that pueblo were a collective person or more specifically a collective masculine subject (a pueblo united "like one, single man"). The poet referred explicitly to struggle as a path to liberation and a way to repossess Tetiz itself: "Recover your dignity and the respect for you that those arrogant, powerful people have forgotten."

After the defeat of the strike and the union's dissolution, organizers authored a lengthy and detailed account of the struggle, entitled "*La batalla de Tetiz y Hunucmá*" ("The Battle of Tetiz and Hunucmá"). The account recast the defeat as a victory, dramatizing the conflict as a story in which el pueblo was dispossessed of its rights and dignity and thus rose up to demand its liberation through a collective repossession of sorts. After an account of the disappearance of the union, "The Battle" concludes with the pyrrhic victory of the workers, who hold fiestas celebrating the "victory of the dignity, unity, and liberty of an entire pueblo that, like a single man, knew how to struggle and to fall with its head held high and to rise again once more." Here, as in the poem mentioned above, emerges a full-fledged, corporeal, masculine, and virile reification of *el pueblo* in human form. "DZOCU YAHA U CAJI TETIZ," the account continues in Maya, then translating these words as "*el pueblo* of Tetiz has awakened." After crediting workers' optimism to their "dignity" and their faith in miraculous intercessions of the Virgin of Tetiz, the authors conclude that the failure of the independent union movement was just a "brief stop along the road of struggle of el pueblo of Tetiz for its rights." This collective "awakening" amounted to a miraculous repossession of that most precious resource of all—history.

A second illustration of the rhetoric of repossession is in the domain of cultural politics—perhaps most notably in works authored by Anacleto Cetina Aguilar, a teacher, a poet, an opposition political activist, a historian, and a resident of the town of Hunucmá (Eiss in press). Throughout Cetina's poetic and historical work, the theme of possession looms especially large in the copious detail he provides about the nature and origin of the physical structures of el pueblo, which the poet endows with organic attributes, even personality. A 1983 poetry collection entitled *Cahtal K'ay* (Maya for *Song of Life in the Pueblo*; Cetina Aguilar 1983), which Cetina describes as having been written in "the language of *el pueblo*," includes a tribute to the town's clock tower as a "venerable guardian that my grandparents/ placed at the heart/ of my beautiful pueblo." The streets of the pueblo are the "arteries/ through which the life of *el pueblo* courses," and so on. In a later historical and cultural compendium, *Breves datos históricos y culturales del municipio de Hunucmá* (1996), Cetina continues in this vein, adding equally effusive descriptions of popular traditions such as religious processions and holidays, regional music and dance, traditional costume, and use of Maya language. Thus he claims those elements—which are, like Hunucmá's built structures, in some measure the residue of the region's nineteenth- and early-twentieth-century gentry—as cultural resources of el pueblo that serve as landmarks of its history and heritage.

The theme of dispossession also pervades *Breves datos*—not in terms of the loss of communal lands but through the material or cultural disfigurement of el pueblo by what Cetina identifies as forces of "modernization" and "neoliberalism." For Cetina, the destruction of an old kiosk, a baroque altarpiece in the church, and the remnants of an old Mayan road (*sac' be*) in the center of town are evidence of the loss, decay, or disintegration of el pueblo. Parallel to the loss of physical integrity is the dispossession of el pueblo's cultural integrity—the progressive loss of Hunucmá's customs, celebrations, and traditions and especially use of Maya language and traditional dress. Perhaps most significantly, the deterioration of the public clock and its evident inability to keep time accurately seem in Cetina's account to offer direct symbolic reference to el pueblo's unmooring from the progressive or forward-moving sense of time and history that once characterized it (as not only a "traditional" but also a "modern" entity). Cetina links these developments—the loss of both tradition and modernity—to the effects of neoliberal economic reforms (unemployment, migration) and the advent of mass media.

It is here that we can appreciate the political horizon of Anacleto Cetina Aguilar's work. Cetina's cultural compendium is a charter for the repossession of el pueblo through such measures as the return to Maya language use and the revitalization of traditional dress, dances, and festivals. "Such beautiful traditions," he writes, "that are so old—perhaps thousands of years old.... For the day that we lose them, we will lose part of ourselves." Most importantly, he calls for residents of Hunucmá to cease forgetting their history, a task he proposes to assist by providing, in *Breves datos*, a history of Hunucmá's martyrdom and struggles for liberation from the colonial era forward. Against the assaults of neoliberalism, Cetina offers the *Breves datos* as a conscious repossession or reassemblage of el pueblo out of what for him are its most important, although undervalued, resources: its built environment, traditions, and history.

Finally, in religious life and especially in the gremio system and religious fiestas, the theme of repossession is perhaps most salient for pueblo residents. The widely recounted story of the Virgin and her miracle (Carrillo y Ancona 1895; Eiss 2002a), however, offers the best example of the importance of repossession in structuring el pueblo as a spiritual entity. In the winter of 1730, as the story goes, the Virgin of Tetiz journeyed across the ocean to Spain, where, clad in a mendicant's tattered garb, she sought out a Franciscan friar and begged for alms to rescue her son and her from the torments of poverty. Himself impoverished, Fray Francisco could find only a single Spanish peso, which he gave to her. In return, she assured him that they would see each other again, declaring that one day he would witness the "miserable state" of her "humble shanty." "Then you will know my entire history, and you will do for me everything that the holy charity that burns in your heart inspires." Subsequently, Francisco rose through the church hierarchy and traveled to the New World, eventually becoming bishop of Yucatán. One day, during a pastoral visit, he decided to stop in the pueblo of Tetiz. There, followed by a procession of Indians, he entered a building that "less than a temple, less than a church, was a hut on the point of collapse." Before him he found the very image of the woman who had visited him, but now carved in wood and dressed in tattered and stained silk and covered in coins and other offerings. As he drew closer to kiss the fringe of her dress reverently, Francisco recognized, hanging on the figure amid the other offerings, the coin that he had given away in Seville. Overcome by the coin's miraculous reappearance, Francisco fell to his knees and determined to make good on the "sacred debt" he had contracted with the mendicant, by directing church resources into the revival of Tetiz's confraternities and into the construction of a new sanctuary for the Virgin.

In the story of the Virgin, the tropes of possession and dispossession are as clear as they are in the 1915 petition, the documents and history produced by the egg strikers in 1990, and the work of Cetina Aguilar. The former appears in the form of the Virgin herself and the coins and other precious offerings that hang around her neck; the latter, in the Virgin's tattered clothing, the dilapidated state of her shrine, and the impoverishment of Tetiz's religious confraternities and indigenous population. The resolution of the story of Francisco's gift, however, structures it as a story not of possession or dispossession but of repossession. The miracle stems not simply from the Virgin's trip to Seville or even from Francisco's reencounter with the coin, but rather from the church's dedication of vast sums to the building of a church in Tetiz and the revival of the confraternities dedicated to the Virgin's worship. The miraculous reencounter with Francisco's coin brings about el pueblo's repossession—of material wealth, grace, and Tetiz's "entire history." Yet this repossession, unlike the repossessions referred to above (in the context of conflicts over land, labor, and culture), constitutes el pueblo not merely as an entity grounded in land or other material resources but rather as a spiritual one, above and beyond the realms of wealth and politics.

The Virgin's story, like those that precede it, shows that even as the resources through which el pueblo is defined differ radically—from land to labor, from traditions to clothing, from language to grace—the paradigm of repossession remains a constant, structuring community through and in relationship to those changing resources and making possible the construction of el pueblo as an embodied entity in space and time. Moreover, the nature and outcome of the "repossession" at stake may vary greatly according to context, but the means of repossession is the same. It is the recovery of history—of historical consciousness or of its signifiers, such as dress, language, or a coin—that makes possible the reclamation of el pueblo as legacy, identity, and destiny. This history, always on the verge of loss yet always somehow inalienable, both the source of things and their final destination, is both the first resource of el pueblo and its last recourse.

"NO" PLACE

It is here that we may return to the story of Hunucmá's origins and read that story as one structured as a narrative of repossession. Dispossessed of gold, land, and lives following the conquest, the people of Hunucmá find their repossession as el pueblo in the assumption of a name, and with this name, the assumption or recognition of the history that this name reveals. This, the story suggests, is a treasure greater than any pile of gold—greater, in fact, than any of the other resources that el pueblo has claimed: from woodlands and salt pools, to language and tradition, and perhaps even to the Virgin's grace. Yet what kind of a history can this story offer for an entity so mutable, contested, and heterogeneous as el pueblo?

The tale of "Nuc ma ti'," when read alongside other contemporary texts, such as the story of the Virgin of Tetiz, "La batalla de Tetiz y

Hunucmá," and *Breves datos*, reveals that the construction of el pueblo takes place not so much through a reduplicative kind of historical memory as through *allegoresis*—"other stories" (Clifford 1986). These are "other" stories in that el pueblo is never constructed only from within, but also from without and across its boundaries—in the moment of the conquest, in the journey of the Virgin to Seville, in the presence of exploiters in "The Battle," and in the presence and agencies of state throughout Hunucmá's history.

These are also "other" stories in that their significance is driven by a structure distinct from their specific content. Despite the radical difference in the content of these "stories" of el pueblo, all are structured explicitly or implicitly according to a common thematics: possession, dispossession, repossession. Yet this allegoresis is not just about a kind of emplotment whose form provides meaning to content (White 1990). What I have tried to demonstrate is that the allegorical construction of el pueblo in political discourse bears within it the traces of concrete histories and experiences of possession, dispossession, and repossession that ultimately lend these thematics both their formal structure and their power. The presence of these histories, even if occluded, works to constitute el pueblo as at once abstract and concrete, both generic and particular, as a collective body embedded in diverse material and cultural resources and shaped by the allegoresis through which these relationships are "storied," as histories that inscribe and "read" el pueblo from within and from without.

Read in this way, the "Nuc ma ti'" story thus is not an "epitomizing event" but rather is structured as an epitomizing allegory, not just in the limited sense of the ways in which that story might refer to or make intelligible other domains in which el pueblo is made or experienced, but also in a wider sense, in that el pueblo—and not just in Hunucmá—might itself always be an inherently allegorical and inherently historical construct. The power of el pueblo as subject and object and its power to possess peoples and places, resources and politics, might derive in some measure from the thematic of its histories. That allegorical structure joins place, people, and politics and lends to the resulting entity—el pueblo—a specific and progressive temporality.

But the story of "Nuc ma ti'" suggests one additional feature of the history of el pueblo that I have left unexplored to this point—that of negation. Anthropological analyses of historical narrative have tended to stress the "uses" of history (Appadurai 1981), and we can imagine that this story, in some contexts, might be a "useful" one to tell. But in itself, this is a story about the refusal of use. It is about a pueblo, as well as a history, that refuses to be made into a resource for others. To stress the dimension of negation in the making of el pueblo is to suggest that el pueblo is a relational rather than an insular construct—its claims are dialectical rather than foundational, and it is so often objectified in instrumental ways. But el pueblo's deepest history may reside in its refusal to be used. In short, what Laclau (2005) has recently identified as the constitutive "emptiness" of "the people" as a transcendental signifier may rather be a sign of refusal and contestation, one that appears "empty" but may nonetheless be charged with historical significance. The power of el pueblo derives from the fact that once, or now, or at some point el pueblo did, does, and will say "No!"—and in that moment, names itself and claims a history that may not be fully known but cannot be denied.

Thus the claim Hunucmá has on el pueblo and the claim that el pueblo has over Hunucmá may relate as much to what el pueblo denies as to what it asserts. Here, perhaps, reside its power and its promise as a collective way to reclaim the past, challenge the present, and imagine the future differently. In this sense, Hunucmá, el pueblo, the people who answered no, is—like utopia—quite literally no place, but also every place. This is the last of el pueblo's claims and the last of its possessions: a possession of, by, and for its spirit. The story of "Nuc ma ti'" may serve, in the last instance, as a reminder of the ghostly presence of el pueblo: a spirit that ever returns to possess those who are grouped under its name and a specter that ever returns to haunt those who are not.

Notes

1. This story was published as the introduction to a collection of poetry authored by Anacleto Cetina Aguilar (1983).

2. The literature involved is so large that I will not attempt to cite it here. A few analysts offer approaches that are quite suggestive, along the lines I am trying to sketch out here. See, for instance, Nugent 2005; Rappaport 1994; and G. Smith 1989.

3. Hardt and Negri (2004:xiv, 79) consider the term *the people* to impose a fallacious unity on diverse political subjects. Hence they reject it, instead embracing *multitude* as a way of capturing both the scope of differences and the possibilities of difference as an enabling condition of liberatory political action. Ernesto Laclau (2005), in a study of populist politics, considers "the people" to be a discursive and rhetorical construct, one that emerges as an "empty signifier" that gives expression to the heterogeneous social spaces and diverse demands and identities of opposition politics. According to Laclau, it is precisely this rhetorical "emptiness" of "the people"

as a signifier that facilitates the logic of collective identifications both with "the people" as a subject of politics and with particular leaders as affective foci for those politics.

4. It is important to note that even today, Maya speakers retain the use of *cah* when referring to what Spanish speakers call *pueblo*.

5. For evidence from Hunucmá in the mid-1890s, see correspondence confiscated from the prison cells of men convicted of banditry regarding commitments to gremios and the payment of masses in 1893 (AGEY-J 1893). On popular spirituality in the nineteenth century, see Rugeley 2001.

6. My use of the term *possession* here might be situated in relation to at least three interrelated areas of anthropological literature. In addition to property, which has been a foundational and abiding concern of the discipline (see Verdery and Humphrey 2004), there is the somewhat broader category of "possessions," encompassing commodities and other objects, as well as intangibles and items of spiritual or cultural value that may or may not be considered properties (Appadurai 1986; Ferry 2005a; Handler 1988; Weiner 1992) and the anthropology of "value" (see Coronil 1997; Eiss and Pedersen 2002; Graeber 2001).

7. Such histories clearly intersected with wider populist political discourse but also may have resonated with long-standing Mayan prophetic and millennial traditions built around dual linear and cyclical conceptions of time. See Bricker 1981; Farriss 1987.

9

Material Resources of the Historical Imagination

Documents and the Future of the Past in Post-Suharto Indonesia

Karen Strassler

It is characteristic of political transitions that received historical wisdoms become unsettled, opening up new opportunities for rewriting national histories. This process was particularly acute in Indonesia following General Suharto's resignation in May 1998 because of the harnessing of historical narratives to state purposes during his thirty-two-year authoritarian regime, the New Order (1966–1998). At a moment when enshrined historical narratives were newly subject to intensive public questioning, the problem and practice of documentation became a focal point of imaginings of a new "awareness of history" (*kesadaran sejarah*) on which a democratic future would depend. In exploring documents as resources for a future history of Indonesia, this chapter analyzes the contradictory impulses of an emergent post-Suharto public sphere. In the immediate post-Suharto period, the rethinking of history enabled and disseminated by a newly free press generated both anxiety about the proliferation of competing accounts and optimism about a more participatory and open society.[1]

That historical debates often coalesced around questions of the authenticity, authority, authorship, and location of documents suggests that documents are not merely the raw materials of professional history. They are also potent resources in the public imagination that crystallize concerns about how historical truth claims are secured, where history might be located, and who might control it. Scholars have investigated the use of documents as sources for professional history (Axel 2002; Certeau 1988; Chandler, Davidson, and Harootunian 1994; Dirks 1993; Ginzburg 1989, 1994, 1999; Grafton 1997; Stoler 1992). But despite calls to attend to historical production outside the academy (D. Cohen 1994, 1997; Samuel 1994; Trouillot 1995), less attention has been paid to the "social life" of historical documents as they are copied, circulated, and contested in the public domain. The failure to consider questions of documentation outside the realm of professional history tends to reinforce an untenable opposition in which archival practice is precisely what defines "history" against an unofficial realm of popular "memory" (Nora 1989). Such oppositions efface a whole range of popular engagements with historiography's evidentiary forms and documentary procedures (Papailias 2005).

Here, I am interested in how documents as materially embodied and imaginatively engaged objects give concrete form to popular conceptions of what history is and might be. Describing documents as resources of the historical imagination calls attention to the ways in which documents were conceived as valuable resources to be mined, conserved, and developed in the making of new, post-Suharto national histories. In some cases, documents ideally led back to an original source—an author—from whom historical truth would issue. In others, the quest for documents was oriented not to a recovered past as much as to an envisioned future in which new kinds of documents would provide the material basis for a more truthful and democratic history.

This conceptualization of documents as "resources" was clearly conditioned by what Ferry and Limbert call, in their introduction to this volume, a "resource imagination" that is widely at work in contemporary Indonesia. The Indonesian state has long asserted its role (not uncontested, to be sure) as guardian of national resources, from the management of oil and other natural resources to the preservation of ecological and cultural diversity (see Lowe, chapter 5) and the development of "human resources" (*sumber daya manusia*) through education and social policy. More specifically, in Indonesian museums, monuments, and official historical discourses, the past (particularly the past of "revolutionary struggle") is framed as an inheritance to be managed for the benefit of future generations and as a resource to be mobilized in the making of young citizens (Strassler 2006).

Documents were also imagined as resources in the sense that they were envisioned as specifically *national* possessions in need of conservation, stewardship, and development. As long as they remained in private hands or monopolized by a single group, their potential as resources remained unrealized; they became actualized as resources for new histories at the moment they entered the public domain. The process of imagining documents as national resources was also part of transforming them into, ideally, politically neutral national possessions, naturalized in the sense that the ideological and interested content of the documents themselves was effaced.

In considering documents as material resources of the historical imagination, I want to suggest, too, that the *materiality* of documents—their artifactual qualities, as well as their content—mattered in the debates about the future of Indonesian history. Anthropologists have encouraged attention to texts as objects whose material and formal qualities are central to their social efficacy (Hull 2003; Messick 1993; Pellegram 1998; Tarlo 2003). In the Indonesian debates, considerations such as whether the documents in question were printed or handwritten; spoken, photographic, or textual; and originals or copies shaped the authority they were deemed to have and the claims made in their name. Affecting the *imagining* of documents, these formal qualities and the physical movements of documents become resources for broader social imaginaries about the nature of history itself. Thus documents were material resources of the *imagination* in the sense, to put it simply, that documents are "good to think." Alternately imagined as authentic or false, lost or at risk, secreted away or publicly circulating, altered or destroyed, documents offered a concrete locus for concerns about national memory and its future stewardship, about the unstable relationship between the past and its representation, and about the dangers and possibilities of generating new histories.

DOCUMENTATION AS A MARK OF THE MODERN

On July 30, 2000, a discussion was held at a cultural center in the Javanese city of Yogyakarta about Milan Kundera's *The Book of Laughter and Forgetting*. Dr. Faruk, a prominent literary critic who was one of the featured speakers, explained to the audience that although Kundera wrote about politically "orchestrated forgetting" (*lupa yang direkayasa*), in Indonesia the problem of forgetting must be seen "in a natural context, cultural, as opposed to a political context" (*Bernas*, July 31, 2000). A newspaper article paraphrases Dr. Faruk's comments:

> Our society…does not have a culture of writing and reading. We don't have the tools to remember with certainty. Meanwhile, the flow of information rushes by. Information follows and overtakes other information. This makes people forget what came before.
> (*Bernas*, July 2000)

Dr. Faruk offered a naturalizing interpretation of Indonesian failures to grapple with the past: "Our forgetting is more 'natural' [*natural*]. It is a forgetting that is natural [*alamiah*] because almost all of our society at an individual and a collective level forgets easily." Forgetting in Indonesia is "a technological problem. Meaning, we don't have a tradition of remembering by writing." Unlike countries such as Japan, which possess "a culture of writing" and "have technology" and thus can keep up with the dynamic pace of the modern age, Indonesians "are slow....If we move fast, we forget. So I tend to see this [forgetting] in a natural context, [a] cultural [context], rather than a political context." In other words, Indonesians forget because they are in, but not culturally or technologically prepared for, the fast pace of modernity.

Given that the manipulation of history was so prevalent a topic in public discourse after Suharto's resignation, the reduction of the problem of memory and forgetting to a question of "technology" seems, at first glance, surprising. Yet Dr. Faruk's denial of the politics of memory (at least as portrayed in the newspaper's rendering of his comments) epitomized a common tendency to treat the problem of history as if it were a problem of underdevelopment. Reiterating worn distinctions between orality and literacy as the divide between tradition and modernity, the idea that Indonesia lacked a "culture of documentation" (*budaya dokumentasi*) or archival traditions was often articulated in everyday conversation as well as in the pages of the news media. People often told me, "We do not *yet* have a culture of documentation," or "We *still* do not have awareness of documentation." In line with the evolutionary logic that situates the non-Western world as temporally behind and spatially marginal to the Euro-American center (Fabian 1983; Gupta and Ferguson 1992)—as well as the Asian center of Japan, always an important referent in Indonesian discourses of modernity and nationalism—the absence of a culture of documentation was not simply a lack but a failure to reach a certain point along a presumed trajectory.

The ideal of historical awareness based on the practice of documentation that elite commentators like Dr. Faruk proposed was intimately attached to a vision of Indonesia as a modern if (incompletely realized) state figured in opposition to its origins in Javanese and other "traditional" cultures. Opposing traditional, irrational, and personally motivated myth to the modern, rational, expert knowledge of history, numerous historians drew a parallel between Suharto's self-aggrandizing and self-legitimating historical "myths" and those produced by Java's traditional rulers (*Bernas* July 2, 1999, September 29, 1999; *Kedaulatan Rakyat*, April 1, 2000). Such forms of history writing were not in keeping, as historian P. J. Suwarno (director of the Center for the Study and Documentation of Indonesian History, Sanata Dharma University, Yogyakarta) put it, in "the era of modern Indonesia, the writing of history should follow the scientific principles [*kaidah ilmu*] of a history that is critical so that it can give real knowledge of events of the past" (*Kompas*, March 2, 1999). One historian states that the "confusion of history" (*kebingungan sejarah*) has reached such a point that people no longer know "which is history and which is fairytale, which is truth and honesty and which, on the other hand, is falsehood and lies" (*Bernas*, September 30, 1999).[2]

The embrace of a rational, objective history based on documentary sources was, then, closely tied to a vision of Indonesia as a secular, modern nation moving forward in linear, progressive time.[3] These ideas of history and modern statehood, not coincidentally often articulated by historians trained in Europe or America and certainly well versed in Euro-American historiography, presuppose both a community of scholar-experts who work independent of the state and a particular kind of public that is the audience for these histories. They also assume a secular nation bound together by awareness of a shared history rather than by charismatic leadership, religious unity, or some other form of community. But if, on the one hand, the regressive, "indoctrinating history" (*sejarah indoktrinatif*) of the New Order was to be rejected (*Kompas*, December 30, 1998), enthusiasm about popular practices of documentation also threatened to undermine the rule of experts (Mitchell 2002) and such technocratic visions of historical knowledge production.

THE DOCUMENTARY FETISH: THE SUPERSEMAR CONTROVERSY

What I know is that now there is much controversy, first about the dictum of Supersemar itself, and about the loss of the original document....This has to do with the authenticity of Supersemar....A document that should have become historical evidence [*bukti sejarah*], gone just like that?!

—*Rachmawati Sukarnoputri*, Bernas, *March 11, 2000*

Within post-Suharto public discussions of the need to "straighten out history," the document often figured as a fetishized re-source—a means of return to a recoverable source or author. As fetish, the document simultaneously crystallized a desire to fix historical truth and stimulated anxiety about the impossibility of achieving such fixity. The documentary fetish, I argue, arises from the profound instability of history in a moment of political transition, when received wisdoms have lost their authoritative grip. It is the material facticity of the document that makes it so convincingly appear to embody and secure the truth of the past. At the same time, however, the materiality of the document renders it vulnerable to manipulation, falsification, and destruction. These "hazards" of materiality (Keane 1997) push against the document's promise of recovery and bring to the fore the malleability of history.

The historical controversy surrounding Supersemar, the founding document of the New Order, exemplifies the workings of the documentary fetish. Supersemar is the name of the "letter of instruction" signed by President Sukarno on March 11, 1966, in the tumultuous aftermath of an alleged communist coup attempt that took place on September 30, 1965, and in which six high-ranking generals were killed.[4] The document served to legitimate the handover of authority by President Sukarno to General Suharto, paving the way for Suharto's banning of the Communist Party, the killing and imprisonment of hundreds of thousands of alleged communists and communist sympathizers, and his own rise to the presidency. Yet Supersemar's foundational status is troubled by the fact that the original of this originary document has been lost. Moreover, several different "official" copies are in circulation. In the post-Suharto era, this document came to embody not the legitimacy of the New Order regime but its illegitimate and uncertain origins.

Several key issues surround the "mystery," as it was often called, of Supersemar. First, how could the original manuscript, in the indignant words of Sukarno's daughter quoted above, be "gone just like that?" Was it intentionally hidden away somewhere, or destroyed? And why? The second problem arises from the circulation of several different "official" copies of Supersemar (*Bernas*, July 9, 1999).[5] In a particularly striking instance, when the government published a book commemorating the thirtieth year of Indonesia's independence, it contained two slightly different versions of Supersemar printed on different pages (Sekretaris Negara 1978). The proliferation of various "official" copies stimulates questions about the actual content of the original document. What in fact did it say? Was it intended to be a mandate to rule, as Suharto claimed, or merely a temporary measure?

A third question concerned the conditions under which Sukarno signed the document and its actual authorship. The version of Supersemar most often identified as the authentic copy by the state and reproduced in school history texts indicates the place of signing as Jakarta, even though it is well known that Sukarno was at his presidential palace in Bogor on the night of March 11, 1966. Was Sukarno given a prewritten document and forced to sign it? If the original was written on military stationery, rather than paper with the presidential letterhead, was it intentionally destroyed to conceal its embarrassing provenance within military quarters, as some have suggested (*Kedaulatan Rakyat,* March 2, 2000; *Kompas,* March 8, 2000)? Was Sukarno, as a former personal adjutant later claimed, threatened with a gun before conceding to sign?[6] Did he dictate the letter himself, as another assistant insisted (*Kompas,* March 8, 2000)? Was the lost original handwritten in Bogor, with official versions later typed up in Jakarta?[7]

The disappearance of the original manuscript and the existence of divergent copies indicate some willful manipulation, but how significant is Supersemar? In fact, the differences in the various extant copies of Supersemar are small, and all contain the provision that Suharto must submit reports on his actions subject to approval by Sukarno, a clear indication that the mandate was intended to be temporary rather than to shift power fully to Suharto. (In speeches after March 11, 1966, Sukarno repeatedly insisted that as president for life, he remained the nation's ultimate authority.) Clearly, the process by which Suharto usurped Sukarno's authority was a long and complex one, involving many maneuvers, of which the signing of Supersemar was just one. Why, then, the fixation upon this lost original document?

That the authenticity of Supersemar became a central concern of post-Suharto historical discourse was in direct proportion to its fetishization by the New Order regime itself.[8] Supersemar functioned in New Order narratives as an origin continually recalled as a way to insist on the legality of the transfer of power to Suharto and, one suspects, to deflect memory of the New Order's bloody beginnings. New Order school textbooks emphasize the foundational status of the document as the legal basis for the New Order, typically describing the letter with legalistic words such as *proof* (*bukti*), *legitimate* (*sah*), *legal* (*legal*), and *law* (*hukum*). One history textbook for high school seniors describes Supersemar as

> an admission in a legitimate way from the formally legal government of the Old Order that it didn't have authority and was no longer able to overcome the crisis of the Indonesian people in all sectors. Thus, in a manner both de facto and de jure, the Old Order government gave over its tasks to Suharto. (Badrika 1997:44–45)

Later, this same text depicts the process by which Suharto became president as a "process by law" (*proses hukum*) that was "rational-objective"

(*rasional-objektif*). Often reproducing the document as an illustration, textbooks stress the material facticity of the document and draw attention to
Sukarno's familiar (and highly fetishized) signature.

Yet for all this rhetoric of law and evidence, there was another dimension to the New Order fetishization of the Supersemar document as a
source of Suharto's authority. The catchy name *Supersemar* combines *super*
(with the same connotations as the English word) with *Semar*, the name of
a much beloved Javanese shadow puppet figure revered as the protector of
Java. (The name is actually an abbreviated form of Surat Perintah Sebelas
Maret, or Letter of Instruction of March 11.) The humorless and lacklus-
ter Suharto attempted throughout his presidency to identify himself with
this funny, irreverent, and mystical folk hero. Naming the document
Supersemar was a way to give it authority deriving not only from legalistic
evidentiary regimes but also from popular trust in mythic figures. Indeed,
other textbooks describe Supersemar in quasi-religious terms, as if the document itself were both an act of God and an entity capable of agency on its
own. A textbook for junior high school students (figure 9.1) reads:

> Thanks to the greatness of God the Almighty...there was born
> the famous Letter of Instruction of March 11, 1966. The Letter
> of Instruction...was born as the opening of the new life of the
> people and state of Indonesia. The Letter of Instruction of
> March 11 is the historical milestone marking the beginning of
> the new life we know as the New Order, the order of renewal of
> the Indonesian people. (Lubis et al. 1984:122–123)

This emphasis on the sacredness and efficacy of Supersemar qua document both effaces the process of its production and transforms Supersemar
into a New Order *pusaka*, an object that contains and emanates power. The
passing of Supersemar from Sukarno to Suharto is not merely an allegedly
legal mandate to rule within the formal procedures of a modern nation-
state; it is also represented in conventional Javanese terms as the transmit-
tal of power, embodied in an object, from an old ruler in decline to a new
ruler in ascendance. The "modern" authority of documentary evidence
and the "traditional" power of the pusaka combine to form a powerful
fetish of New Order origins.

Given Supersemar's status in New Order histories, it is not surprising
that in the immediate post-Suharto period, considerable public discourse
swelled around the question of its authenticity and the mysterious loss of
its original. Supersemar became effective as a condensed symbol of the

PRESIDEN
REPUBLIK INDONESIA

SURAT PERINTAH 11 MARET

I. **Mengingat:**
1. Tingkatan Revolusi sekarang ini, serta keadaan politik baik Nasional maupun Internasional.
2. Perintah Harian Panglima Tertinggi Angkatan Bersenjata/Presiden/Pemimpin Besar Revolusi pada tanggal 8 Maret 1966.

II. **Menimbang:**
1. Perlu adanya ketenangan dan kestabilan Pemerintahan dan jalannya Revolusi.
2. Perlu adanya jaminan keutuhan Pemimpin Besar Revolusi, ABRI, dan Rakyat untuk memelihara kepemimpinan dan kewibawaan Presiden/ Panglima Tertinggi/Pemimpin Besar Revolusi serta segala ajaran-ajarannya.

III. **Memutuskan/Memerintahkan:**
Kepada : Letnan Jenderal Soeharto, Menteri Panglima Angkatan Darat.
Untuk : Atas nama Presiden/Panglima Tertinggi/Pemimpin Besar Revolusi.
1. Mengambil segala tindakan yang dianggap perlu, untuk terjaminnya keamanan dan ketenangan serta kestabilan jalannya Pemerintahan dan jalannya Revolusi, serta menjamin keselamatan pribadi dan kewibawaan Pimpinan Presiden/Panglima Tertinggi/Pemimpin Besar Revolusi/Mandataris MPRS demi untuk keutuhan Bangsa dan Negara Republik Indonesia dan melaksanakan dengan pasti segala ajaran Pemimpin Besar Revolusi.
2. Menggunakan koordinasi pelaksanaan perintah dengan Panglima-Panglima Angkatan-Angkatan lain dengan sebaik-baiknya.
3. Supaya melaporkan segala sesuatu yang bersangkut paut dalam tugas dan tanggung jawabnya seperti tersebut di atas.

IV. **Selesai.**

Jakarta, 11 Maret 1966

Presiden/Panglima Tertinggi/Pemimpin
Besar Revolusi/Mandataris MPRS

Soekarno

Teks lengkap SUPERSEMAR

FIGURE 9.1

Supersemar document reproduced in a 1984 textbook. The caption reads: "Complete text of Supersemar." Although it uses an orthographic system adopted after 1966 and thus is clearly not a copy of the original document, the illustration nevertheless looks like a reproduction of the document, complete with Sukarno's signature and official letterhead (Lubis et al. 1984).

manipulation of history and a focal point of the profound doubts and conspiracy theorizing that attended official explications of both historical and contemporary events. Concern with locating the authentic document and determining its original contents replicated in a Reformasi idiom the New Order fetishization of the document. In numerous accounts of the "search" for Supersemar, it was as if this single document were the source that would reveal the true history of the New Order. In an article in the national news magazine *Tempo*, for example, then speaker of the house Akbar Tanjung noted: "From this document it is hoped it can be determined whether the shift in power from Sukarno to Suharto was legitimate [*sah*] or not, whether it really was an official giving over of power or only the giving of a temporary mandate" (*Tempo*, March 13–19, 2000, p. 22).[9]

Commentary about Supersemar also revealed anxiety about the threat posed to the state's authoritative historical resource, the national archive, by the loss of the original. The question of who was responsible for storing the document and in whose hands it might have ended up received heavy press coverage during this period. Newspaper articles reminded readers of a ten-year prison sentence for deliberately losing or withholding from the archives a document of national importance.[10] The director of the national archive, Mukhlis Paeni, publicly sought information from a variety of important national figures, all said at one time to have been in possession of the original Supersemar (*Bernas*, July 9, 1999). As in a game of hot potato, each pointed a finger at someone else, denying that he had held the document last or had held it at all (*Bernas*, March 11, 2000; *Kedaulatan Rakyat*, March 14, 2000; *Kompas*, March 17, 2000; *Tempo*, March 13–19, 2000). Only Suharto (and the dead) remained silent.

Finding the document would restore "history," rescuing it from private possession, to its rightful place in the national archive, and it would also halt the dangerous proliferation of versions of history unanchored by an authoritative source. The anxiety about copies circulating untethered from authentic originals is exemplified in Mukhlis Paeni's statement: "The existence of the authentic manuscript is greatly needed because if things are just left alone, there will be ever-more versions of Supersemar that circulate, and now there are already four versions of Supersemar that are each different from the other" (*Bernas*, March 11, 2000; see also March 18, 2000). Another article paraphrases a complaint by the head of the Yogyakarta branch of the Legal Aid Society: "The absence of the authentic letter of instruction of March 11, 1966, gives rise to different opinions among the people and confuses the children studying at school" (*Kedaulatan Rakyat*, March 10, 1999). The problem of the proliferation of accounts occurs not only in the differing copies of the document that circulate in various texts but also in the divergent "testimonies" about the event of its signing emerging from different historical actors. "A number of mysteries surrounding Supersemar up until now still have not been revealed," notes one commentator. "It's true that many historical actors have given their testimonies. But they tend to tell the story of Supersemar according to their own versions, of course, each with their own interests" (*Bernas*, March 11, 2000). Recovery of the authentic document would silence the clamor of interested accounts in favor of a single authoritative and credible national history.

THE ABSENT AUTHOR: THE GENERAL ATTACK CONTROVERSY

If the problem at the center of the Supersemar controversy was a document of dubious authenticity, another post-Suharto historical controversy hinged on the absence of documents altogether. Suharto's alleged manipulation of the history of the General Attack of March 1, 1949, also figured prominently in calls to "straighten out" the New Order's "crooked" histories. As president, Suharto had burnished his revolutionary and heroic credentials by continually recalling his association with this celebrated event in revolutionary history. The General Attack occurred in a moment of desperation for the fledgling republic. The republic's capital, Yogyakarta, was under Dutch control, its president and vice president were jailed, and its army had been forced into the hills. The Dutch were claiming de facto victory. In an effort to prove to the UN and the international community that the Indonesian Revolution had not been defeated, the Indonesian army launched a daring attack on the Dutch-held capital and managed to hold the city for six hours. That Suharto was the field commander of the attack was never in question. Rather, post-Suharto public debates centered on whether Suharto had also been the author of the plan, as he claimed. Many believed that the true mastermind was the late sultan of Yogyakarta, Hamengkubuwono IX, a prominent nationalist and a revered traditional ruler. The problem was a lack of documentary evidence that might settle the question.

In Suharto's autobiography (1988) and in a number of history books (Sekretaris Negara 1978), as well as in the "historical" films *Janur Kuning* (*Young Coconut Leaf*, 1979) and *Serangan Fajar* (*Dawn Attack*, 1981), Suharto's role in the attack as its commander and initiator were put forward as historical fact (K. Sen 1994). As one commentator wrote, "The General Attack of March 1st—especially among school children—became identical with the figure of Suharto. Moreover, children witnessed the

General Attack of March 1 as if it were really in front of their eyes through the film *Janur Kuning*" (*Kompas*, March 1, 1999).[11] As with Supersemar, this historical controversy did not begin with Suharto's fall; Suharto's claims to have initiated the attack were contradicted in a biography of the sultan based on interviews with him (published in 1982) and had been contested by several witnesses even during Suharto's regime (*Kompas*, March 1, 1999). But following Suharto's ouster, the question of the plan's authorship generated a frenzy of press coverage, especially as the date of its annual commemoration approached, with calls for witnesses to come forward and historians to rewrite accounts of this event.

Attention focused on whether there might exist "authentic documents" that could prove once and for all that the sultan was the author of the attack. The prominent political figure Permadi (a former dissident and a psychic) claimed to have once seen in the sultan's possession a set of letters exchanged between the sultan and General Soedirman (commander of the Indonesian Republican Army during the revolution), in which the sultan proposed the attack and Soedirman approved and suggested Suharto as the field commander. One article reported:

> Permadi claims to have seen for himself proof in the form of letters between Sultan HB IX and General Sudirman in planning the attack. All of this historical proof was stored in a leather bag and kept inside a metal cabinet that was in Sultan HB IX's house on Prapatan Street in Jakarta. "From those documents, I saw that on the Seventh of February 1949, General Soedirman sent a letter to the Sultan HB IX. Between the two of them then flowed communication where letters were sent back and forth two or three times," said Permadi. (*Kedaulatan Rakyat*, March 1, 2000)

In response to Permadi's statement, in the same article, the historian G. Moedjanto is quoted as saying, "If these letters between the Sultan and Pak 'Dirman can be found, then the course of history of the March 1, 1949, General Attack will be straightened out."

Discussion about the possible fate of these alleged documents served as what Eiss (chapter 8) calls an "allegory" of "possession, dispossession, repossession." On the same day and in the same newspaper, the sultan's palace of Yogyakarta issued a statement, responding to Permadi's claims, to the effect that as guardian of the sultan's belongings, the palace possessed no such documents (*Kedaulatan Rakyat*, March 1, 2000). A spokesperson for the palace claimed that it fervently wished to help "uncover the true history," but "not all the documents that are needed are there." But the statement also insinuated that such documents might have existed at one time and been intentionally disappeared. The spokesman pointedly stated that servants of the palace were not allowed to inspect the sultan's home in Jakarta until seven days after his burial. The article recounts:

> When the metal cabinet [described by Permadi] was inspected, it turned out it was already empty. There were no documents whatsoever. Only photographs that were strewn about. As if rifled through. And at that point there was an order from the Secretary of State that the family of the Sultan move out [of the house] right away.... "So we don't have left any documents at all."
> (*Kedaulatan Rakyat*, March 1, 2000)

The Suharto regime's manipulation of history came thus to be figured in the vivid image of a metal cabinet turned upside down, its precious documents stolen.

In March 2000, however, there were exultant reports that "authentic proof" (*bukti otentik*) of the sultan's authorship, which would finally "straighten out this history," had been found (*Bernas*, March 10, 2000). A BBC interview with the sultan from the 1980s had been located. In it, he claimed to have authored the attack.[12] News reports emphasized its documentary rather than oral quality, calling it a "written interview" and noting that it had been "signed by the Sultan himself." Moreover, the claim that this was an "official document" with the status of "historical evidence" was buttressed by the fact that the interview had been found filed away in the national archive (*Kedaulatan Rakyat*, March 10, 2000). Another article referred to the interview account as "authentic documents owned by the National Archive" (*Kompas*, March 11, 2000). The emphasis on their written status and location in the national archive serves further to establish their authority, for, as Emma Tarlo writes, "'paper truths,' despite their flimsiness and elasticity, despite their potential to be forged or destroyed, nonetheless have authority, belonging as they do to the world of the modern state where the written word reigns supreme" (2003:75).

Of course, as one historian pointed out, the sultan's after-the-fact account was no more an "authentic source" than Suharto's autobiography; both were "assertions by historical actors" (*Kedaulatan Rakyat*, April 1, 2000). Yet what is significant is that people wanted to treat this finding, which confirmed popular belief, as proof that would resolve the controversy. To constitute the radio interview as proof, it needed to be detached from its oral source and given the authority of a written document. Historical truth is ideally located in the modern form of a document rather than in the more obviously interested and less authoritative oral form of testimony.

As with the case of Supersemar, the significance accorded to the General Attack in Reformasi historical debates recodes the New Order narratives that enshrined this event as a key turning point in the revolution. Ultimately, the debates question Suharto's role but not necessarily the centrality of the event itself. Like Supersemar, the General Attack of March 1 may not have been the turning point it was portrayed to be in official histories of the revolution. It had been made so in part through an official historiography that promoted the military's decisive role in the struggle for independence (McGregor 2007). In this way, these two historical controversies central to the post-Suharto discourse on straightening out history were not at a deep level disruptive to nationalist historical narratives. Much like Reformasi itself, these efforts might unseat Suharto, transforming a story of service and glory into one of betrayal and calumny, without fundamentally challenging established structures.

DOCUMENTING UNCOMFORTABLE HISTORIES

Discussions of "straightening out" the history of Supersemar and the General Attack of March 1, 1949, imagined authentic documents as lost or withheld but recoverable resources, holding out the promise that finding them would put to rest lingering questions as to what had "really" happened. But there was not a great deal at stake in resolving these controversies, I have suggested. In centering on narrow questions of authorship, historical debate remained fixated on personal responsibility, pitting Suharto against the figures of Sukarno and the sultan. A popular consensus condemning Suharto was already in place, as was nostalgic idealization of both Sukarno and Sultan Hamengkubuwono IX. The desire to locate authentic documents was essentially a desire to confirm what people already believed or wanted to believe, and the energy directed to these narrow historical questions deflected attention away from the more unsettling prospect of reckoning with Indonesia's violent history of deep social and political conflict.

Calls to "straighten out" the history of G30S/PKI (the September 30 Movement/Indonesian Communist Party), the alleged coup attempt that was blamed on the Indonesian Communist Party and became the pretext for the killing of at least a half million alleged communists in the years 1965–1967, received a far more ambivalent reaction. For the most part, public discussions of the historical controversy of G30S/PKI remained narrowly focused on the events of the night of September 30 and on the identity of the mastermind of the coup attempt (see *Bernas*, September 29, 1999, September 30, 1999; *Kedaulatan Rakyat*, October 2, 1999). As with the "controversies" of Supersemar and the General Attack, the post-Suharto rewriting of G30S/PKI often simply inverted the terms of New Order discourse in its search for the *dalang* (shadow puppeteer) behind the event, reducing complex social and historical processes to a problem of authorship. Although Suharto had branded the PKI the dalang of the coup attempt, now the implication was that Suharto himself had masterminded the coup. Just as New Order historical accounts and commemorations had obsessively retold the story of the coup attempt while remaining silent about the killings that followed, so these attempts to uncover the conspiracy behind the September 30 Movement deflected attention away from the far more challenging task of accounting for and acknowledging the vast numbers killed and wrongfully imprisoned in its aftermath.[13]

But when historians called for a reevaluation of the historical record of the killings (*Kedaulatan Rakyat*, October 2, 1999) and former political prisoners began to insist that their suppressed accounts be heard, efforts to rewrite history—and to produce new documents in the form of memoirs (Latief 2000; Sulami 1999) and forensic evidence—were met with hostility from a variety of quarters. Islamic groups and New Order political and military figures directly involved in the purges issued warnings against efforts by "communists" to "overturn the facts of G/30S proven by history" and spark a new communist movement (*Bernas*, March 18, 2000; *Kedaulatan Rakyat*, March 20, 2000; *Kompas*, April 22, 1999). Ominous suggestions that a desire for "revenge" animated these calls to rewrite history replayed New Order narratives about the cyclical recurrence of communist rebellion conceived as a generational family affair (*Bernas*, April 27, 1999; *Kompas*, October 26, 1999). This notion of regenerating generational violence had legitimized the state's discriminatory practices against entire families of those implicated in the alleged coup and helped make plausible the idea of the "latent danger" of communism so often mobilized by the New Order regime against its enemies.[14]

In April 1999, Sulami, a former political prisoner, formally established the Organization to Investigate the Victims of Murder of 1965–1966 (Yayasan Penelitian Korban Pembunuhan 1965–1966, or YPKP).[15] This organization was dedicated to documenting human rights abuses against alleged communists and to finding mass graves and other evidence of massacres. The history that the YPKP sought to document could not be reduced to a single author or a singular event. It implicated both the army and large groups of civilians (often organized religious organizations) as perpetrators, involved hundreds of thousands of victims, and occurred over an extended period. In searching for mass graves located in rural areas, rather than singular, authored documents, YPKP sought a kind of material historical evidence that could not easily be disentangled from wider social entailments.

Moreover, YPKP's emphasis was not on recovery of lost documents but on filling in the gaps of a fundamentally undocumented history by generating a new archive of New Order abuses. Such efforts, articulated primarily in the idiom of human rights and led by a former political prisoner, were immediately perceived as interested or "political," rather than falling within the ideally neutral domain of historical inquiry. To counter the perception that they were a political group, members of YPKP repeatedly appealed to the legitimated and depoliticized discourse on straightening out history. Rather than seek to "give rise to a communist movement," they promised, their goal was simply to help in "the writing of Indonesian history" (*Kedaulatan Rakyat*, October 4, 1999; see also *Jateng Pos*, October 5, 1999). In one instance, the Purbalingga branch of YPKP brought 440 former political prisoners to the regional parliament to request rehabilitation and compensation; the organization had had them fill out forms documenting their experiences. The head of the local organization insisted that the goal of this activity was "not political" but "humanitarian" and historical: "The long-term goal of YPKP is to give information that is correct about events during the years of 65/66 to the next generation. They need to know that there are many manipulated histories that have to be straightened out in the opening up of this incident" (*Kedaulatan Rakyat*, April 1, 2000). Despite these attempts to cast YPKP's work in this legitimated and safe idiom, the hostile reaction to its efforts suggests the limits, when confronted with a truly divisive, unresolved past, of an ideology that treated documents as nonpartisan resources to be mined for an ideally neutral and uncontroversial national history.

ARCHIVING THE FUTURE PAST

Whereas some post-Suharto historical discussions were oriented to the past, many imagined the present as an endangered future history. Here, the question of historical documents was treated as a problem of resource conservation and management. Where were vital national historical resources to be housed, who would control access to them, and who was to be charged with their preservation? Amid heightened attention to New Order manipulations of the past and sensitive to the widespread destruction of documents that had accompanied the transition to the New Order, many expressed concern about archiving the present for the benefit of the future. The fear that archives might not be "safe" sites of storage was in part a response to the material conditions of state archives and libraries, where lack of funding and infrastructural supports such as air-conditioning and trained personnel left microfilms to succumb to the ravages of mold, acidic papers to crumble into dust, and documents to be stored in haphazard fashion. But the primary concern was their vulnerability to political manipulation and erasure. One newspaper article noted, "In order to avoid there being efforts to obscure and manipulate the facts of the history of Indonesia, the archival documents from the period of the New Order government...and the Reformasi Cabinet have to be safeguarded" (*Kedaulatan Rakyat*, January 30, 2000).[16]

Anxious to recover their authority and overcome their discredited status as pliant servants of political power, state archival institutions were quick to reassert their role as the (professional and therefore politically neutral) custodians of national history. The head of the Office of the National Archive of Central Java expressed hope that by properly archiving Reformasi documents, "the course of history of the Indonesian people won't be lost" (*Bernas*, February 14, 2000). Mukhlis Paeni, director of the national archive in Jakarta, who spearheaded the highly public search for Supersemar, warned of the danger facing Indonesian history in this moment of transition. Noting that "there is a tendency among the people and government agencies to erase their tracks [*menghilangkan jejak*] by burning a number of documents," he observed: "If we are not quick to chase down [documents produced during the New Order] we will lose that evidence [bukti] of the history of this people" (*Bernas*, July 9, 1999).

The national archive and other state-run historical institutions also sought to collect materials from private individuals that could be transformed, through relocation in state archives, into resources for national history. For example, a letter of July 1998 from the head of the Benteng Vredeberg Museum in Yogyakarta, a museum dedicated to the history of the national struggle (*perjuangan*), requested permission from the Department of Education and Culture to collect from the public "priceless" "historical documents" pertaining to "the change of era from the New Order...to the era of Reformasi" (Budihardja 1998):

> [The] Museum Benteng Vredeberg Yogyakarta, as one of the institutions given the task of gathering, taking care of, studying and communicating historical materials to the public, hopes that public figures [*tokoh-tokoh*], freedom fighters [*pejuang*], heads of

> organizations/agencies and the general public will be so kind as
> to give reformasi documents, posters, photos and banners that
> remain and that form authentic proof of the course of an event
> in the history of the life course of the Indonesian state, so that
> these can become part of the material collection of the history of
> the struggle of the nation.(Budihardja 1998)

Embodied in such efforts to collect materials from the public was a vision
of state-run institutions, guided by ideally neutral expert-professionals acting as the guardians of national history.

DREAMS OF THE PUBLIC ARCHIVE: POPULAR
PRACTICES OF DOCUMENTATION AND WITNESSING

Yet among students, journalists, and middle-class intellectuals and
activists, a desire to break the state's monopoly on history and an interest
in more open, public archives had also taken hold. Popular practices of
documentation were celebrated as the key to securing the future history of
the present and, more broadly, a genuinely democratic society. Indeed, the
recording and anticipated recollection of Reformasi were integral to the
movement itself.[17] Student photographers began documenting their
demonstrations against the Suharto regime in late 1997 and early 1998,
convinced that the mainstream press, still constrained by official censorship, would never cover the violence directed at them and fearful that their
struggle might be disappeared from the historical record. Students often
spoke of their images as historical documents (*dokumentasi sejarah*) that
would serve as "authentic proof," an antidote to the Suharto's regime's
"thirty-two years of lies" and a guarantee that future regimes could not
efface or distort the history of the student movement. Following the relax-
ation of press controls after Suharto's resignation, images of Reformasi
demonstrations flooded the public domain via television, newspapers,
visual chronicles of Reformasi, calendars, and photo exhibitions. The experience of consuming these photographs of political violence and demonstrations—"authentic data [*data otentik*] for today's generation and the
future"—ratified the public's sense of participation in a new era of openness and freedom (*Kedaulatan Rakyat*, December 20, 1998).

Given the importance of "transparency" as a governing trope of
Reformasi, it is little surprise that photographs were particularly privileged
documents (Strassler 2004). Articulating this sense of the superior value of
photographic documentation, a student photographer told me: "That is

the power of photography, it can become a historical file....If you see a photograph, you straight away know, the history was like that. It was just like that, the event." Students and other commentators on photographs of the Reformasi demonstrations often celebrated their inherent truthfulness as "objective facts," in explicit contrast to written words, which were deemed more vulnerable to corruption, manipulation, and propaganda. Writings on Reformasi photo exhibitions echoed these assumptions: "Photos are valued for their straightforwardness [*kejujuran*], because photos do not bear words. Precisely because of this, [photos] are more able to express an event just as it is" (*Solo Pos*, October 26, 1999). Another critic reviewing an exhibition wrote:

> If what one searches for is black-on-white proof [*bukti*] for the validity [*keabsahan*] of something, the fifty-seven black-and-white photographs that are shown [in this exhibit] form mute witnesses [*saksi-saksi*] of a new historical era of this republic....This is the black and white of history. Not like the empty word-spewing tongues of leaders [*tokoh*]...which can glitter [*berkelit*], turn facts inside out, and make meaning follow the dominant wave. (*Suara Pembaruan*, July 5, 1998)

Here, it was the black and white of the photograph, rather than the printed page, that was imagined to provide reliable documentary proof.

Frequently, exhibition catalogs, newspaper articles, and other statements accompanying displays of Reformasi photographs emphasized that the images now on view had formerly been secreted away in private collections, unable, because of censorship, to be published during Suharto's rule. The flyer for one exhibit of a photojournalist's photographs noted that because many of the images could not be published when they were first taken, they had "entered into [the photographer's] private documentation."[18] Another exhibition showed both contemporary photojournalism and photographs from the 1960s and 1970s; its promotional material likewise emphasized that many of the photographs had languished in private collections.[19] As one organizer of the exhibition told me, by showing "these historical witnessings...we want to reopen the album of history." This notion of release from the realm of the private into public exposure lent an aura of Reformasi authenticity to the exhibitions; it also echoed the discourse surrounding the hoped-for recovery of documents such as Supersemar. Imagined to be secreted away in private hands, these documents would be transformed into resources for national history by their public release. Their proper home would not be the files of the national archive but a more diffused, extrastate, public location in the institutions of the newly free press.[20]

These imaginings of photographs as resources for a future history of the present, like the effort to "straighten out history" by recovering lost documents, displaced the work of historical representation onto a fetishized material form that seemed to promise a stable locus of truth and transparent access to the past. But the emphasis on *popular acts* of documentation and witnessing also articulated a vision of history distinct from the documentary fetish animating the search for Supersemar and the author of the General Attack of March 1, 1949. Students and journalists saw themselves as participants in the making of a vast, multiply authored photographic archive. Those attending the exhibitions repeatedly remarked on the images' status as material for a new kind of history that would no longer be subject to state control. As one visitor jotted in a comment book: "Have these exhibitions often so that the Indonesian people's history will no longer be monopolized." Another commentator at a screening of videotapes of Reformasi demonstrations articulated a sense of urgency about gathering up otherwise dispersed and private acts of seeing into one publicly accessible archive of Reformasi witnessing: "This video, this witnessing...is only from one set of eyes. That has to be stressed. There are still many witnessings that have to be witnessed...it will be richer, and the public will know more, if we are open to other witnessings, too." Such commentaries articulated an emerging vision of a history located outside the state. Generated and disseminated by students and journalists, this history would be authenticated by ordinary people through acts of public witnessing.

THE ART OF CLIPPING

In November 1999, an artist named Wary Wirana exhibited large-scale collages made from newspaper clippings—he called them clipping art—at a major cultural institution in Yogyakarta (figure 9.2). In the catalog to the exhibition, titled *The Tragedy of Democracy*, Wary Wirana wrote:

> The weakness of our people that is most fundamental is a result of not wanting to "study history." History up to this point has only been read as memorization, not studied as a past that has a connection with the present and the future. As a result, history always repeats itself as events whose faces and shapes are different, but whose substance is the same. Thus while many other peoples are already at the stage of "free people," we are still known as a clump of humanity that is "still uncivilized."

FIGURE 9.2

Wary Wirana with one of his "clipping art" collages, Solo, April 2000 (courtesy Karen Strassler).

Echoing Dr. Faruk, the literary critic quoted earlier in this chapter, Wary Wirana linked Indonesia's "still uncivilized" (*masih biadab*) status to a failure of historical consciousness.[21] In an interview, he elaborated: "We are very much behind the Western world. Because we are weak in documentation. We are just beginning to document." But, he went on, Indonesia is transitioning from an era of "closed documentation" to one of "open documentation"—an era of what he called naked history (*sejarah telanjang*). Whereas Faruk attributed Indonesian forgetting to technological lack, Wary Wirana proposed "clipping" as the solution. His collages of clipped images, headlines, and articles aimed to counter the instant obsolescence of information in the news media, pull thematic threads from its cacophonous disorder, and promote reflection. As his exhibition pamphlet noted, the goal was thereby "to strengthen awareness of history."

Wary Wirana's clipping art had ironic precedents in New Order historiographic practices. Learning to present neatly glued and properly labeled clippings (*kliping*) once formed an integral part of formal education from elementary through high school in Indonesian classrooms.[22] Reading the press as a public archive in order to read against the grain of state narratives was precisely what Indonesian schoolchildren were taught *not* to do in these assignments. Under conditions of a censored press and controlled public discourse and in a classroom environment in which there was a "right" answer to all questions, clipping tended to be a tautological exercise in confirming official narratives. Museums and state agencies even sponsored "clipping contests" in commemoration of various events in national history.[23] Clipping thus taught history as a practice of quoting from authoritative sources, in which the students' engagement was not with content but with form; the main criteria for judging student clippings seems to have been how neat they were. But the success of such pedagogical strategies is always uncertain. Wary Wirana emphasized that he began to make his clipping art in 1997, well before Suharto's fall; his point was that even under conditions of censorship, the press treated as a public archive can have counterhegemonic effects.

Wirana's project sought to halt the incessant, amnesia-producing "flow of information" in the press. Clipping, he believed, would engender new habits of historical awareness by keeping issues in the public eye. "If these were hung in schools," he told me, gesturing to the collages on the walls, "every day [students] would see this open documentation, which in a direct way would strengthen their 'memory' [*memori*] or recollection [*ingatan*]." He went on: "Most people's critical feelings will be awakened if every day they are aroused [*greget*]. Which is what we hope will come from open documentation. Photographs, clippings." Set apart and accorded the status of documents, collected and visually juxtaposed, clippings accumulate discursive and affective power, creating a more lasting impact than the fleeting impressions of the ephemeral media. Through extended exposure, public events become embedded in collectively shared but individually inscribed memories. "When it is shown in a visual way as a work of art," Wirana wrote in his pamphlet, "it is hoped that it can arouse people to make demands based on facts that are factual and 'authentic' [*fakta-fakta yang faktual dan 'otentik'*]."

Wirana conceived his art of "open documentation" as a way not only to put history on public view but also to elicit popular participation in its making. With clipping art, "everyone can be an artist," he told me, envisioning a future in which Indonesians would actively create their own thematically organized and publicly displayed clippings. Wary Wirana's dream of a future of open documentation and historical awareness exemplifies hopes lodged in popular *practices* of documentation as a means of bringing about a more participatory future and points to the crucial role of the newly free press in fostering the utopian visions of a post-Suharto history. Here, the free press is imagined as the ideal resource for an "open" history. No longer defined by singularity, originality, and authorship, the authenticity of these "documents" (which, as clippings, are always already copies) derives from their availability for popular collection and display.

CONCLUSION: LIMITS OF HISTORY

In post-Suharto Indonesia, documents and documentary practices offered both imaginative and material resources for diverse engagements with the problem of history. Appeals to documents as resources for a new history registered both the profound anxieties and the optimism unleashed by the new climate of political openness. The treatment of documents as scarce and valuable national resources could, on the one hand, perpetuate the idea that history might be "straightened out"—that controversy and indeterminacy might ultimately be resolved and that history itself might be returned from the unruly domain of public discourse into the authoritative hands of state institutions and experts. But others—artists, journalists, students, activists—imagined documents as a sustainable resource that promised a more inclusive, participatory history. Rather than fantasize locating historical truth in the form of a singular, authoritative document, they envisioned the emergence of a new, participatory public realm characterized by popular practices of documenting and witnessing history.

These imaginings of history were prompted not only by the content of particular documents but also by their form and material "disposition" (Hull 2003). The material conditions of historical documents as objects—handwritten or signed, printed or copied, photographic or textual, public or secret, manipulated or pristine, durable or fragile, lost or recovered—are central to the signifying work they do, whether the documents in question actually exist or are merely imagined to, whether those who debate them so passionately actually hold them in their hands or merely invoke them as possible anchors for the unstable ground of history in a time of political transition. Conceived as precious resources to be mined for rewriting the past, endangered resources to be conserved for a future history of the present, national resources rescued from private interests, and public resources to be developed for the benefit of future generations, documents held the key to a new democratic future founded on a new relationship to history.

The post-Suharto debates about history circulated widely within the discursive spaces opened up by new freedoms of expression, forming a lively debate in the press and in some public arenas. A final anecdote suggests the limits of these documentary dreams, however. On June 7, 1999, the day of Indonesia's first free elections since 1955, a friend and I rode around on a motorcycle to different polling places to sense people's moods as they placed their votes. Both of us carried cameras. At one polling station in a quiet neighborhood, a middle-aged man wearing a sarong and faded button-down shirt asked us what we were doing. My friend, a middle-class college graduate, conspicuous in this conservative neighborhood for his longish hair, explained that he was taking pictures because "this is part of our history [*sejarah*]." He used the inclusive form of *our* [*kita*], invoking his and the man's common ownership of national history. But the man rejected this inclusion as he affirmed a lingering New Order ideology in which "the masses" stand apart from the national elite, whose task it is to steward the nation on its journey. He slapped his forehead with his palm as he burst out laughing: "History! As far as documentation, we still...we don't think of it....We, the little people [*wong cilik*], we just think about the economy....History doesn't even occur to us!" Implicit in his statement was an assertion of a different temporal orientation: "your" concern with the nation's past and its future, he seemed to be saying, is a luxury "we"—caught in the more urgent present of need—cannot afford.

Notes

An earlier draft of this chapter was presented at the Association of Asian Studies meetings in Washington, DC, April 2001. Henk Schulte Nordholt, Webb Keane, and Patricia Spyer, as well as members of the audience, offered valuable comments and critiques. For their insightful readings of more recent drafts, thanks are due to Jennifer Cole, Kenneth George, Smita Lahiri, Ann-Marie Leshkowich, Janet McIntosh, Mary Steedly, Ann Laura Stoler, Ajantha Subramanian, and Christine Walley. I am also grateful to the members of the SAR advanced seminar, Paul Eiss, Elizabeth Ferry, Richard Handler, Mandana Limbert, Celia Lowe, Erik Mueggler, and Paul Nadasdy, for their excellent comments. I am solely responsible for the chapter's limitations.

1. Reformasi was a student-led movement for reform that culminated in Suharto's resignation. I use the term "immediate post-Suharto period" to refer to the period of transitional governments between 1998 and 2001, led first by Suharto's protégé and vice president, B. J. Habibie (May 1998–October 1999), followed by Abdurrachman Wahid (also known as Gus Dur; October 1990–July 2001). This chapter draws on articles from newspapers published in the Javanese city of Yogyakarta

(*Kedaulatan Rakyat, Bernas*), as well as regional and national newspapers collected during my fieldwork in Yogyakarta between November 1998 and May 2000 and during a subsequent research trip in 2004. On the press in Indonesia, see Romano 2003 and Sen and Hill 2000. Numerous scholars within and outside Indonesia have written on the state of history in the New Order and post-Suharto efforts to rewrite it. On the latter, see Curaming 2003; Karsono 2005; Klinken 2005; Purwanto 2006; Schulte Nordholt 2004. I have focused here not on the many academic articles and conference papers produced by Indonesian historians in the aftermath of Suharto's rule but on press reporting on various historical controversies, because my interest is in how questions of history were disseminated to a broader Indonesian public under new conditions of press freedom. On nationalist history in Indonesia, see Leigh 1991; McGregor 2007; Reid 1979; Soedjatmoko 1960. As Karsono (2005) points out, it would be wrong to suggest that debates about "straightening out" history began with the demise of the New Order; attempts to rectify history and accusations of falsification and distortion are as old as the republic itself and have flared particularly in other periods of regime change.

2. On the problem of historical "awareness" and "confusion" about history, see *Bernas*, March 23, 2000; see also the formation of the Team for the Straightening Out of History and Values of Struggle (Tim Pelurusan Sejarah dan Nilai-Nilai Perjuangan) in Jakarta, calling for misguided history books to be taken out of circulation (*Kedaulatan Rakyat*, March 27, 2000).

3. On documents as "artifacts of modern knowledge" and markers of modern statecraft, see Riles 2006. There is, of course, a long genealogy linking documentary bureaucratic practices to the emergence of modern states, leading back to Weber (1968). For further discussion of "developmental national time" in Indonesia, see Lowe, chapter 5.

4. On the 1965 alleged coup attempt, see Anderson, McVey, and Bunnell 1971; Cribb 1990; Crouch 1978; Roosa 2006.

5. According to another article, the archive holds four copies of the manuscript. One was published by the Pusat Penerangan Angkatan Darat (Center of Intelligence for the Armed Services); another was published by the State Department. Between just those two manuscripts, there are twenty-five differences in content, typing, commas, spelling, and the signature (*Kompas*, March 17, 2000; see also February 9, 2001).

6. In 1998 Wilardjito, a former adjutant of Sukarno, came forward to say that he had been present at the signing of Supersemar and that the generals bearing the document had pulled guns on Sukarno, forcing him to sign. Wilardjito was promptly sued by the police for "spreading lies"; his case was taken up by the Yogyakarta Legal Aid Society and received heavy coverage in the local press. See, for example, *Bernas*,

July 26, 1999, July 28, 1999, September 6, 1999, March 12, 2000; *Kedaulatan Rakyat*, June 3, 1999, August 25, 1999, March 13, 2000.

7. There are also questions about how the original document was reproduced. Although one witness claims that the document was brought to an army office and "multiplied" (*diperbanyak*), it is unlikely that the office in question had a photocopy machine at the time. See *Kompas*, March 8, 2000.

8. Emphasis on "authentic documents" (as well as public concerns about manipulated or manufactured documentary evidence) was clearly a feature of New Order historical discourse as well. On the questioning of Sukarno's authorship of Pancasila—the state ideology—see Brooks 1995. The crisis of September 30, 1965, was itself precipitated in part, in the weeks prior to the alleged coup attempt, by the circulation of the "Gilchrist document," a document of uncertain authenticity, allegedly leaked from the British embassy. This suggested that an anticommunist group of generals sympathetic to the United States and Britain aimed to overthrow Sukarno.

9. The controversy continued well past the immediate post-Suharto period under discussion in this chapter. But it seemed to be on the verge of ending in April 2005, when the family of General M. Jusuf, who had been present at Bogor on March 11 and who died in September 2004, announced that the original document was in the family's possession, kept in storage in an undisclosed bank. Yet amid assurances that the "misteri" of Supersemar would now be resolved, remaining some questions suggested that the controversy was not about to end after all: the authenticity of the document had not yet been checked, the "original" document might turn out to be a carbon copy [*tembusan*] or a photocopy, and those commenting on its enormous significance for the history of Indonesia had not actually seen it yet. The contents of the document, it was promised, would be revealed in a forthcoming book, composed by several prominent historians (see *Jawa Pos*, April 5, 2005; *Kedaulatan Rakyat*, April 6, 2005; *Kompas*, April 5, 2005).

10. The law in question is UU 11/1974, cited in *Kedaulatan Rakyat*, June 3, 1999. Other articles cite a 1971 law on archives (UU 7/1971) (*Bernas*, March 2, 2000; *Kompas*, March 3, 2000).

11. Films were an important element in the arsenal of New Order official histories. Most influential was the government-sponsored docudrama on the 1965 "coup"— *G30S/Pengkhianatan PKI* (*The September 30 Movement/Communist Treason*), which first appeared in 1985 and was aired on television on the anniversary of the alleged coup every year until 1998.

12. None of the reports gives a specific date for the interview, but one describes it as from the 1980s (*Kompas*, March 11, 2000).

13. The appeals to documentary evidence so prevalent in the discussions of

Supersemar and the General Attack, moreover, were relatively absent from public discourse on G30S/PKI. Ironically, key documents related to the coup attempt that could have been called upon to "straighten out" this history do exist. These include autopsy reports on the murdered generals, which clearly indicate that they were not sexually tortured and thereby challenge one of the most inflammatory accusations in New Order accounts of the alleged communist coup attempt (Anderson 1987). Several articles do mention the autopsy reports (for example, *Bernas*, September 29, 1999). Nevertheless, another article in the same newspaper recounts the old story that the generals were "kidnapped and then sadistically tortured" and describes President Habibie's commemorative visit to a diorama showing the torture of the generals (*Bernas*, October 20, 1999).

14. The uproar that greeted (and defeated) President Wahid's attempt to revoke a 1966 law banning the teaching of Marxist-Leninist ideas illustrated how much the specter of communism remained a potent political weapon. On the threat of communism making a "comeback," see *Jateng Pos*, October 4, 1999; *Kedaulatan Rakyat*, October 2, 1999, October 5, 1999, October 20, 2000, March 31, 1999, and April 8, 2000. Additionally, radical student activists and progressive political groups such as the People's Democratic Party (PRD) were continually compared to the Communist Party, alongside dire reminders that "as can be seen from the course of Indonesian history, communist movements will arise every thirty years" (*Kedaulatan Rakyat*, October 8, 1999).

15. Sulami had been an officer in Gerwani (Gerakan Wanita Indonesia, or the Women's Movement of Indonesia), an organization affiliated with the Communist Party and particularly demonized in the aftermath of the events of September 30–October 1, 1965. On the history of Gerwani and representations of the coup, see Wieringa 2002.

16. On the intentional destruction of documents during the 1960s, see *Kompas*, February 9, 2001; *Tempo*, October 21–27, 2003.

17. See Eiss's similar argument that "'event-making' might take place in advance of the event itself, shaping its commitment to memory before and during its occurrence as much as in its aftermath" (2002b:108). For more extensive discussion of the phenomenon of student photography during Reformasi, see Strassler 2003, 2005.

18. The "Kesaksianku [My Witnessing]" exhibition (February 9–14, 1999, Yogyakarta) showed the photographs of *Kedaulatan Rakyat* photojournalist Eko Boediantoro.

19. "Presenting Three Orders of Yogyakarta–Solo Photojournalists" (April 10–18, 1999) was sponsored by photojournalists representing Yogyakarta and Solo newspapers. The exhibition displayed photographs from the "three orders" of postcolonial

Indonesian history: Sukarno's Old Order, Suharto's New Order, and the Reformasi era.

20. The idea of a "free" press had enormous symbolic weight as a marker of Reformasi's achievements and a new era. In practice, the press of the post-Suharto era has come under new forms of extrastate censorship, such as violent attacks by extremist religious groups and hired thugs (defending the interests of officials and businessmen accused of corruption).

21. *Biadab* also means "uncultured," "uneducated," "barbaric," or "savage."

22. One third-grade textbook contains this assignment: "Collect photographs of heroes. Then put them into groups, Revolutionary Heroes and National Heroes" (Tim Penulis Buku Prestasi 1989:43). A textbook for eighth graders assigns students to clip images about the Communist Party from newspapers, magazines, or books and to write an explanation of the images (Tim Penyusun Sejarah 1995:169). Another textbook calls on students to put together an album of photographs about "development activities in different regions" (Rasita et al. 1991:109).

23. See, for example, *Kedaulatan Rakyat*, September 20, 1990, July 19, 1992.

References

ARCHIVAL REFERENCES

Archivo General del Estado de Yucatán—Colonial, Tierras (AGEY-C)

1815   Informe que hace el procurador de los naturales Agustín Crespo ante el gobernador sobre el litigio de tierras entre los pueblos de Umán y Abalá. Caja 31, vol. 1, exp. 20, f. 14r–17v.

Archivo General del Estado de Yucatán—Justicia (AGEY-J)

1853   Queja de George Uc contra el juez de paz segundo de Tetiz, D. Anastacio Castilla. Caja 56, exp. 41.

1856a   Causa por acusación de Doña Juana Peña contra el casique Pascual Chac. Caja 78, exp. 20.

1856b   Queja contra el juez de paz 1 de Hunucmá Don Deciderio Escalante por abuso de autoridad. Caja 77, exp. 14.

1857   Causa seguida al cacique de Hunucmá Pascual Chac por talar un monte propiedad de Juana Peña. Caja 80, exp. 50.

1861   Diligencias contra el juez de paz de Kinchil por abusos de autoridad. Caja 95, exp. 62.

1889   Diligencias muerte de Ricardo Aguilar Brito. 170-C, reel 244.

1891   Expediente formado con motivo de un oficio del C. Gobernador del estado, acompañando un número de "La Revista de Mérida" en que se denuncian varios abusos cometidos en algunas fincas rústicas del C. José D. Rivero Figueroa. Caja 7, exp. 26.

1892   Causa seguida a Isidro Tzuc y socios, por homicidio y lesiones inferidas a Hilario Sosa. Caja 16, exp. 29.

1893   Causa seguida a Florentino Poot por incendio y homicidio. Caja 23, exp. 23.

Archivo General del Estado de Yucatán—Poder Ejecutivo, Gobernación (AGEY-PE-G)

1915   José Pío Chuc et al. to Exmo. Señor Gobernador, May 2, 1915. Box 479.

Archivo General del Estado de Yucatán—Poder Ejecutivo, Tierras (AGEY-PE-T)

1837   Información de la república de indígenas del pueblo de Kinchil, en justificación de los perjuicios por la mensura de las tierras concedidas al C. Felipe Peña. Caja 38, vol. 1, exp. 32.

Archivo General de la Nación—Bienes nacionales (AGN-B)

1819   Petición de justicia de los naturales para que se les pague la madera para construcción de casa que venden al convent. Vol. 26, exp. 55, f. 19–20.

REFERENCES

Archivo General de la Nación—Tierras (AGN-T)

1815   Transunto de un convenio de uso común de tierras entre Umán, Chocholá, Abalá y las parcialidades de Dzibikal, Dzibikak, y Abalá, 15 de marzo de 1815. Vol. 1419, exp. 2, f. 56r–v.

1819   Venta de tierras realangas denunciadas por don Julián del Castillo y Cámara. Vol. 1421, exp. 13.

Archivo de la Secretaría de la Reforma Agraria (ASRA)

1937   Lázaro Cárdenas, Resolución Presidencial, September 16, 1937. Hunucmá, Expediente de Dotación.

Foreign Office

1905   Shi Hongshao to *waiwubu*. Public Records Office, Kew. FO 228/1604.

1906   Report by Mr. Litton (sent home by Mr. Ottewill) on Journey from Tengyueh to Upper Salwen. Public Records Office, Kew. FO 881/8682.

India Office Records Archive

Muscat State Affairs Including Boundaries, Subsidies, Tariffs, Visits, Treaties, Supply of Arms and Ammunition. Gulf States: Records of the Bushire, Bahrain, Kuwait, Muscat and Trucial States Agencies 1763–1951. British Library, London.

Royal Botanic Garden

1913   Forrest to Williams, July 17, George Forrest Collection, Edinburgh.

1917a   Forrest to Smith, July. George Forrest Collection, Edinburgh.

1917b   Forrest to Balfour, November 1. George Forrest Collection, Edinburgh.

1918a   Forrest to Balfour, July 7, George Forrest Collection, Edinburgh.

1918b   Forrest to Balfour, May 2, George Forrest Collection, Edinburgh.

1918c   Forrest to Chittenden, June 20, George Forrest Collection, Edinburgh.

1918d   Forrest to Balfour, March 26, George Forrest Collection, Edinburgh.

1918e   Forrest to Chittenden, August 25, George Forrest Collection, Edinburgh.

1919a   Forrest to Williams, July 31, George Forrest Collection, Edinburgh.

1919b   Forrest to Chittenden, August 23, George Forrest Collection, Edinburgh.

1921a   Forrest to Smith, August 19, George Forrest Collection, Edinburgh.

1921b   Forrest to Balfour, August 30, George Forrest Collection, Edinburgh.

1921c   Forrest to Balfour, September 3, George Forrest Collection, Edinburgh.

1921d   Forrest to Cory, September 7, George Forrest Collection, Edinburgh.

1922a   Forrest to Balfour, March 23, George Forrest Collection, Edinburgh.

1922b   Forrest to Cory, August 4, George Forrest Collection, Edinburgh.

BOOKS AND OTHER REFERENCES

Adler, Judith

2006   Cultivating Wilderness: Environmentalism and Legacies of Early Christian Asceticism. Comparative Studies in Society and History 48(1):4–37.

Alexander's Gas and Oil Connection

2003   Omani Oil Production Falls despite Increase in Reserves. Electronic document, http://www.gasandoil.com/goc/news/ntm33632.htm, accessed December 6, 2007.

Alonso, Ana María

1994   The Politics of Space, Time and Substance: State Formation, Nationalism and Ethnicity. Annual Review of Anthropology 23:379–405.

Anderson, Benedict

1983   Imagined Communities: Reflections on the Origin and Spread of Nationalism. London: Verso.

1987   How Did the Generals Die? Indonesia 43:109–113.

1990   A Time of Darkness and a Time of Light: Transposition in Early Indonesian Nationalist Thought. *In* Language and Power: Exploring Political Cultures in Indonesia. Ithaca, NY: Cornell University Press.

1991   Imagined Communities: Reflections on the Origin and Spread of Nationalism. Rev. edition. New York: Verso.

2003a   ANP Position Papers. Electronic document, http://web.uvic.ca/~anp/Public/posish_pap.html, accessed December 6, 2007.

2003b   Responses. *In* Grounds of Comparison: Around the Work of Benedict Anderson. Jonathan Culler and Pheng Cheah, eds. Pp. 225–246. London: Routledge.

Anderson, Benedict R. O'G., Ruth McVey, and Frederick Bunnel

1971   A Preliminary Analysis of the October 1, 1965, Coup in Indonesia. Interim Report Series. Ithaca, NY: Cornell Modern Indonesia Project.

Appadurai, Arjun

1981   The Past as a Scarce Resource. Man 16(2):201–19.

1986   The Social Life of Things: Commodities in Cultural Perspective. Cambridge: Cambridge University Press.

Asad, Talal

1987   Are There Histories of People without Europe? Comparative Studies in Society and History 29(3):594–607.

Asch, Michael

1989   Wildlife: Defining the Animals the Dene Hunt and the Settlement of Aboriginal Rights Claims. Canadian Public Policy 15(2):205–219.

ASPO USA

2007   2007 Houston World Oil Conference. Electronic document, http://www.aspousa.org/aspousa3/index.cfm, accessed December 6, 2007.

Austen, Jane

1992[1811]   Sense and Sensibility. New York: Knopf.

Axel, Brian, ed.

2002   From the Margins: Historical Anthropology and Its Futures. Durham, NC: Duke University Press.

REFERENCES

Ayers, Edward
1984   Vengeance and Justice: Crime and Punishment in the Nineteenth-Century
        American South. New York: Oxford University Press.

Badrika, Wayan
1997   Sejarah Nasional Indonesia dan Umum. Vol. 3. Jakarta: Penerbit Erlangga.

Baños Ramírez, Othón
1990   Yucatán: Ejidos sin campesinos. Mérida, Mexico: Ediciones de la Universidad
        Autónoma de Yucatán.
1996   Neoliberalismo, reorganización y subsistencia rural: El caso de la zona
        henequenera de Yucatán, 1980–1992. Mérida, Mexico: Universidad Autónoma
        de Yucatán.

Barkan, Elazar, and Ronald Bush
1995   Prehistories of the Future: The Primitivist Project and the Culture of
        Modernism. Stanford, CA: Stanford University Press.

Baudrillard, Jean
1994   The Illusion of the End. Stanford, CA: Stanford University Press.

Benjamin, Thomas
2000   La Revolución: Mexico's Great Revolution as Memory, Myth and History.
        Austin: University of Texas Press.

Benjamin, Walter
1968   Illuminations: Essays and Reflections. Edited and with an introduction by
        Hannah Arendt. Harry Zohn, trans. New York: Schocken Books.
1999   Unpacking My Library: A Talk about Collecting. *In* Walter Benjamin, Selected
        Writings. Michael W. Jennings, Howard Eiland, and Gary Smith, eds. Pp.
        486–493. Cambridge, MA: Harvard University Press.

Bergson, Henri
1910   Time and Free Will: An Essay on the Immediate Data of Consciousness.
        F. L. Pogson, trans. New York: Macmillan.

Berlant, Lauren
1996   The Face of America and the State of Emergency. *In* Disciplinarity and Dissent
        in Cultural Studies. Cary Nelson and Dilip Parameshwar Gaonkar, eds. Pp.
        397–440. New York: Routledge.

Berman, Marshall
1982   All That Is Solid Melts into Air: The Experience of Modernity. New York:
        Simon and Schuster.

Birth, Kevin
1999   Any Time Is Trinidad Time. Gainesville: University Press of Florida.
2004   Finding Time: Studying the Concepts of Time Used in Daily Life. Field
        Methods 16(1):70–84.
2006   The Immanent Past: Culture and Psyche at the Juncture of Memory and
        History. Special issue, Ethos 34(2):169–191.

Blaikie, Piers M., and H. Brookfield, eds.

1987   Land Degradation and Society. London: Methuen.

Bloch, Maurice

1977   The Past and the Present in the Present. Man, n.s., 12:278–92.

Bourdieu, Pierre

1963   The Attitude of the Algerian Peasant toward Time. *In* Mediterranean Countrymen. J. Pitt-Rivers, ed. Pp. 55–72. Westport, CT: Greenwood.

1977   Outline of a Theory of Practice. R. Nice, trans. Cambridge: Cambridge University Press.

Boyarin, Jonathan

1994   Remapping Memory: The Politics of Timespace. Minneapolis: University of Minnesota Press.

Bracamonte y Sosa, Pedro

1994   La memoria enclaustrada: Historia indígena de Yucatán, 1750–1915. Mexico City: CIESAS.

2003   Los mayas y la tierra: La propiedad indígena en el Yucatán colonial. Mexico City: Miguel Angel Porrua.

Brading, David

1971   Miners and Merchants in Bourbon Mexico, 1763–1810. Cambridge: Cambridge University Press.

Braun, Bruce, and Noel Castree, eds.

1998   Remaking Reality: Nature at the Millennium. New York: Routledge.

Bricker, Victoria

1981   The Indian Christ, the Indian King: The Historical Substrate of Maya Myth and Ritual. Austin: University of Texas Press.

Brightman, Robert

1987   Conservation and Resource Depletion: The Case of the Boreal Forest Algonquians. *In* The Question of the Commons: The Culture and Ecology of Communal Resources. B. McCay and M. Acheson, eds. Pp. 121–141. Tucson: University of Arizona Press.

1993   Grateful Prey: Rock Cree Human–Animal Relationships. Los Angeles: University of California Press.

Brooks, Karen

1995   The Rustle of Ghosts: Bung Karno in the New Order. Indonesia 60:89–93.

Brosius, J. Peter

1999   Analyses and Interventions: Anthropological Engagements with Environmentalism. Current Anthropology 40(3):277–309.

Budihardja

1998   Laporan Pameran. Exhibition report. Yogyakarta, Indonesia: Museum Benteng Vredeberg.

REFERENCES

Bugbee, Henry G.
1974   Wilderness in America. Journal of the American Academy of Religion
        42(4):614–620.

Callon, Michel
1979   L'État face à l'innovation technique. Le cas du véhicule électrique. Revue
        française de science politique 29(3):426–447.

Callon, Michel, John Law, and Arie Rip, eds.
1986   Mapping the Dynamics of Science and Technology: Sociology of Science in the
        Real World. Basingstoke, UK: MacMillan.

Canguilhem, Georges
1991   The Normal and the Pathological. Boston: Zone Books.

Carrillo y Ancona, Crescencio
1895   El obispado de Yucatán. Historia de su fundación y de sus obispos desde el
        siglo XVI hasta el XIX. Tomo II. Mérida, Mexico: Imprenta y Litografía R.
        Caballero.

Certeau, Michel, de
1988   The Writing of History. New York: Columbia University Press.

Cetina Aguilar, Anacleto
1983   Cahtal K'ay: Canto a mi pueblo. Mérida, Mexico: Talleres Gráficos del Sudeste,
        SA.
1996   Breves datos históricos y culturales del municipio de Hunucmá. Mérida,
        Mexico: Talleres Gráficos del Sudeste, SA.

Chandler, James, Arnold I. Davidson, and Harry Harootunian, eds.
1994   Questions of Evidence: Proof, Practice, and Persuasion across the Disciplines.
        Chicago: University of Chicago Press.

Chaudhury, Kiren
1997   The Price of Wealth: Economies and Institutions in the Middle East. Ithaca,
        NY: Cornell University Press.

Cheah, Pheng
2003   Spectral Nationality: Passages of Freedom from Kant to Postcolonial
        Literatures of Liberation. New York: Columbia University Press.

Cheng, Anne Anlin
2001   The Melancholy of Race. Oxford: Oxford University Press.

Childs, Courtney
2005   Racism Got Your Tongue? The Discourse of "Self-Segregation" at the
        University of Virginia. Fourth-year thesis, Department of Anthropology,
        University of Virginia, Charlottesville.

Clifford, James
1986   On Ethnographic Allegory. In The Writing of Culture: The Poetics and Politics
        of Ethnography. James Clifford and George E. Marcus, eds. Pp. 98–121.
        Berkeley: University of California Press.

Cohen, Bernard

1996   Colonialism and Its Forms of Knowledge: The British in India. Princeton, NJ: Princeton University Press.

Cohen, David

1994   The Combing of History. Chicago: University of Chicago Press.

1997   Further Thoughts on the Production of History. *In* Between History and Histories: The Making of Silences and Commemorations. Gerald Sider and Gavin Smith, eds. Pp. 300–310. Toronto: University of Toronto Press.

Conklin, Beth, and Laura Graham

1995   The Shifting Middle Ground: Brazilian Indians and Eco-politics. American Anthropologist 97(4):695–710.

Cooper, Frederick

2005   Colonialism in Question: Theory, Knowledge, History. Berkeley: University of California Press.

Cooper, Frederick, and Ann Laura Stoler, eds.

1997   Tensions of Empire: Colonial Cultures in a Bourgeois World. Berkeley: University of California Press.

Coronil, Fernando

1997   The Magical State: Nature, Money and Modernity in Venezuela. Chicago: University of Chicago Press.

Council for Yukon Indians

1993   Umbrella Final Agreement between the Government of Canada, the Council for Yukon Indians, and the Government of the Yukon. Ottawa: Minister of Indian Affairs and Northern Development.

Crapanzano, Vincent

2003   Reflections on Hope as a Category of Social and Psychological Analysis. Cultural Anthropology 18(1):13–32.

Cribb, Robert, ed.

1990   The Indonesian Killings, 1965–1966: Studies from Java and Bali. Monash Papers on Southeast Asia. Clayton, Australia: Monash University.

Cronon, William

1983   Changes in the Land: Indians, Colonists and the Ecology of New England. New York: Hill and Wang.

1991   Nature's Metropolis: Chicago and the Great West. New York: W. W. Norton.

1995   The Trouble with Wilderness, or, Getting Back to the Wrong Nature. *In* Uncommon Ground: Toward Reinventing Nature. New York: W. W. Norton.

Cronon, William, ed.

1995   Uncommon Ground: Toward Reinventing Nature. New York: W. W. Norton.

Crouch, Harold

1978   The Army and Politics in Indonesia. Ithaca, NY: Cornell University Press.

Cruikshank, Julie

1990   Life Lived like a Story: Life Stories of Three Yukon Native Elders. Lincoln: University of Nebraska Press.

1998   The Social Life of Stories: Narrative and Knowledge in the Yukon Territory. Lincoln: University of Nebraska Press.

Cruz-Torres, Maria Luz

2004   Lives of Dust and Water: An Anthropology of Change and Resistance in Northwestern Mexico. Tucson: University of Arizona Press.

Crystal, Jill

1990   Oil and Politics in the Gulf: Rulers and Merchants in Kuwait and Qatar. Cambridge: Cambridge University Press.

Culotta, Elizabeth

2005   Battle Erupts over the "Hobbit" Bones. Science 307:1179.

Curaming, Rommel

2003   Towards Reinventing Indonesian Nationalist Historiography. Kyoto Review 2. Electronic document, http://kyotoreview.cseas.kyoto-u.ac.jp/issue2/article_245.html, accessed July 17, 2007.

Dalton, Rex

2005a   Fossil Finders in Tug of War over Analysis of Hobbit Bones. Nature 434:5.

2005b   More Evidence for Hobbit Unearthed as Diggers Are Refused Access to Cave. Nature 437:934–935.

Davis, John

1987   Libyan Politics Tribe and Revolution: An Account of the Zuwaya and Their Government. London: I. B. Tauris.

Delaney, Carol

1995   Father State, Motherland, and the Birth of Modern Turkey. *In* Naturalizing Power: Essays in Feminist Cultural Analysis. Sylvia Yanagisako and Carol Delaney, eds. Pp. 177–200. New York: Routledge.

Deléage, Jean-Paul

1994   Eco-Marxist Critique of Political Economy. *In* Is Capitalism Sustainable? Political Economy and the Politics of Ecology. Martin O'Connor, ed. Pp. 37–52. New York: Guilford.

Dirección General de Estadística

1901–   Censo general de la Republica Mexicana verificado el 28 de octubre de 1900.
1905   Mexico City: Dirección General de Estadística.

Dirks, Nicholas B.

1993   Colonial Histories and Native Informants: Biography of an Archive. *In* Orientalism and the Postcolonial Predicament: Perspectives on South Asia. Carol Breckenridge and Peter van der Veer, eds. Pp. 279–213. Philadelphia: University of Pennsylvania Press.

2001   Castes of Mind: Colonialism and the Making of Modern India. Princeton, NJ: Princeton University Press.

Dobson, Andrew

1990   Green Political Thought: An Introduction. London: Unwin Hyman.

Douglas, Mary, and Aaron Wildavsky

1982   Risk and Culture: An Essay on the Selection of Technical and Environmental Dangers. Berkeley: University of California Press.

Durkheim, Émile

1994   The Elementary Forms of the Religious Life. Karen Fields, trans. and ed. New
[1924]   York: Simon and Schuster.

1915   The Elementary Forms of the Religious Life. London: Allen and Unwin.

Easton, Norman

2002   "It's Hard Enough to Control Yourself; It's Ridiculous to Think You Can Control Animals": Competing Views on "the Bush" in Contemporary Yukon. Paper presented at the annual meetings of the Alaska Anthropological Association, Anchorage, April 4–7.

Eckersley, Robin

1992   Environmentalism and Political Theory: Toward an Ecocentric Approach. Albany, NY: SUNY.

Eder, Klaus

1996   Social Construction of Nature: A Sociology of Ecological Enlightenment. London: Sage.

Eickelman, Dale

1983   Omani Village: The Meaning of Oil. *In* The Politics of Middle Eastern Oil. John E. Peterson, ed. Pp. 211–219. Washington, DC: Middle East Institute.

Eiss, Paul K.

2002a   Hunting for the Virgin: Meat, Money and Memory in Yucatán. Cultural Anthropology 17(3):291–330.

2002b   Redemption's Archive: Remembering the Future in a Revolutionary Past. Comparative Studies of Society and History 44(1):106–136.

2003   The War of the Eggs: Event, Archive and History in Yucatán's Independent Union Movement, 1990. Ethnology 42(2):87–108.

2008   To Write Liberation: Time, History and Hope in Yucatán. *In* Small Worlds: Method, Meaning, and Narrative in Microhistory. James F. Brooks, Christopher R. N. DeCorse, and John Walton, eds. Pp. 53–76. Santa Fe, NM: SAR Press.

Eiss, Paul K., and David Pedersen

2002   Introduction: Values of Value. Cultural Anthropology 17(3):283–290.

Eliade, Mircea

1978   The Forge and the Crucible: The Origins and Structure of Alchemy. Chicago: University of Chicago Press.

Ennami, 'Amr K.

1972   Studies in Ibadism. Tripoli: University of Libya.

REFERENCES

Erdmann, M. V., and R. L. Caldwell
2000   How New Technology Put a Coelacanth among the Heirs of Piltdown Man.
        Nature 406:343.

Errington, Shelly
1998   The Death of Authentic Primitive Art and Other Tales of Progress. Berkeley:
        University of California Press.

Escobar, Arturo
1999   After Nature: Steps to an Antiessentialist Political Ecology. Current
        Anthropology 40(1):1–30.

Espiritu, Yen Le
1992   Asian American Panethnicity. Philadelphia: Temple University Press.

Evans-Pritchard, E. E.
1940   The Nuer, a Description of the Modes of Livelihood and Political Institutions
        of a Nilotic People. Oxford: Clarendon.

Fabian, Johannes
1983   Time and the Other: How Anthropology Makes Its Object. New York:
        Columbia University Press.

Fajans, Jane
1997   They Make Themselves: Work and Play among the Baining of Papua New
        Guinea. Chicago: University of Chicago Press.

Fallaw, Ben
2001   Cárdenas Compromised: The Failure of Reform in Postrevolutionary Yucatán.
        Durham, NC: Duke University Press.

Farriss, Nancy
1984   Maya Society under Colonial Rule. Princeton, NJ: Princeton University Press.
1987   Remembering the Future, Anticipating the Past: History, Time, and
        Cosmology among the Maya of Yucatán. Comparative Studies in Society and
        History 29(3):566–593.

Feit, Harvey A.
1998   Reflections on Local Knowledge and Wildlife Resource Management:
        Differences, Dominance and Decentralization. In Aboriginal Environmental
        Knowledge in the North. L.-J. Dorais, M. Nagy, and L. Müller-Wille, eds. Pp.
        123–148. Quebec: GÉTIC.

Ferguson, James
1990   The Anti-Politics Machine: "Development," Depoliticization, and Bureaucratic
        Power in Lesotho. Cambridge: Cambridge University Press.
1999   Expectations of Modernity: Myths and Meanings of Urban Life on the
        Zambian Copperbelt. Berkeley: University of California Press.

Ferry, Elizabeth Emma
2005a   Not Ours Alone: Patrimony, Collectivity and Value in Contemporary Mexico.
        New York: Columbia University Press.

2005b   Geologies of Power: Value Transformations of Minerals from Guanajuato, Mexico. American Ethnologist 23(3):420–436.

2006   Memory as Wealth, History as Commerce: Uses of Patrimony in a Central Mexican City. Ethos: The Journal of Psychological Anthropology 34(2):297–324.

Fienup-Riordan, Ann

1990   Original Ecologists? The Relationship between Yup'ik Eskimos and Animals. *In* Eskimo Essays: Yup'ik Lives and How We See Them. New Brunswick, NJ: Rutgers University Press.

Finn, Janet

1998   Tracing the Veins: Of Copper, Culture, and Community from Butte to Chuquicamata. Berkeley: University of California Press.

Fish and Wildlife Management Board

2000   Fifth Annual Report. Whitehorse, YT: Yukon Fish and Wildlife Management Board.

Florida, Nancy K.

1995   Writing the Past, Inscribing the Future: History as Prophecy in Colonial Java. Durham, NC: Duke University Press.

Fogelson, Raymond D.

1989   The Ethnohistory of Events and Nonevents. Ethnohistory 36(2):133–147.

Forrest, George

1908   Journey on the Upper Salwen, October–December, 1905. Geographical Journal 32(3):239–266.

1920   A Lecture by Mr. George Forrest on Recent Discoveries of Rhododendrons in China. Rhododendron Society Notes 2:3–23.

Foster, John B.

2000   Marx's Ecology: Materialism and Nature. New York: Monthly Review.

Foster, Robert J.

2005   Commodity Futures: Labour, Love and Value. Anthropology Today 21(4):8–12.

Freud, Sigmund

1976[1919]The "Uncanny." New Literary History 7(3):619–645.

Fujimura, Joan

1992   Crafting Science: Standardized Packages, Boundary Objects, and "Translation." *In* Science as Practice and Culture. A. Pickering, ed. Pp. 168–211. Chicago: University of Chicago Press.

Gabbert, Wolfgang

2004   Becoming Maya: Ethnicity and Social Inequality in Yucatán since 1500. Tucson: University of Arizona Press.

Gaonkar, Dilip Parameshwar, ed.

2001   Alternative Modernities. Durham, NC: Duke University Press.

REFERENCES

García-Guinea, Javier, Matthew Harffy, and Mark D. Bateman
1998 Museums: A Palliative or Solution for Declining Historical Mines? Episodes 21(1):32–36.

Geertz, Clifford
1973 Person, Time and Conduct in Bali. *In* The Interpretation of Cultures. New York: Basic Books.

Gell, Alfred
1992 The Anthropology of Time: Cultural Constructions of Temporal Maps and Images. Oxford: Berg.

Gezon, Lisa L.
2006 Global Visions, Local Landscapes: A Political Ecology of Conservation, Conflict, and Control in Northern Madagascar. Lanham, MD: AltaMira.

Giddens, Anthony
1995 A Contemporary Critique of Historical Materialism. Houndmills, UK: MacMillan.

Ginzburg, Carlo
1989 Clues, Myths, and the Historical Method. Baltimore: Johns Hopkins University Press.
1994 Checking the Evidence: The Judge and the Historian. *In* Questions of Evidence: Proof, Practice, and Persuasion across the Disciplines. James Chandler, Arnold I. Davidson, and Harry Harootunian, eds. Pp. 290–303. Chicago: University of Chicago Press.
1999 History, Rhetoric, and Proof. Hanover, NH: University Press of New England.

Glacken, Clarence
1967 Traces on the Rhodian Shore: Nature and Culture in Western Thought from Ancient Times to the End of the Eighteenth Century. Berkeley: University of California Press.

Goffman, Erving
1963 Stigma: Notes on the Management of Spoiled Identity. Englewood Cliffs, NJ: Prentice-Hall.

Goodstein, David
2004 Out of Gas: The End of the Age of Oil. New York: W. W. Norton.

Gorz, André
1982 Farewell to the Working Class. London: Pluto.

Graeber, David
2001 Toward an Anthropological Theory of Value: The False Coin of Our Own Dreams. New York: Palgrave.

Grafton, Anthony
1997 The Footnote: A Curious History. Cambridge, MA: Harvard University.

Greenhouse, Carol
1996 A Moment's Notice: Time Politics across Cultures. Ithaca, NY: Cornell University Press.

Groom, Martha, Gary Meffe, and C. Ronald Carroll

2006   Principles of Conservation Biology. Sunderland, MA: Sinauer.

Grosz, Elizabeth

2004   The Nick of Time: Politics, Evolution, and the Untimely. Durham, NC: Duke University Press.

Guan Xuexuan

1743   Lijiang fu zhi lüe. Lijiang, China: Lijiang Naxizu Zizhixian xian shi zhi bian wei hui ban gong shi.

Güémez Pineda, Arturo

1994   Liberalismo en tierras del caminante: Yucatán, 1812–1840. Zamora, Mexico: El Colegio de Michoacán.

Guha, Ramachandra

1990   The Unquiet Woods: Ecological Change and Peasant Resistance in the Himalaya. Berkeley: University of California Press.

Gullaba, Alberto

2004   Diversity at Virginia: A Student Narrative. Fourth-year thesis, Department of Politics, University of Virginia, Charlottesville.

Gupta, Akhil

1998   Postcolonial Developments: Agriculture and the Making of Modern India. Durham, NC: Duke University Press.

2004   Postcolonial Developments: Agriculture and the Making of Modern India. Berkeley: University of California Press.

Gupta, Akhil, and James Ferguson

1992   Beyond "Culture": Space, Identity, and the Politics of Difference. Cultural Anthropology 7(1):6–23.

Gurvitch, Georges

1963   Social Structure and the Multiplicity of Times. *In* Sociological Theory, Values, and Sociocultural Change. A. Tiyakian, ed. Pp. 171–184. New York: Free Press.

1964   The Spectrum of Social Time. M. Korenbaum, trans. Dordrecht, Netherlands: D. Reidel.

Guyer, Jane I.

2007   Prophecy and the Near Future. American Ethnologist 34(3):409–421.

Hacking, Ian

1990   The Taming of Chance. Cambridge: Cambridge University Press.

1999   The Social Construction of What? Cambridge, MA: Harvard University Press.

Halliday, Fred

1974   Arabia without Sultans. New York: Penguin Books.

Hallowell, A. Irving

1937   Temporal Orientation in Western Civilization and in a Preliterate Society. American Anthropologist 39(4):647–670.

REFERENCES

1960   Ojibwa Ontology, Behavior, and Worldview. *In* Culture in History: Essays in Honor of Paul Radin. S. Diamond, ed. Pp. 19–52. New York: Columbia University Press.

Handler, Richard

1988   Nationalism and the Politics of Culture in Quebec. Madison: University of Wisconsin Press.

1991   Who Owns the Past? History, Cultural Property, and the Logic of Possessive Individualism. *In* The Politics of Culture. Brett Williams, ed. Pp. 63–74. Washington, DC: Smithsonian Institution Press.

Handler, Richard, and Eric Gable

1997   The New History in an Old Museum: Creating the Past at Colonial Williamsburg. Durham, NC: Duke University Press.

Handler, Richard, and Daniel Segal

1990   Jane Austen and the Fiction of Culture: An Essay on the Narration of Social Realities. Tucson: University of Arizona Press.

Hann, C. M., ed.

1998   Property Relations: Renewing the Anthropological Tradition. Cambridge: Cambridge University Press.

Hansen, Thomas Blom, and Finn Stepputat, eds.

2001   States of Imagination: Ethnographic Explorations of the Postcolonial State. Durham, NC: Duke University Press.

Haraway, Donna

1991   Simians, Cyborgs, and Women: The Reinvention of Nature. London: Routledge.

Harding, Susan

2005   Living Prophecy at Heaven's Gate. *In* Histories of the Future. Daniel Rosenberg and Susan Harding, eds. Pp. 297–320. Durham, NC: Duke University Press.

Hardt, Michael, and Antonio Negri

2004   Multitude: War and Democracy in the Age of Empire. New York: Penguin.

Harris, Olivia

1988   The Earth and the State: The Sources and Meanings of Money in Northern Potosí, Bolivia. *In* Money and the Morality of Exchange. Jonathan Parry and Maurice Bloch, eds. Pp. 232–268. Cambridge: Cambridge University Press.

Harvey, David

1974   Population, Resources and the Ideology of Science. Economic Geography 50(3):256–277.

1990   The Condition of Postmodernity: An Enquiry into the Origins of Cultural Change. Oxford: Blackwell.

1996   Justice, Nature and the Geography of Difference. Oxford: Blackwell.

Hays, Samuel P.

1959   Conservation and the Gospel of Efficiency: The Progressive Conservation

Movement, 1890–1920. Cambridge, MA: Harvard University Press.

He Wanbao and He Jiaxiu, eds.

1999   Naxi Dongba gu ji yi zhu quan ji (An Annotated Collection of Naxi Dongba
         Manuscripts). 100 vols. Kunming, China: Yunnan renmin chubanshe.

He Zhiwu and Guo Dalie

1985   Dongba jiao de paixi he xianzhuang (The Schools and Current State of
         Dongba Religion). *In* Dongba wenhua lunji (Collected Essays on Dongba
         Culture). Guo Dalie and Yang Shiguang, eds., 38–54. Kunming, China: Yunnan
         renmin chubanshe.

Heidegger, Martin

1977   The Question Concerning Technology and Other Essays. New York: Harper
         and Row.

Herzfeld, Michael

1991   A Place in History: Social and Monumental Time in a Cretan Town. Princeton,
         NJ: Princeton University Press.

1992   The Production of Indifference: Exploring the Symbolic Roots of Western
         Bureaucracy. Chicago: University of Chicago Press.

Hill, Jane, and Bruce Mannheim

1992   Language and World View. Annual Review of Anthropology 21:381–406.

Hill, Jonathan, ed.

1988   Rethinking History and Myth: Indigenous South American Perspectives on the
         Past. Urbana: University of Illinois Press.

Hobsbawm, Eric, and Terence Ranger, eds.

1983   The Invention of Tradition. Cambridge: Cambridge University Press.

Hoffman, Valerie J.

2001   Nineteenth- and Early Twentieth-Century Ibadi Discussions on Religious
         Knowledge and Muslim Sects. Paper presented at the Annual Middle East
         Studies Association Conference, San Francisco, November 18.

2004   The Articulation of Ibadi Identity in Modern Oman and Zanzibar. Muslim
         World 94:201–216.

Hong Congwen

1997   Cong Banhong shijian kan Yunnan bianjiang guanli jigou de yunzuo,
         Zhongguo bianjiang shidi yanjiu 3:69–79. [clarification of reference (title and
         name of journal) to come from Mueggler]

Hsu, Elizabeth

1998   Moso and Naxi: The House. *In* Naxi and Moso Ethnography: Kin, Rites,
         Pictographs. Michael Oppitz and Elizabeth Hsu, eds. Pp. 47–80. Zurich:
         Völkerkundemuseum Zürich.

Hughes, Francis

1987   Oil in Oman: A Short Historical Note. *In* Oman: Economic, Social and
         Strategic Developments. B. R. Pridham, ed. Pp. 168–176. London: Croom
         Helm.

REFERENCES

Hull, Matthew S.
2003   The File: Agency, Authority, and Autography in a Pakistan Bureaucracy.
        Language and Communication 23:287–314.

Implementation Review Group (IRG)
2007   Yukon First Nation Final and Self-Government Agreement Implementation
        Reviews. Report prepared for the governments of Canada, Yukon, and Yukon
        First Nations and the Council of Yukon First Nations. Whitehorse, YT:
        Implementation Review Group.

International Monetary Fund (IMF)
1998   IMF Concludes Article IV Consultation with Oman. Electronic document,
        http://www.imf.org/external/np/sec/pn/1998/pn9851.htm, accessed
        December 6, 2007.

Irvine, Judith
2004   Say When: Temporalities in Language Ideology. Journal of Linguistic
        Anthropology 14(1):99–109.

Iskander, Dodi R.
1988   Pendidikan Sejarah Perjuangan Bangsa SMA Kelas III. Bandung, Indonesia:
        Ganeca Exact.

Ivy, Marilyn
1995   Discourses of the Vanishing: Modernity, Phantasm, Japan. Chicago: University
        of Chicago Press.

Jacoby, Karl
2001   Crimes against Nature: Squatters, Poachers, Thieves, and the Hidden History
        of American Conservation. Berkeley: University of California Press.

Janert, Klaus L., ed.
1984   Nachitextedition. 15 vols. Wiesbaden, Germany: F. Steiner.
1965   Na-khi Manuscripts, part 2. Wiesbaden, Germany: F. Steiner.

Joseph, Gilbert M.
1988   Revolution from Without: Yucatán, Mexico and the United States, 1880–1924.
        Durham, NC: Duke University Press.

Kantorowicz, Ernst
1997   The King's Two Bodies: A Study in Medieval Political Theology. Princeton, NJ:
[1957] Princeton University Press.

Karsono, Sony
2005   Setting History Straight? Indonesian Historiography in the New Order.
        Master's thesis, Ohio University, Athens.

Keane, Webb
1997   Signs of Recognition. Berkeley: University of California Press.
2005   Signs Are Not the Garb of Meaning. In Materiality. Daniel Miller, ed. Pp.
        182–205. Durham, NC: Duke University Press.

Kelman, Sarah

2006   "Long Pearls and Blonde Hair Highlights—It's So Not Me": How Minority Greeks Negotiate Dialectical Incorporations and Rejections of Whiteness through Identity-Forming Practices at the University of Virginia. Fourth-year thesis, Department of Anthropology, University of Virginia, Charlottesville.

Kerr, Clark

1963   The Uses of the University. Cambridge, MA: Harvard University Press.

Klinken, Gerry van

2005   The Battle for History after Suharto. In Beginning to Remember: The Past in the Indonesian Present. Mary Zurbuchen, ed. Pp. 233–258. Singapore: Singapore University Press and University of Washington Press.

Kluane First Nation

2003a   Kluane First Nation Final Agreement. Ottawa: Minister of Public Works and Government Services Canada.

2003b   Kluane First Nation Final Agreement Implementation Plan. Ottawa: Minster of Public Works and Government Services Canada.

Koselleck, Reinhart

1985   Futures Past: On the Semantics of Historical Time. Cambridge, MA: MIT Press.

2002   The Practice of Conceptual History: Timing History, Spacing Concepts. Stanford, CA: Stanford University Press.

Krech, Shepard

1999   The Ecological Indian: Myth and History. New York: W. W. Norton.

Kurin, Richard

2006   The Hope Diamond: The Legendary History of a Cursed Gem. New York: Smithsonian Institution and Harper Collins.

Laclau, Ernesto

2005   On Populist Reason. London: Verso.

Landen, Robert Geran

1967   Oman since 1856: Disruptive Modernization in a Traditional Arab Society. Princeton, NJ: Princeton University Press.

Landes, David

2000   Revolution in Time: Clocks and the Making of the Modern World. 2nd edition. Cambridge, MA: Harvard University Press.

Latief, Abdul

2000   Pleidoi Kolonel A. Latief: Soeharto Terlibat G30S. Jakarta: Institut Studi Arus Informasi.

Latour, Bruno

1987   Science in Action: How to Follow Scientists and Engineers through Society. Cambridge, MA: Harvard University Press.

1988   The Pasteurization of France. Cambridge, MA: Harvard University Press.

REFERENCES

1993   We Have Never Been Modern. Cambridge, MA: Harvard University Press.
1999   Circulating Reference: Sampling the Soil in the Amazon Forest. *In* Pandora's
        Hope: Essays on the Reality of Science Studies. Cambridge, MA: Harvard
        University Press.
2004   Politics of Nature: How to Bring the Sciences into Democracy. Cambridge,
        MA: Harvard University Press.
2005   Reassembling the Social: An Introduction to Actor-Network Theory. Oxford:
        Clarendon.

Law, John, and John Hassard
1999   Actor Network Theory and After. Oxford: Blackwell.

Le Goff, Jacque
1980   Time, Work, and Culture in the Middle Ages. Chicago: University of Chicago
        Press.

Leach, Edmund
1961   Rethinking Anthropology. London: Athlone.

Leigh, Barbara
1991   Making the Indonesian State: The Role of School Texts. Review of Indonesian
        and Malaysian Affairs 25(1):17–43.

Leopold, Aldo
1933   Game Management. New York: Scribner's.

Lewicki, Tadeusz
1971   The Ibadites in Arabia and Africa. Cahiers D'Histoire Mondiale 13(1):3–130.

Li, Tania
2000   Articulating Indigenous Identity in Indonesia: Resource Politics and the Tribal
        Slot. Comparative Studies in Society and History 42(1):149–179.

Li Xi, ed.
2001   Jin shen zhi lu: Naxi zu Dongba shen lu tu (A Road Approaching the Gods: A
        Naxi Dongba Painting of a Spirit Road). Kunming, China: Yunnan meishu
        chubanshe.

Locke, John
2003   Two Treatises of Government, and, A Letter Concerning Toleration. London:
[1690] Yale University Press.

**Lovins, Amory B., E. Kyle Datta, Odd-Even Bustnes, Jonathan G. Koomey, and
Nathan J. Glasgow**
2005   Winning the Oil Endgame: Innovation for Profits, Jobs and Security.
        Snowmass, CO: Rocky Mountain Institute.

Lowe, Celia
2004   Making the Monkey: How the Togean Macaque Went from "New Form" to
        "Endemic Species" in Indonesians' Conservation Biology. Cultural
        Anthropology 19(4):491–516.
2006   Wild Profusion: Biodiversity Conservation in an Indonesian Archipelago.
        Princeton, NJ: Princeton University Press.

Lubis, Husin, Gatot Suraji, S. Harijadi Judha, Sudarmadji, Jacobus Rinussa, and St. Negoro
1984   Pendidikan Sejarah Perjuangan Bangsa. Jakarta: Yudhistira.

Ludden, David
1992   India's Development Regime. *In* Colonialism and Culture. Nicholas Dirks, ed. Pp. 245–287. Ann Arbor: University of Michigan Press.

Lukes, Steven
1977   Power and Structure. *In* Power. S. Lukes, ed. Pp. 3–29. New York: Columbia University Press.

Lupton, Deborah
1999   Risk. London: Routledge.

Al-Maamiry, Ahmed Hamoud
1980   Oman and Ibadism. New Delhi: Lancers Books.

Maass, Peter
2005   The Breaking Point. New York Times Magazine, August 21:30–35, 50, 56, 59.

Maclean, Brenda
2004   George Forrest, Plant Hunter. Edinburgh: Antique Collectors' Club.

Maine, Henry
1986   Ancient Law: Its Connections with the Early History of Society, and Its Relation
[1864]   to Modern Ideas. Tucson: University of Arizona Press.

Manzo, Kate
1991   Modernist Discourse and the Crisis of Development Theory. Studies in Comparative International Development 26(2):3–36.

Marks, Stuart
1984   The Imperial Lion: Human Dimensions of Wildlife Management in Central Africa. Boulder, CO: Westview.

Martin, Emily
1995   Working across the Human-Other Divide. *In* Reinventing Biology: Respect for Life and the Creation of Knowledge. Ruth Hubbard and Linda Birke, eds. Pp. 261–275. Bloomington: Indiana University Press.

Marx, Karl
1994   Economic and Philosophic Manuscripts. *In* Selected Writings. Lawrence
[1844]   Simon, ed. Pp. 54–81. New York: Hackett.
1993   The Grundrisse: Foundations of the Critique of Political Economy. Martin
[1857]   Nicolaus, trans. New York: Penguin Classics.
1967[1867] Capital. Vol. 1. Friedrich Engels, ed. New York: International Publishers.

Marx, Leo
2000   The Machine in the Garden: Technology and the Pastoral Ideal in America.
[1964]   New York: Oxford University Press.

Mason, Arthur
2007   The Rise of Consultant Forecasting in Liberalized Natural Gas Markets. Public Culture 19(2):367–379.

REFERENCES

Maurer, William

2002   Repressed Futures: Financial Derivatives' Theological Unconscious. Economy and Society 31(1):15–36.

McCabe, Heather, and Janet Wright

2000   Tangled Tale of a Lost, Stolen, and Disputed Coelacanth. Nature 406:114.

McClellan, Catharine

1975   My Old People Say: An Ethnographic Survey of Southern Yukon Territory. 2 vols. Ottawa: National Museum of Man.

McGregor, Katharine

2002   Commemoration of 1 October: "Hari Kesaktian Pancasila": A Post-mortem Analysis? Asian Studies Review 26(1):39–72.

2007   History in Uniform: Military Ideology and the Construction of Indonesia's Past. Singapore: Singapore University Press, University of Hawaii Press, KITLV, and the Asian Studies Association of Australia.

Mckhann, Charles

1992   Fleshing Out the Bones: Kinship and Cosmology in Naqxi Religion. PhD dissertation, University of Chicago.

McPherson, C. B.

1962   The Political Theory of Possessive Individualism: Hobbes to Locke. Oxford: Clarendon.

Meadows, Donella H., Dennis Meadows, Jørgen Randers, and William W. Behrens III

1972   The Limits to Growth; A Report for the Club of Rome's Project on the Predicament of Mankind. New York: Universe Books.

Merchant, Carolyn

1980   The Death of Nature: Women, Ecology, and the Scientific Revolution. San Francisco: Harper and Row.

Messick, Brinkley

1993   The Calligraphic State: Textual Domination and History in a Muslim Society. Berkeley: University of California Press.

Middle East Economic Survey (MEES)

2003   Middle East Crude Oil Production and Exports. MEES, October 6.

Miller, Daniel

1987   Material Culture and Mass Consumption. Oxford: Basil Blackwell.

2005   Materiality. Durham, NC: Duke University Press.

Ministry of Information, Sultanate of Oman

1995   The Royal Speeches of H. M. Sultan Qaboos bin Said, 1970–1995. Muscat, Oman: Ministry of Information.

Mintz, Sidney

1974   Worker in the Cane: A Puerto Rican Life History. New York: W. W. Norton.

1985   Sweetness and Power: The Place of Sugar in Modern History. New York: Viking.

Mitchell, Don

1996   The Lie of the Land: Migrant Workers and the California Landscape. Minneapolis: University of Minnesota Press.

Mitchell, Timothy

1991   The Limits of the State: Beyond Statist Approaches and Their Critics. American Political Science Review 85(1):77–96.

2002   Rule of Experts: Egypt, Techno-politics, Modernity. Berkeley: University of California Press.

Miyazaki, Hirokazu

2003a   Economy of Dreams: The Production of Hope in Anthropology and Finance. Working paper. Center for the Study of Economy and Society, Cornell University, Ithaca, NY.

2003b   The Temporalities of the Market. American Anthropologist 105(2):255–265.

2006   Economy of Dreams: Hope in Global Capitalism and Its Critiques. Cultural Anthropology 21(2):147–172.

Miyazaki, Hirozaku, and Annelise Riles

2005   Failure as an Endpoint. In Global Assemblages: Technology, Politics, and Ethics as Anthropological Problems. Aihwa Ong and Stephen J. Collier, eds. Pp. 320–331. Malden, MA: Blackwell.

Morris, James

1957   Sultan in Oman: Venture into the Middle East. New York: Pantheon Books.

Morrow, Phyllis, and Chase Hensel

1992   Hidden Dissension: Minority–Majority Relationships and the Use of Contested Terminology. Arctic Anthropology 29(1):38–53.

Mrazek, Rudolph

2002   Engineers of Happyland: Technology and Nationalism in a Colony. Princeton, NJ: Princeton University Press.

Muckenheim, Stephanie

1998   The Importance of Fishing and Fish Harvesting to Yukon First Nations People. Whitehorse, YT: Yukon Fish and Wildlife Management Board.

Mumford, Lewis

1962[1934] Technics and Civilization. New York: Harcourt, Brace, and World.

Munn, Nancy

1977   The Spatiotemporal Transformations of Gawan Canoes. Journale de la Société des Oceanistes 33:39–53.

1992   The Cultural Anthropology of Time: A Critical Essay. Annual Review of Anthropology 21:93–123.

Nadasdy, Paul

2003   Hunters and Bureaucrats: Power, Knowledge, and Aboriginal–State Relations in the Southwest Yukon. Vancouver, BC: UBC Press.

2005a   The Anti-politics of TEK: The Institutionalization of Co-management Discourse and Practice. Anthropologica 47(2):215–232.

2005b   Transcending the Debate over the Ecologically Noble Indian: Indigenous
          Peoples and Environmentalism. Enthohistory 52(2):291–331.
2007   The Gift in the Animal: The Ontology of Hunting and Human-Animal
          Sociality. American Ethnologist 34(1):25–43.
In press "We Don't *Harvest* Animals; We *Kill* Them": Agricultural Metaphors and the
          Politics of Wildlife Management in the Yukon. *In* Knowing Nature,
          Transforming Ecologies: Science, Power, and Practice. M. Goldman, P.
          Nadasdy, and M. Turner, eds. Chicago: University of Chicago Press.

Nash, June
1979   We Eat the Mines and the Mines Eat Us: Dependency and Exploitation in
          Bolivian Tin Mines. New York: Columbia University Press.

Natcher, David, Susan Davis, and Clifford Hickey
2005   Co-management: Managing Relationships, Not Resources. Human
          Organization 64(3):240–250.

Needham, Joseph
1959   Science and Civilization in China. Vol. 3. Cambridge: Cambridge University Press.

Nelson, Richard K.
1983   Make Prayers to the Raven: A Koyukon View of the Northern Forest. Chicago:
          University of Chicago Press.

Neu, Dean
2000   "Presents" for the "Indians": Land, Colonialism, and Accounting in Canada.
          Accounting, Organizations, and Society 25:163–184.

Nguyen, Huong
2005   Problematizing Progress. Fourth-year thesis, Department of Anthropology,
          University of Virginia, Charlottesville.

Nora, Pierre
1989   Between Memory and History: Les Lieux de Memoire. Representations 26:7–25.

Notzke, Claudia
1994   Aboriginal Peoples and Natural Resources in Canada. North York, ON: Captus
          University Publications.

Nugent, David
2005   Modernity at the Edge of Empire State, Individual, and Nation in the
          Northern Peruvian Andes, 1885–1935. Berkeley: University of California Press.

O'Connor, James
1998   Natural Causes: Essays in Ecological Marxism. New York: Guilford.

Ortner, Sherry
1973   On Key Symbols. American Anthropologist 75(5):1338–1346.

Özyürek, Esra
2006   Nostalgia for the Modern: State Secularism and Everyday Politics in Turkey.
          Durham, NC: Duke University Press.

Papailias, Penelope
2005   Genres of Recollection: Archival Poetics and Modern Greece. New York: Palgrave.

Parker, Priya
2004   Student Racial Climate: An Analysis and Assessment. Fourth-year thesis, Program in Political and Social Thought, University of Virginia, Charlottesville.

Parmentier, Richard J.
1985   Times of the Signs: Modalities of History and Levels of Social Structure in Belau. *In* Semiotic Mediation: Sociological and Psychological Perspectives. Elizabeth Mertz and Richard Parmentier, eds. Pp. 131–154. Orlando, FL: Academic Press.
2007   It's about Time: On the Semiotics of Temporality. Language and Communication 27(3):272–277. 2

Patch, Robert
1993   Maya and Spaniard in Yucatán, 1648–1812. Stanford, CA: Stanford University Press.
2002   Maya Revolts and Revolutions in the Eighteenth Century. New York: M. E. Sharpe.

Paulson, Susan, Lisa L. Gezon, and Michael Watts
2003   Locating the Political in Political Ecology. Human Organization 62(3):205–217.

Peel, J. D. Y.
1984   Making History: The Past in the Ijesha Present. Man 19(1):111–132.

Pellegram, Andrea
1998   The Message in Paper. *In* Material Cultures. Daniel Miller, ed. Pp. 103–120. Chicago: University of Chicago Press.

Peluso, Nancy Lee
1991   Rich Forests, Poor People: Resource Control and Resistance in Java. Berkeley: University of California Press.

Pemberton, John
2004   On the Subject of "Java." Ithaca, NY: Cornell University Press.

Peterson, John E.
1978   Oman in the Twentieth Century. London: Croom Helm.

Petroleum Development of Oman
2003   Annual Report for 2003 to His Majesty Sultan Qaboos bin Said Sultan of Oman. Electronic document, www.pdo.co.om/PDO/NewsandLibrary/PublicationsandReport/Annual_Reports.htm, accessed September 2005.

Piore, Michael, and Charles Sabel
1984   The Second Industrial Divide: Possibilities for Prosperity. New York: Basic Books.

Platts
2007   Platts. Electronic document, www.platts.com, accessed December 6, 2007.

Plumwood, Val
1986   Ecofeminism: An Overview and Discussion of Positions and Arguments.
        Australasian Journal of Philosophy 64:120–138.

Pocock, J. G. A.
1985   Virtue, Commerce, and History: Essays on Political Thought and History,
        Chiefly in the Eighteenth Century. Cambridge: Cambridge University Press.

Pomian, Krzysztof
1996   Collectors and Curiosities: Paris and Venice, 1500–1800. Cambridge, UK:
        Polity.

Postone, Moishe
1993   Time, Labor, and Social Domination: A Reinterpretation of Marx's Critical
        Theory. Cambridge: Cambridge University Press.

Povinelli, Elizabeth
1995   Do Rocks Listen? The Cultural Politics of Apprehending Australian Aboriginal
        Labor. American Anthropologist 97(3):505–518.

Power, Michael
1997   The Audit Society: Rituals of Verification. Oxford: Oxford University Press.

Purwanto, Bambang
2006   Gagalnya Historiografi Indonesiasentris? Yogyakarta, Indonesia: Ombak.

Raffles, Hugh
2002   In Amazonia: A Natural History. Princeton, NJ: Princeton University Press.

Rappaport, Joanne
1994   Cumbe Reborn: An Andean Ethnography of History. Chicago: University of
        Chicago Press.

Rasita, Iit, Bambang Sumbogo, and T. Hasanuddin
1991   Cintaku Negaraku: Buku Pelengkap PSPB Untuk Kelas 3 SMP. Klaten,
        Indonesia: PT Intan Pariwara.

Redfield, Robert
1941   The Folk Culture of Yucatan. Chicago: University of Chicago Press.

Reid, Anthony
1979   The Nationalist Quest for an Indonesian Past. In Perceptions of the Past in
        Southeast Asia. Anthony Reid and David Marr, eds. Pp. 281–299. Singapore:
        Heinemann.

Restall, Matthew
1997   The Maya World: Yucatec Culture and Society, 1550–1850. Stanford, CA:
        Stanford University Press.
1998   Maya Conquistador. Boston: Beacon.

Richards, J.
1993   Primula. London: B. T. Batsford.

Rigby, Peter
1983   Time and Historical Consciousness: The Case of Ilparakuyo Maasai.

Comparative Studies in Society and History 25(3):428–456.

Riles, Annelise, ed.

2006   Documents: Artifacts of Modern Knowledge. Ann Arbor: University of
        Michigan Press.

Robbins, Joel

2004   Becoming Sinners: Christianity and Moral Torment in a Papua New Guinea
        Society. Berkeley: University of California Press.

Roberts, Paul

2004   The End of Oil: On the Edge of a Perilous New World. New York: Mariner
        Books.

Rock, Joseph Francis

1937   Studies in Naxi Literature, vol. II: The Na-khi Ha zhi p'i, or the Road the Gods
        Decide. Bulletin de l'École Française d'Extrême-Oriente 37:40–119.

1947   Ancient Naxi Kingdom of Southwest China. Cambridge, MA: Harvard
        University Press.

1952   The Na-khi Naga Cult and Related Ceremonies. Rome: Istituto Italiano per il
        Medio ed Estremo Oriente.

1955   The Zhi-mä Funeral Ceremony of the Na-khi of Southwest China, Described
        and Translated from Na-khi Manuscripts. Vienna-Mödling: St. Gabriel's
        Mission.

1963   A Na-khi–English Encyclopedic Dictionary. Rome: Instituto Italiano per il
        Medio ed Estremo Oriente.

1965   Na-khi Manuscripts. Part 2. Klaus L. Janert, ed. Wiesbaden, Germany: Franz
        Steiner Verlag GMBH.

Rofel, Lisa

1999   Other Modernities: Gendered Yearnings in China after Socialism. Berkeley:
        University of California Press.

Romano, Angela

2003   Politics and the Press in Indonesia: Understanding an Evolving Political
        Culture. London: Routledge Curzon.

Roosa, John

2006   Pretext for Mass Murder: The September 30th Movement and Suharto's Coup
        d'Etat in Indonesia. Madison: University of Wisconsin Press.

Rose, Nikolas

1999   Powers of Freedom: Reframing Political Thought. Cambridge: Cambridge
        University Press.

2006   The Politics of Life Itself: Biomedicine, Power, and Subjectivity in the Twenty-
        First Century. Princeton, NJ: Princeton University Press.

Rosen, Lawrence

1984   Bargaining for Reality: The Construction of Social Relations in a Muslim
        Community. Chicago: University of Chicago Press.

REFERENCES

Rosenberg, Daniel, and Susan Harding, eds.
2005   Histories of the Future. Durham, NC: Duke University Press.

Rostow, Walt
1960   Stages of Economic Growth: A Non-Communist Manifesto. New York: Cambridge University Press.

Rotenberg, Robert
1992   The Power to Time and the Time to Power. *In* The Politics of Time. Vol. 4. H. Rutz, ed. Pp. 18–36. Washington, DC: American Anthropological Association.

Roys, Ralph
1957   The Political Geography of the Yucatan Maya. Washington, DC: Carnegie Institution.

Rugeley, Terry
1996   Yucatán's Maya Peasantry and the Origins of the Caste War. Austin: University of Texas Press.
2001   Of Wonders and Wise Men: Religion and Popular Cultures in Southeast Mexico, 1800–1876. Austin: University of Texas Press.

Rutz, Henry, ed.
1992   The Politics of Time. Washington, DC: American Anthropological Association.

Sahlins, Marshall
1972   Stone Age Economics. Chicago: Aldine-Atherton.
1985   Islands of History. Chicago: University of Chicago Press.
2002   Waiting for Foucault, Still. Chicago: Prickly Paradigm.

Samuel, Raphael
1994   Theatres of Memory: Past and Present. London: Verso.

Schulte Nordholt, Henk
2004   Decolonizing Indonesian Historiography. Working Paper 6. Center for East and Southeast Asian Studies, Lund University, Sweden. Electronic document, www.ace.lu.se, accessed July 17, 2007.

Scott, James
1998   Seeing like a State: How Certain Schemes to Improve the Human Condition Have Failed. New Haven, CT: Yale University Press.

Segal, Daniel
1991   Can You Tell a Jew When You See One? or Thoughts on Meeting Barbra/Barbie at the Museum. Judaism 48:234–241.
2000   "Western Civ" and the Staging of History in American Higher Education. American Historical Review 105:770–805.

Sejati Foundation
1994   Bajau. Jakarta: Sejati Foundation.

Sekretaris Negara

1978   Tiga Puluh Tahun Indonesia Merdeka 1945–1949. Jakarta: State Department.

Sen, Amartya

1983   Poverty and Famines: An Essay on Entitlements and Deprivation. Oxford: Oxford University Press.

Sen, Krishna

1994   Indonesian Cinema: Framing the New Order. London: Zed Books.

2007   Sen, Krishna, and David Hill. Media, Culture and Politics in Indonesia. Jakarta:
[2000]   Equinox Press.

Shapin, Steven, and Simon Schaffer

1989   Leviathan and the Air-Pump: Hobbes, Boyle, and the Experimental Life. Princeton, NJ: Princeton University Press.

Siegreied, Nikolaus A.

2000   Legislation and Legitimation in Oman: The Basic Law. Islamic Law and Society 7(2):359–397.

Silver Institute

2007a   Demand and Supply in 2006. Electronic document, http://www.silverinstitute. org/supply/index.php#demand, accessed December 5, 2007.

2007b   Silver Facts. Electronic document, http://www.silverinstitute.org/facts/ index.php, accessed December 5, 2007.

Simon, Julian Lincoln

1981   The Ultimate Resource. Princeton, NJ: Princeton University Press.

Sindicato Independiente de Trabajadores de la Industria Avícola (SITIA)

1990   La batalla de Tetiz y Hunucmá: Los ciento cuarenta días que conmovió a Yucatán. Mérida, Mexico: SITIA.

Slater, Candace

1995   Reinventing Eden: Western Culture as a Recovery Narrative. *In* Uncommon Ground. William Cronon, ed. Pp. 114–131. New York: W. W. Norton.

Smith, Gavin

1989   Livelihood and Resistance: Peasants and the Politics of Land in Peru. Berkeley: University of California Press.

Smith, Neil

1984   Uneven Development: Nature, Capital, and the Production of Space. New York: Blackwell.

Smith, Neil, and Phil O'Keefe

1980   Marx, Geography and the Concept of Nature. Antipode 12(2):30–39.

Soedjatmoko

1960   An Approach to Indonesian History: Towards an Open Future. An Address before the Seminar on Indonesian History, Gadjah Mada University, Jogjakarta, December 14, 1947. Ithaca, NY: Cornell University Southeast Asia Program.

Soeharto [Suharto]

1988   Pikiran, Ucapkan, dan Tindakan Saya: Otobiografi seperti dipaparkan kepada G. Dwipayana dan Ramadhan K. H. [My Thoughts, Speech, and Acts: Autobiography as told to G. Dwipayana and Ramadhan K. H.], G. Dwipayana and Ramadhan K. H., eds. Jakarta: PT Citra Lamtoro Gung Persada.

Spirn, Anne Whiston

1995   Constructing Nature: The Legacy of Frederick Law Olmsted. *In* Uncommon Ground: Toward Reinventing Nature. William Cronon, ed. Pp. 91–113. New York: W. W. Norton.

Squatriti, Paolo, ed.

2007   Natures Past: The Environment and Human History. Ann Arbor: University of Michigan Press.

Stevenson, Marc

2006   The Possibility of Difference: Rethinking Co-management. Human Organization 65(2):167–180.

Stewart, Kathleen, and Susan Harding

1999   Bad Endings: American Apocalypsis. Annual Review of Anthropology 28:285–310.

Stewart, Susan

1993   On Longing: Narratives of the Gigantic, the Miniature, the Souvenir, the Collection. Durham, NC: Duke University Press.

Stoler, Ann Laura

1985   Capitalism and Confrontation in Sumatra's Plantation Belt, 1870–1979. New Haven, CT: Yale University Press.

1992   In Cold Blood: Hierarchies of Credibility and the Politics of Colonial Narratives. Representations 37:151–189.

2002   Carnal Knowledge and Imperial Power: Race and the Intimate in Colonial Rule. Berkeley: University of California Press.

Stonich, Susan C.

1993   "I Am Destroying the Land": The Political Ecology of Poverty and Environmental Destruction in Honduras. Boulder, CO: Westview.

Strassler, Karen

2003   Refracted Visions: Popular Photography and the Indonesian Culture of Documentation in Postcolonial Java. PhD dissertation, University of Michigan, Ann Arbor.

2004   Gendered Visibilities and the Reformasi Dream of Transparency: The Chinese-Indonesian Rape Debates in Post-Suharto Indonesia. Gender and History 16(3):689–725.

2005   Material Witnesses: Photographs and the Making of Reformasi Memory. *In* Beginning to Remember: The Past in Indonesia's Present. Mary Zurbuchen, ed. Pp. 278–311. Singapore: Singapore National University Press and University of Washington Press.

2006   Reformasi through Our Eyes: Children as Witnesses of History in Post-Suharto
            Indonesia. Visual Anthropology Review 22(2)53–70.

Strathern, Marilyn

1999   Property, Substance, and Effect: Anthropological Essays on Persons and Things.
            Chicago: Athlone.

2000   Audit Cultures: Anthropological Studies in Accountability, Ethics, and the
            Academy. New York: Routledge.

Suharto. *See* **Soeharto**

Sulami

1999   Perempuan-Kebenaran dan Penjara. Jakarta: Cipta Lestari.

Sustained Dialogue

2007   Welcome to Sustained Dialogue. Electronic document, http://www.student.
            virginia.edu/~sduva/, accessed December 11, 2007.

Sweetman, John

1984   War and Administration: The Significance of the Crimean War for the British
            Army. Edinburgh: Scottish Academy Press.

Tanner, Adrian

1979   Bringing Home Animals: Religious Ideology and Mode of Production of the
            Mistassini Cree Hunters. New York: St. Martin's Press.

Tarlo, Emma

2003   Unsettling Memories: Narratives of the Emergency in India. Berkeley:
            University of California Press.

Thant Myint-U

2001   The Making of Modern Burma. Cambridge: Cambridge University Press.

Thompson, E. P.

1967   Time, Work-Discipline and Industrial Capitalism. Past and Present 38(1):56–97.

Tim Penulis Buku Prestasi

1989   Pendidikan Sejarah Perjuangan Bangsa Kelas 3 SD. Semarang, Indonesia:
            Aneka Ilmu.

Tim Penyusun Sejarah

1995   Ilmu Pengetahuan Sosial Sejarah Nasional dan Umum untuk Kelas 3 SMP.
            Jakarta: PT Tiga Pustaka Mandiri.

Tournadre, Nicholas, and Sangda Dorje

2003   Manual of Standard Tibetan Language and Civilization. Ithaca, NY: Snow Lion.

Traweek, Sharon

1988   Beamtimes and Lifetimes: The World of High-Energy Physicists. Cambridge,
            MA: Harvard University Press.

Trouillot, Michel-Rolph

1995   Silencing the Past: Power and the Production of History. Boston: Beacon.

REFERENCES

Tsing, Anna
2005   Friction: An Ethnography of Global Connection. Princeton, NJ: Princeton
         University Press.

Tully, James
1993   An Approach to Political Philosophy: Locke in Contexts. Cambridge:
         Cambridge University Press.

Turner, M. Rick
2005   A Disturbing Trend. Visions: A Newsletter for the Parents of African-American
         Students (Office of African-American Affairs, University of Virginia) 10(1):1–2.

Turner, Terence
1995   Social Body and Embodied Subject: Bodiliness, Subjectivity and Sociality
         among the Kayapó. Cultural Anthropology 10(2):143–179.

United Nations Statistics Division
2007   Oman—Data Availability. Electronic document, http://unstats.un.org/unsd/
         snaama/countryAvailability.asp?Code=512, accessed December 6, 2007.

University of Virginia
2003–   President's Report. Electronic document, http://www.virginia.edu/president/
  2004   report04/president.html, accessed December 11, 2007.
2004   UVA Top News Daily. Electronic document, http://www.virginia.edu/
         topnews/06_11_2004/smith_davis.html, accessed December 11, 2007.

Urciuoli, Bonnie
1996   Exposing Prejudice: Puerto Rican Experiences of Language, Race, and Class.
         Boulder, CO: Westview.

1999   Producing Multiculturalism in Higher Education: Who's Producing What for
         Whom? Qualitative Studies in Education 12(3):287–298.

2003   Excellence, Leadership, Skills, Diversity: Marketing Liberal Arts Education.
         Language and Communication 23(1):385–408.

2005a   The Language of Higher Education Assessment: Legislative Concerns in a
         Global Context. Indiana Journal of Global Legal Studies 12(3/4):183–204.

2005b   Team Diversity: An Ethnography of Institutional Values. In Auto-ethnogra-
         phies: The Anthropology of Academic Practices. Anne Meneley and Donna
         Young, eds. Pp. 159–172. Toronto: Broadview.

Usher, Peter
1986   The Devolution of Wildlife Management and the Prospects for Wildlife
         Conservation in the Northwest Territories. Ottawa: Canadian Arctic Resources
         Committee.

Vassberg, David
1984   Land and Society in Golden Age Castile. Cambridge: Cambridge University Press.

Velasco, Horacio
1989   Signos y sentidos de la identidad de los pueblos castellanos: El concepto de

pueblo y la identidad. *In* Iberian Identity: Essays in the Nature of Identity in Portugal and Spain. Richard Herr and John H. R. Polt, eds. Pp. 81–97. Berkeley: University of California Press.

Verdery, Katherine

1992   The "Etatization" of Time in Ceausescu's Romania. *In* The Politics of Time. H. Rutz, ed. Pp. 37–61. Washington, DC: American Anthropological Association.

Verdery, Katherine, and Caroline Humphrey

2004   Introduction: Raising Questions about Property. *In* Property in Question: Value Transformation in the Global Economy. Katherine Verdery and Caroline Humphrey, eds. Pp. 1–28. Oxford: Berg.

Villalba, Margarita

1999   Valenciana: Expansión y Crisis en el Siglo XVIII. Master's thesis, Universidad Nacional Autónoma de México.

Villanueva Mukul, Eric, ed.

1990   El henequén en Yucatán: Industria, mercado y campesinos. Mérida, Mexico: Maldonado Editores.

Volkman, Toby Alice

1990   Visions and Revisions: Toraja Culture and the Tourist Gaze. American Ethnologist 17(1):91–108.

Watts, Michael

1998   Nature as Artifice and Artifact. *In* Remaking Reality: Nature at the Millennium. B. Braun and N. Castree, eds. Pp. 243–268. London: Routledge.

Weber, Max

1946   Bureaucracy. *In* From Max Weber: Essays in Sociology. H. H. Gerth and C. W. Mills, eds. Pp. 196–244. New York: Oxford University Press.

1958   The Protestant Ethic and the Spirit of Capitalism. New York: Charles Scribner's Sons.

1968   Bureaucracy. *In* On Charisma and Institution Building. Chicago: University of Chicago Press.

Weinberg, Samantha

2000   A Fish Caught in Time. New York: Harper Collins.

Weiner, Annette

1992   Inalienable Possessions: The Paradox of Keeping-While-Giving. Berkeley: University of California Press.

Wells, Allen

1985   Yucatán's Gilded Age: Haciendas, Henequen, and International Harvester, 1860–1915. Albuquerque: University of New Mexico Press.

Wells, Allen, and Gilbert M. Joseph

1996   Summer of Discontent, Seasons of Upheaval: Elite Politics and Rural Insurgency in Yucatán, 1876–1915. Stanford, CA: Stanford University Press.

REFERENCES

White, Hayden
1990   The Content of the Form: Narrative Discourse and Historical Representation. Baltimore: Johns Hopkins University Press.

Whorf, Benjamin Lee
1956   Language, Thought and Reality: Selected Writings of Benjamin Lee Whorf. Cambridge, MA: MIT Press.

Wieringa, Saskia E.
2002   Sexual Politics in Indonesia. New York: Palgrave MacMillan.

Wilkinson, John C.
1987   The Imamate Tradition of Oman. Cambridge: Cambridge University Press.

Williams, Raymond
1973   The Country and the City. Oxford: Oxford University Press.
1976   Keywords: A Vocabulary of Culture and Society. Oxford: Oxford University Press.

Willis, J. C.
1915   The Endemic Flora of Ceylon, with Reference to Geographical Distribution and Evolution in General. Philosophical Transactions of the Royal Society of London. Series B, Containing Papers of a Biological Character, 206:307–342.
1916a   The Distribution of Species in New Zealand. Annals of Botany 30(3):437–457.
1916b   The Evolution of Species in Ceylon, with reference to the Dying Out of Species. Annals of Botany 3(1)0:1–23.

Wolf, Eric
1955   Types of Latin American Peasantry: A Preliminary Discussion. American Anthropologist 57(3):452-471.
1982   Europe and the People without History. Berkeley: University of California Press.

Woodman, Dorothy
1962   The Making of Burma. London: Cresset.

Worster, Donald
1993   The Wealth of Nature: Environmental History and the Ecological Imaginations. Oxford: Oxford University Press.

Xie Benshu
2000   Cong Pianma shijian dao Banhong shijian: Zhong Mian bianjie lishi yange wenti. Yunnan shehui kexue 4:72–81.

Xu Hongzu
1999   Xu Xiake you ji xiao zhu. Zhu Huirong, ed. Kunming, China: Yunnan renmin chubanshe.

Yeats, John
1887   The Natural History of the Raw Materials of Commerce. London: G. Philip.

al-Yousef, Mohamed bin Musa
1995   Oil and the Transformation of Oman, 1970–1995. London: Stacey International.

Yukon Department of Renewable Resources

1997   Sport Fishing Regulations Summary 1997–1998. Whitehorse, YT: Yukon
        Territorial Government.

Zaloom, Caitlin

2004   The Productive Life of Risk. Cultural Anthropology 19(3):365–391.

Zemsky, Robert, G. R. Wegner, and W. F. Massy

2005   Today's Colleges Must Be Market Smart and Mission Centered. Chronicle
        Review, July 15: B6–7.

Index

Addison, Joseph, 23–24n27
Africa, and connections to Oman, 43–46
agriculture: and land tenure in Yucatán, 197–98, 203, 206; and metaphors in wildlife management, 76–77; and natural cycles of time, 76
al-nahda, and contemporary Omani renaissance, 31, 47n6
Alvarado, Salvador, 204
Anderson, Benedict, 29, 47n4, 80, 82, 83, 113, 124, 125, 126, 127, 128n1, 192
anthropology: and cultural embeddedness of temporality, 23n23; and notions of cyclical time, 75–76; and perspectives of "non-Western cultures," 136; and social construction of concept of time, 88, 101; stress on "uses" of history in analyses of historical narratives, 211; and studies of temporality, 52–54; and texts as objects, 217
anxiety, and race as psychological space at University of Virginia, 183–84
appropriation, concept of labor as, 8–9
archives, of national historical resources in Indonesia, 230–34
Asch, Michael, 80
Asian Americans, and politics of student diversity at University of Virginia, 177–78, 179, 184–85
Asian Student Union (ASU), 171
Austen, Jane, 13
Avicolas Fernández (Yucatecan poultry company), 206–207

Bajau people (Indonesia), 121–24, 128n4
Balfour, Isaac Bailey, 137, 160
barasti, and image of past in Oman, 39–40
Barkan, Elazar, 124

Baudrillard, Jean, 70
Benjamin, Walter, 28, 70, 80
Benteng Vredeberg Museum (Indonesia), 231–32
Bergson, Henri, 52, 104n9
Berman, Marshall, 23n22
biodiversity, and politics of conservation biology in Indonesia, 118
Birth, Kevin, 23n24, 53, 61
Bloch, Maurice, 12, 14, 23n23, 52–53
body, and corporate life of mineral specimens, 68
botany, and collection of plant specimens in Yunnan, 129–64
Bourdieu, Pierre, 53, 83
Braun, Bruce, 10
Breves datos históricos y culturales del municipio de Hunucmá (Cetina Aguilar 1996), 208, 209, 211
Brightman, Robert, 81
British Empire, and India Survey, 130–31, 133–34, 165n4
bureaucracy: and concepts of space and time, 103–104n7; and rise of capitalism, 85–87; and wildlife management in Yukon, 89, 90–102
Bureimi War (Oman, 1950s), 33, 34
Burma, and British survey of borders, 130–31, 165n4
Bush, Ronald, 122, 124

Cahs, and el pueblo in Yucatán, 194, 195–96, 197, 198, 199, 200, 201, 202, 203, 213n4
Cahtal K'ay (*Song of Life in the Pueblo*, Cetina Aguilar 1983), 208
Canada, and debates about wildlife as renewable resource in Yukon, 75–102

School for Advanced Research Advanced Seminar Series

PUBLISHED BY SAR PRESS

CHACO & HOHOKAM: PREHISTORIC
REGIONAL SYSTEMS IN THE AMERICAN
SOUTHWEST
Patricia L. Crown & W. James Judge, eds.

RECAPTURING ANTHROPOLOGY: WORKING IN
THE PRESENT
Richard G. Fox, ed.

WAR IN THE TRIBAL ZONE: EXPANDING
STATES AND INDIGENOUS WARFARE
*R. Brian Ferguson &
Neil L. Whitehead, eds.*

IDEOLOGY AND PRE-COLUMBIAN
CIVILIZATIONS
*Arthur A. Demarest &
Geoffrey W. Conrad, eds.*

DREAMING: ANTHROPOLOGICAL AND
PSYCHOLOGICAL INTERPRETATIONS
Barbara Tedlock, ed.

HISTORICAL ECOLOGY: CULTURAL
KNOWLEDGE AND CHANGING LANDSCAPES
Carole L. Crumley, ed.

THEMES IN SOUTHWEST PREHISTORY
George J. Gumerman, ed.

MEMORY, HISTORY, AND OPPOSITION UNDER
STATE SOCIALISM
Rubie S. Watson, ed.

OTHER INTENTIONS: CULTURAL CONTEXTS
AND THE ATTRIBUTION OF INNER STATES
Lawrence Rosen, ed.

LAST HUNTERS–FIRST FARMERS: NEW
PERSPECTIVES ON THE PREHISTORIC
TRANSITION TO AGRICULTURE
*T. Douglas Price &
Anne Birgitte Gebauer, eds.*

MAKING ALTERNATIVE HISTORIES:
THE PRACTICE OF ARCHAEOLOGY AND
HISTORY IN NON-WESTERN SETTINGS
Peter R. Schmidt & Thomas C. Patterson, eds.

SENSES OF PLACE
Steven Feld & Keith H. Basso, eds.

CYBORGS & CITADELS: ANTHROPOLOGICAL
INTERVENTIONS IN EMERGING SCIENCES AND
TECHNOLOGIES
Gary Lee Downey & Joseph Dumit, eds.

ARCHAIC STATES
Gary M. Feinman & Joyce Marcus, eds.

CRITICAL ANTHROPOLOGY NOW:
UNEXPECTED CONTEXTS, SHIFTING
CONSTITUENCIES, CHANGING AGENDAS
George E. Marcus, ed.

THE ORIGINS OF LANGUAGE: WHAT
NONHUMAN PRIMATES CAN TELL US
Barbara J. King, ed.

REGIMES OF LANGUAGE: IDEOLOGIES,
POLITIES, AND IDENTITIES
Paul V. Kroskrity, ed.

BIOLOGY, BRAINS, AND BEHAVIOR: THE
EVOLUTION OF HUMAN DEVELOPMENT
*Sue Taylor Parker, Jonas Langer, & Michael
L. McKinney, eds.*

WOMEN & MEN IN THE PREHISPANIC
SOUTHWEST: LABOR, POWER, & PRESTIGE
Patricia L. Crown, ed.

HISTORY IN PERSON: ENDURING STRUGGLES,
CONTENTIOUS PRACTICE, INTIMATE
IDENTITIES
Dorothy Holland & Jean Lave, eds.

THE EMPIRE OF THINGS: REGIMES OF VALUE
AND MATERIAL CULTURE
Fred R. Myers, ed.

CATASTROPHE & CULTURE: THE
ANTHROPOLOGY OF DISASTER
*Susanna M. Hoffman &
Anthony Oliver-Smith, eds.*

URUK MESOPOTAMIA & ITS NEIGHBORS:
CROSS-CULTURAL INTERACTIONS IN THE ERA
OF STATE FORMATION
Mitchell S. Rothman, ed.

REMAKING LIFE & DEATH: TOWARD AN
ANTHROPOLOGY OF THE BIOSCIENCES
Sarah Franklin & Margaret Lock, eds.

TIKAL: DYNASTIES, FOREIGNERS,
& AFFAIRS OF STATE: ADVANCING
MAYA ARCHAEOLOGY
Jeremy A. Sabloff, ed.

GRAY AREAS: ETHNOGRAPHIC ENCOUNTERS
WITH NURSING HOME CULTURE
Philip B. Stafford, ed.

PLURALIZING ETHNOGRAPHY: COMPARISON
AND REPRESENTATION IN MAYA CULTURES,
HISTORIES, AND IDENTITIES

American Arrivals: Anthropology Engages the New Immigration
Nancy Foner, ed.

Violence
Neil L. Whitehead, ed.

Law & Empire in the Pacific: Fiji and Hawai'i
Sally Engle Merry & Donald Brenneis, eds.

Anthropology in the Margins of the State
Veena Das & Deborah Poole, eds.

The Archaeology of Colonial Encounters: Comparative Perspectives
Gil J. Stein, ed.

Globalization, Water, & Health: Resource Management in Times of Scarcity
Linda Whiteford & Scott Whiteford, eds.

A Catalyst for Ideas: Anthropological Archaeology and the Legacy of Douglas W. Schwartz
Vernon L. Scarborough, ed.

The Archaeology of Chaco Canyon: An Eleventh-Century Pueblo Regional Center
Stephen H. Lekson, ed.

The Gender of Globalization: Women Navigating Cultural and Economic Marginalities
Nandini Gunewardena & Ann Kingsolver, eds.

Community Building in the Twenty-First Century
Stanley E. Hyland, ed.

Afro-Atlantic Dialogues: Anthropology in the Diaspora
Kevin A. Yelvington, ed.

Copán: The History of an Ancient Maya Kingdom
E. Wyllys Andrews & William L. Fash, eds.

The Seductions of Community: Emancipations, Oppressions, Quandaries
Gerald W. Creed, ed.

The Evolution of Human Life History
Kristen Hawkes & Richard R. Paine, eds.

Imperial Formations
Ann Laura Stoler, Carole McGranahan, & Peter C. Perdue, eds.

Opening Archaeology: Repatriation's Impact on Contemporary Research and Practice
Thomas W. Killion, ed.

New Landscapes of Inequality: Neoliberalism and the Erosion of Democracy in America
Jane L. Collins, Micaela di Leonardo, & Brett Williams, eds.

Small Worlds: Method, Meaning & Narrative in Microhistory
James F. Brooks, Christopher R. N. DeCorse, & John Walton, eds.

Memory Work: Archaeologies of Material Practices
Barbara J. Mills & William H. Walker, eds.

Figuring the Future: Globalization and the Temporalities of Children and Youth
Jennifer Cole & Deborah Durham eds.

Writing Culture: The Poetics and Politics of Ethnography
James Clifford & George E. Marcus, eds.

The Collapse of Ancient States and Civilizations
Norman Yoffee & George L. Cowgill, eds.

Partcipants in the School for Advanced Research short seminar "The Politics of Resources and their Temporalities," Santa Fe, New Mexico, October 26–28, 2005. Seated (from left): Mandana Limbert, Elizabeth Emma Ferry. Standing (from left): Paul Eiss, Karen Strassler, Celia Lowe, Erik Mueggler, Paul Nadasdy, Richard Handler.